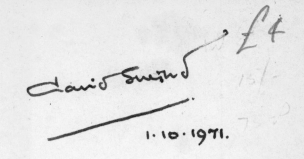

David Smith £4

15/-

1·10·1971.

THE SINEWS OF PEACE

SAVROLA
THE STORY OF THE MALAKAND FIELD FORCE
THE RIVER WAR
LONDON TO LADYSMITH VIA PRETORIA
IAN HAMILTON'S MARCH
LORD RANDOLPH CHURCHILL
MY AFRICAN JOURNEY
LIBERALISM AND THE SOCIAL PROBLEM
THE WORLD CRISIS:
        1911-1914
        1915
        1916-1918
        AFTERMATH
        THE EASTERN FRONT
MY EARLY LIFE
THOUGHTS AND ADVENTURES
MARLBOROUGH, 4 VOLS.
GREAT CONTEMPORARIES
STEP BY STEP: 1936-1939
ARMS AND THE COVENANT
INTO BATTLE
THE UNRELENTING STRUGGLE
THE END OF THE BEGINNING
ONWARDS TO VICTORY
THE DAWN OF LIBERATION
VICTORY
SECRET SESSION SPEECHES

THE
SINEWS OF PEACE

POST-WAR SPEECHES
BY
WINSTON S. CHURCHILL

Edited by
RANDOLPH S. CHURCHILL

CASSELL
AND COMPANY LTD.
LONDON, TORONTO, MELBOURNE
SYDNEY, WELLINGTON

First published . . 1948

PRINTED IN LUXEMBOURG
BY IMPRIMERIE BOURG-BOURGER
40, AVENUE DE LA GARE

F 648

INTRODUCTION

This volume of Mr. Churchill's speeches covers the eighteen-month period from the fall of the Caretaker Government in June, 1945, to the close of the year 1946. The previous seven volumes of Mr. Churchill's speeches, *Into Battle, The Unrelenting Struggle, The End of the Beginning, Onwards to Victory, Victory* and *Secret Session Speeches*, cover the period of the war years and contain all the speeches which he made as Prime Minister of the victorious National Coalition Government. In the period covered by the current volume, Mr. Churchill is no longer Prime Minister but Leader of His Majesty's Opposition.

Britain is now at peace, but the whole world is once again confronted with many of the dangers which marked the period from 1933 to 1939. It is natural, therefore, that the accents of warning and the undertones of alarm contained in *Arms and the Covenant* and the first part of *Into Battle* should once more recur.

The national unity, which was forged in the stresses of war, dissolved with the break-up of the Coalition Government. It is inevitable therefore that the twenty-nine speeches contained in this volume should not have received the almost unanimous agreement of his fellow countrymen which greeted Mr. Churchill's wartime speeches. The discriminating reader may yet conclude that the literary and oratorical quality of the speeches in this volume is as high as anything that has fallen from Mr. Churchill in the past; he may also conclude that the farsighted prescience and sure-footed judgement, unheeded at the time, which all to-day acclaim in the pre-war speeches, will be increasingly recognized in those contained in this volume.

There is however one characteristic which will be found common to all three sets of speeches, namely the quality of moral leadership. A son may perhaps not always be regarded as the most objective judge of such qualities in a father and I am therefore happy to place on permanent record the opinion of a distinguished Dutch journalist, Mr. J. H. Huizinga.

Writing in *Time and Tide* a year ago, Mr. Huizinga suggested that in the first two years after the war

v

"the prize for moral leadership should surely go to Mr. Churchill rather than to any of the official leaders. That is the recognition which fairness demands should be given..."

Mr. Huizinga continued: "Who in this country—and indeed in the world—could more legitimately claim to have displayed these virtues [of leadership], at Fulton and after, than Mr. Winston Churchill? Who had enough faith in the Western way of life, not merely to proclaim its superior merits, but to propose that something should be done to safeguard it, regardless of the threats and censure such self-protective measures would evoke from the enemies of liberty? Who showed enough originality of mind to break with the traditional conception of the 'quivering, precarious balance of power' and to plead for the replacement of 'such narrow margins offering temptations to a trial of strength' by a new and infinitely more stable system of retaining a balance of power in hand? Who had enough vision, imagination and insight to realise as early as the beginning of 1946 that it was practical politics to count on the Americans making such a system possible? Who was not afraid to confront the British public as early as November, 1945, when it was still flushed with the pride of victory, with the extremely unpalatable fact—and surely to none more unpalatable than to this proudest of Britons himself— that the leadership in such a novel system would inevitably pass to the Americans? ('The United States may be the necessary leader which is required to build up that great structure of world security.') Who dared to challenge all the popular illusions of the time? Who dared to call a spade a spade, and a Russian an enemy of democracy?* Who did not hesitate to jerk the public out of its cosy intellectual haze, its U.N.O.-worship and its diplomatic make-believe, by warning that 'the time for generalities is past'; that 'our difficulties and dangers will not be removed by closing our eyes to them'; that 'peace will not be preserved by pious sentiments expressed in terms of platitudes or by official grimaces and diplomatic

---

* Mr. Churchill has not, in fact, called the Russians "enemies of democracy". He regards them rather as victims of despotism. It is Soviet Communists whom Mr. Churchill regards as "enemies of Democracy". [R. S. C.]

correctitude'? Who turned the 'cards on the table' face upwards and showed the public what sort of cards they really were more than a year before this salutory revelation received its official blessing in a strictly non-official pamphlet of the same name? In short, who has led and who has followed?"

Most of the speeches in this volume centre around Mr. Churchill's two famous declarations at Fulton and at Zurich. At Fulton he spoke of the Iron Curtain with which the Russians had divided Eastern from Western Europe and urged a fraternal association of the English-speaking peoples to cope with the dangers of Communist expansion. The Fulton speech drew cries of horrified alarm, not only from Communists and their dupes, but from many usually right-minded and sensible politicians and journalists. Re-reading that speech in the light of after-knowledge, many people may wonder what the fuss was all about. They may perhaps conclude that one of the most dangerous and thankless tasks in politics is to tell the truth and to give warning of danger in good time instead of late in the day.

At Zurich, Mr. Churchill developed the theme of a United Europe which he had first broached at Metz. Here again he found himself a good deal in advance of public opinion. Yet today, the cause he pleaded at Zurich is common ground among all non-Communist political parties in all of Western Europe as well as in the United States of America. The moral would seem to be that though the role of the prophet is never an easy one, ultimate acceptance of the truth can usually be counted upon, even if somewhat tardily, in the democracies of the West. We must hope that this fact will encourage public men everywhere increasingly to face the facts of the world in which we live, and to proclaim the truth however unpopular or unrewarding such a process may at the time appear.

RANDOLPH S. CHURCHILL

CONTENTS

THE SINEWS OF PEACE

DEMOBILISATION

SECOND READING OF THE CONSOLIDATED FUND
[No. 1] BILL

A SPEECH TO THE HOUSE OF COMMONS
22 OCTOBER 1945

---

6 *August—First Atomic Bomb dropped on Hiroshima.*
8 *August—Second Atomic Bomb dropped on Nagasaki.*
8 *August—Soviet Union declares war on Japan.*
14 *August—Unconditional surrender of Japan.*
15 *August—Opening of Parliament.*
8 *September—General MacArthur enters Tokyo.*
11 *September—Foreign Ministers of Britain, United States, France and the Soviet Union meet in London to draft Peace Treaties.*
3 *October—Foreign Ministers' Meeting adjourned without agreement.*

[*22 October* 1945

WE have asked for this Debate upon demobilisation, because demobilisation is the foundation upon which, at this moment, everything else stands, and also, because tardy, inadequate demobilisation is the fountain-head of all our domestic difficulties. Whatever view may be taken of Socialism or free enterprise, surely it is common ground between us all, that we should get all the great wheels and the little wheels of life and industry in this country turning as soon as possible. For this we need the men. Without the men, and also the women, now held in the Services, there can be no speedy revival. The woeful shortage of consumer goods will continue. The Government will be afraid to allow people to spend their savings, for fear of undue rise in prices. Scarcity will be used as justification for controls, and controls will become the fatal means of prolonging scarcity. Get all the great wheels turning, and all the little cog wheels too! Let them rotate and revolve, spin and hum, and we shall have taken a long step forward towards our

9

deliverance. In order to get them turning, we must bring the men home, and set the men free.

I am disquieted at the slow rate of demobilisation. I would have been ashamed to be responsible for the earliest declarations of His Majesty's Government on this subject. Even now that these have been markedly improved, I have no hesitation in saying that they fall far below what is both possible and necessary. His Majesty's Ministers have had an enormous windfall in the sudden end of the Japanese war, and of the cessation of fighting and slaughter throughout the world. There are no more enemies to conquer; no more fronts to hold.

[HON. MEMBERS: *Oh!*]

I mean of course in a military sphere. All our foreign foes have been beaten down into unconditional surrender. Now is the time to bring home the men who have conquered, and bring them back to their families and productive work. There is, at this time, no fear of large-scale unemployment. Every industry is clamouring for men. Everywhere are useful and fruitful tasks to be performed. I am sure that the restrictions and controls which would prevent men from getting work, and which would hobble and fetter the life-energies of the nation, will be swept away once the men are back, and the whole great series of wheels will begin to turn. Do not let us be deterred by the fear of shortage of houses. Use billeting to the full wherever necessary; take the land for the houses, if you need it—I say if you need it—as readily as you would have taken it for a gun site in 1940-41. Do whatever is needful and humanly possible to bring the men home and get things started again.

I would not go so far in urging the Government to these extreme efforts—I know their difficulties—if I were not prepared myself to run the risk of trying to make a positive contribution to our problems. There is some risk in a Member of the Opposition making a positive proposal, or set of proposals. I have no longer the power to "press the button" and obtain the exact information on any point. Still I have a general knowledge of our national life-problem as a whole, particularly on its military side. For what it is worth, I am prepared, in good will and in good faith, to offer some definite suggestions to His Majesty's Government. We are told that the return of the troops and the members of the other Services is delayed or regulated by

three conditions—first, our commitments—such is the term
that is used—that is the military necessities; second, transportation; and third, the execution of the Bevin Coalition
Government demobilisation plan.

I will deal with these three. First of all, commitments.
This is a most dangerous ground for anyone not possessed
of the latest information to venture upon. Nevertheless, I
shall try my best, and, if the estimates which I make are
shown to be erroneous, I shall be very ready to be convinced
by the responsible statements of Ministers. I am going to
submit to the House what I think should be the strength of
the United Kingdom Armed Forces, which we should aim
to reach with all possible speed. A year later these strengths
could be reconsidered in closer relation to our long-term
plan. I take the Navy first. On existing plans, allowing
for intake, on December 31st of this year, the strength of
the Navy would be 665,000, of whom 55,000 are women,
so that the Navy would retain 448,000 even at the end of
June, 1946. I am astounded that such figures should be
accepted by His Majesty's Government. I know no reason
why Vote A of the Navy should exceed the figure at which
it stood in the Estimates of 1939, namely, 133,000. We had
a fine Navy at the outbreak of war. I was sent to the
Admiralty, at a few hours' notice on September 3rd, 1939,
and that is what I found, relatively, to the Forces of other
countries against whom we were at that time matched, or
likely to be matched. I have yet to hear any argument
which justifies our planning to maintain, at the present
time—unless it be in connection with the Fleet Air Arm—a
larger naval force in personnel than we had at the beginning
of the late war.

I remember that at the height of the Nelson period, in the
war against Napoleon, we reached a Vote A of 148,000,
and that, oddly enough, was the figure that I was responsible for reaching in August, 1914. Let us take, as a working
figure, 150,000. If there is some entirely new case to be
unfolded because of new commitments which I have not
heard of, the Government should lay that case before the
House. On the whole, although I think we should not be
too precipitate in judging these matters, it would seem that
new conditions might, at any rate in respect of very large
vessels, tell the other way. But, failing some entirely new
situation, of which only the Government can be aware,

definite orders should be given to discharge all men surplus to the 150,000, and to make sure that the enormously swollen shore establishments are reduced equally with those afloat. I hazard the guess that at this time, there are nearly as many men of the Navy ashore as afloat. I should have thought that no great length of time would be needed for this operation, provided orders were given now, and enforced with real authority. At the same time, while this operation is going on, every opportunity should be given to men, entitled to release, to stay on if they volunteer. If there were so many volunteers that the number was exceeded, I think we should face that.

It seems to me that there is a large number of people in the Services who wish to continue voluntarily, and we all think that is a very good thing. After all, though this war has been terrible in many ways, we have not had the awful slaughter of the last war, or the hideous grind of the trenches. There has been movement and drama, and I can quite see that there may be some who would prefer to continue in the profession of arms. I think that if they were offered suitable terms, they would give a further period, voluntarily, of service abroad. But at present I am assured that no plan has been made, and no commanding officer in any of the Services knows how to answer the inquiries which are made of him. So while affirming and enforcing the principle of national service—of which I trust we are to hear from His Majesty's Government—it should surely be our policy to encourage the largest number of men to stay of their own free will. We ought to be very reluctant at this juncture to turn off any trained man who wishes to continue under arms. This digression applies to all three Services; but, returning to the Navy, apart from what I have said about volunteers, I submit that the figure should come down at once, as speedily and as quickly as possible to 150,000 men on Vote A.

I come now to the Royal Air Force. I do not know what the Government's policy is about the Air Force. It may be that what I am going to suggest is more than they have in mind. I consider that the permanent Royal Air Force must be maintained on a very large scale, and in magnificent quality, with the very latest machines, and that they should become the prime factor in our island and Imperial defence. I may say I had thought that 150 to 200 combattant squadrons, with the necessary training establishments, and, of course, with the large auxiliary reserves which can be developed, should be our staple. This would involve about 4,000 machines under constant *construction*, the auxiliary forces being additional. If you have 100 men on the ground for every machine in the air you are making an allowance which, in my opinion, is grossly extravagant and capable of immense revision by competent administration. However, to be on the safe side, I would take that figure. It would seem to me that the personnel for the R.A.F. should be 400,000, as compared with 150,000 for the Royal Navy, and that it should now be brought down to that figure. The present plan for the Air Force contemplates 819,000 men and women being retained up to December 31st, and as many as 699,000 being held as late as June 30th, 1946.

I yield to none in my desire to see preserved this splendid weapon of the Royal Air Force, upon which our safety and our freedom depend, but, for this great purpose, it is all the more necessary to get the life of the nation working again and not to squander our remaining treasure in keeping a large number of men in the Royal Air Force—who are not really wanted either for immediate needs, or for the permanent organisation—and to keep them lolling about at great cost to the public and vexation to themselves. I submit to the Ministers whom I see opposite, that they should fix the figure of the permanent Air Force organisation and then cut down to that with the utmost speed. This also implies decisions being taken about airfields which are now being held and guarded, on a full war-time scale, by such large numbers of men.

I have touched on the Navy and the Royal Air Force. Now I come to the most difficult subject of all, the Army, and if I were to burden the House with all the reasonings which led to my present computation, I should, Mr. Speaker, far outrun the limits of your patience and, no doubt, of my own voice. For the occupation of Germany and the Low Countries a ration strength of 400,000 men should be the maximum. I say ration strength because all calculations in divisions are misleading. There is no need for general organisation in divisional formations, or for such divisions as are maintained to possess the characteristics and the armaments of divisions entering a line of battle in the heat of the struggle against the former German Army in its prime. It is a different task that they have to do, and different organisations are required to meet it. Mobile brigades, military police, armoured car and light tank units, sedentary forces for particular garrison duties—such are the methods to which military thought should be guided by political authority.

The task of holding Germany down will not be a hard one; it will be much more difficult to hold her up. The weight of administration must be thrown upon the Germans. They must be made to bear the burden. We cannot have all our best officers, scientists and engineers organising them, when we, ourselves, have need of those men's services. But I will not expatiate on this point. I say 400,000 ration strength—one half teeth, the other half tail,—would be sufficient. It may well be, also, that apart from this force, training establishments from Great Britain should be set up in Germany, where the young troops would learn their profession on soil which their fathers and elder brothers have at once conquered and liberated. I understand that the United States are keeping about 350,000 troops in Germany, of which, again broadly speaking, one-half are fighting men and one-half administrative services.

In view of all the dangers that there are in North-Eastern Italy, in view of our obligations in Greece and all the difficulties developing in Palestine and the Middle East, I would hazard the figure of another 400,000 ration strength which would be required, at any rate, I think, until the end of 1946, and probably longer, in the Mediterranean theatre. In Palestine, above all, gendarmerie and brigade groups should supersede divisional formations with all their cumbrous apparatus. I would add to these figures, as a margin for War Office establishments in this island and India, as well as fortress garrisons outside the Mediterranean, another 200,000 men, making a total for the Army, in the period which lies immediately before us, of 1,000,000 men. I must emphasise that this 1,000,000 strength is a ration strength of United Kingdom soldiers, and does not take auxiliary or native soldiers into account. I may say that I came to this conclusion before I saw the figures of the late Government's plan which the Minister of Labour put forward, I think, on the 2nd of this month. I find that by June 30th, 1946, His Majesty's Government propose to reduce the Army to 1,156,000 men. There is certainly not much between us on that figure. I would not quarrel about it.

The question however remains, when is this total to be reached? Why should time be wasted in reaching that total? This is the vital point. Any unnecessary men kept by compulsion with the Colours hamper our revival here, and waste the money we shall need to maintain our Armed Forces in the years that are to come. Under the present plan by December 31st there will still be 2,343,000 men and women in the Army, of whom 130,000 will be women. Considering that that will be nearly eight months after the German war ended, I say that the number is far too many. I am told that January and February are months when releases from the Army flag notably. In what way should we be harmed if the Government total of 1,156,900 men aimed at for June 30th, 1946, were, by good and energetic administration, reached by the end of March? Should we not be very much better off? I urge that this new target should be at once declared, namely, to reach the June figure three months earlier. If we add 1,000,000 United Kingdom ration strength for the Army to 400,000 for the Royal Air Force and 150,000 for the Royal Navy, we have a total ration strength of 1,550,000 men, which, I submit to the House, if organised with due economy and contrivance, should suffice for our needs in the immediate future, and should give time for the long term policy to be shaped in closer detail.

Now if we take this figure as a working basis, let us subtract it from the total numbers which will be retained under arms at December 31st by the latest scheme of the Government. I understand that if the whole of this present programme is carried out, they will have 3,842,000 men and women in the Forces at that date. There are, therefore, potentially more than 2,225,000 men who are redundant and surplus, in my view, and who should not be retained in the Services more than one moment longer than is necessary to bring them home, or set them free, if they are here already. These 2,225,000 men who are redundant are unemployed. We publish the unemployment figures each week and rejoice that they are small, but they are an inaccurate return while there is this great pocket, this 2,225,000, unemployed. To have 2,225,000 unemployed, and unemployed under the most wasteful and expensive conditions to the State, and in many cases irritating to the men themselves, is intolerable.

The majority of these men are outside the United Kingdom. Nothing is more costly than holding the dumb-bell at arm's length. Every day counts. Even in June, 1946, eight months from now, and 13 months after the end of the war with Germany, the Government propose, with intake, to hold 2,408,000 persons in uniform in the three Services. I contend that the target to be aimed at should be 1,550,000 and that this smaller figure should be reached earlier. The maintenance of immense numbers of redundant forces overseas, and held here in this island, not only brings ruin to the Exchequer but also makes inroads upon our shipping for the feeding of the Forces overseas. These inroads are of a grievous character, and the most solid justification is needed to defend them. I regard the speedy repatriation and release of these 2,225,000 men as a supreme task which lies before His Majesty's Government at the present time.

I must, however, make one very serious reservation. In my calculations and estimates I have definitely excluded the possibility of a major war in the next few years. If His Majesty's Government consider that this is wrong, then it would not be a case of demobilisation at all but of remobilisation, because what has taken place and is going on has already woefully impaired the immediate fighting efficiency of the enormous Forces we still retain. I believe, however, it may be common ground that this possibility of a major war may rightly be excluded, and that we have an interlude of grace in which mankind may be able to make better arrangements for this tortured world than we have hitherto achieved. Still, I make that reservation.

I shall no doubt be told that there is no transport, and that all our transportation both by sea and air is fully occupied on the existing proposals. So far as sea transportation is concerned, I do not believe it. When I recall to mind the immense magnitude of the supply fleets which were provided and prepared for the Japanese struggle in 1945 and 1946, and the fact that we are relieved of at least three-quarters, if not four-fifths, of the burden of maintaining an aggressive war at the other end of the world, it is incredible that there should not be now enough tonnage available, and that we should not be able to have an incomparably higher scale of transportation than any envisaged in the days when the Bevin scheme was framed, when we contemplated a prolonged war with Japan.

There are various suggestions of a minor character, but cumulatively of some notable consequence, to make about speeding up transportation by more ingenuity in the employment of the merchant vessels now engaged on troop movement. For instance, would it not be possible to bring into service the laid-up escort carriers with skeleton crews? Each of these would carry some 1,500 troops. Why should not the Medloc movement, that is the Mediterranean line of communications movement, which is well below the former planned target, not be doubled? For this purpose, and in order to secure the immediate release of more men from India and the Middle East, it may be necessary to expand the staging camps in Egypt. Surely this should not be delayed another moment? Again, is it not possible to make greater use of the trans-Canada route to bring home our people from the Pacific that way round? If we could do this we should use to the full on their return voyage, at least, the British ships now engaged on repatriating Canadian and American personnel from Europe. Together the measures would even now secure a substantial increase in the movement of troops in the first three months of next year. If these measures had been taken earlier that increase could have been gained on these figures by the end of this year. Surely even now not a moment should be lost in bringing into play these potentialities? There is also the Navy, which could move, with its own resources, some 6,000 men monthly—their own men from the Pacific fleet to Vancouver.

THE FIRST LORD OF THE ADMIRALTY [Mr. A. V. Alexander]: We are doing so.

MR. CHURCHILL: That shows that we are not in dispute in the matter, but we have not heard about it. The right hon. Gentleman may indeed "do good by stealth," but he must not be vexed when he "blushes to find it fame." Are these men now being transported across Canada by the same rolling stock which is being used to take in the opposite direction the Canadian troops who have arrived in Halifax from Europe? These Navy men from the Pacific could then embark for home in ships which carry home to Canada, Canadian troops. Has that been arranged? These

6,000 Naval ratings per month could then be brought home earlier than the plan, even under the present rules. This would entail the release of a much larger corresponding number of the same age and service groups who are kept waiting for their release, and an appreciable acceleration would be brought about. These are points which I give only as instances. No doubt there are many others which should be studied with attention by His Majesty's Government. If they are already approved, it would give us great pleasure to hear that fact and credit the administration with it in the later stages of the Debate. We should be glad also of further information of the mass movement by air from remote areas, which seems to be of the greatest value and importance.

But, after all, the great bulk of the troops and air ground personal are over here at home, or only across the Channel in Europe. Sea transport does not enter into their return to any great extent. Ships of all kinds—well we know it—can carry troops either way across the Channel. No ships at all are needed for those who are now in this country. In the Debate on the Address I asked for the numbers of men in the various depots. They have not been given. There is no reason why they should not be given. We request that they should now be given. Until we have the official figures I cannot, of course, speak with up-to-date accuracy, but I do not expect the assumption on which I am basing my argument will be very far astray.

I believe there are at least 400,000 more men than are needed for any useful purpose in what used to be called the 21st Army Group in Germany and in the Low Countries. That is not including the British Army in Italy or Austria, with which I am not dealing at this moment. Is it not true that there are here at home over a million men, the great majority of whom are absolutely redundant? Is it not true that there are something like, or over, a million men here at home? We expect to know. All these men, so much needed in civil life, are being kept out of the national economic and industrial recovery, not because of any military commitments, nor for any want of transportation, but simply because their turn comes later than that of a far smaller number of men who cannot for a considerable time be brought home from the East and the Far East. This raises grave problems of which I am well aware, but we must ask: Is it sensible, is it necessary, and can it on that basis be defended?

This brings me to the third and last part of this argument. It is a part with which I am deeply familiar, namely the Bevin demobilisation plan. No one, I think, except its author, has more right to speak about it than I, for I was Secretary of State for War and Air during the whole demobilisation period after the last war, and well I know the perils and difficulties which beset that process. I have left on record in my book *The Aftermath* the complexities and shocking misfortunes in which we were involved in those days by the Addison scheme of demobilisation, which was felt by the fighting troops and those who had been out longest to be most unfair, and which was sprung upon them in a manner which gave it the least chance of favourable acceptance. I have, therefore, always been a strong supporter of the Bevin scheme. One must always try to carry the confidence and sense of loyalty and fair play of the troops. It must, however, be stated and remembered that this scheme was based on the assumption that the Japanese war would continue on a great scale for at least 18 months after a German surrender, and perhaps longer, and that large new armies would have to be sent to the Far East, going away from home at the end of this long struggle in Europe, while the process of turning over to peace conditions was in full swing through the country and through a very large part of the Armed Forces.

That problem we have, thank God, been saved. It is not the situation with which we are now confronted. We have a different scene and a different problem. We must do justice to the case as it stands and to the facts as they are. I am sure it was right to frame this Bevin scheme and to make it our foundation and the first floor of our demobilisation. Nevertheless, I am inclined to think that Army opinion as a whole, convinced of the fairness of the intentions of the late and present Governments towards them, will be prepared to accept further considerable modifications in that scheme. Tidiness is a virtue, symmetry is often a constituent of beauty, but it would be a mistake to insist pedantically upon a rigid application of the Bevin scheme in the changed circumstances of to-day.

Let us take an extreme example. If, for instance, 100 men have to be kept idle in England, because 10 men higher up on the list cannot yet be brought home from Hongkong, or Rangoon, or Calcutta, and cannot yet be placed in a category which entitles them to be brought home from these places, everyone would admit that that would be pushing a good principle to absurdity. I would rather address myself to the 10 men and, by substantial additions to their pay or bonus or leave on release, and by special care for their future employment or otherwise, make up to them any disappointments, which they may feel, not because they are not returning as soon as possible but because others lower down on the list have got out before them.

I am sure—and I do not speak without thought or some knowledge—that if the whole position were explained to the Army, and if substantial compensation were forthcoming to those kept longer than their time, with a proper proportion of compassionate cases, the men would understand and would accept the position. After all, does a Briton say to himself, "I am unfortunate: I cannot get home but I can bear it, because I know that 10 or 20 other men are being made unfortunate too, on my account"? That seems to me a sour and morose form of comfort. Might not a man prefer substantial compensation for himself instead of misfortunes needlessly inflicted upon others which can do him no possible good? Suppose every man was given double pay for every day that he was kept beyond his proper priority that would be a small cost to the State compared with the enormous waste of keeping hundreds and hundreds of thousands of men out of productive work.

MR. EVELYN WALKDEN [Doncaster]: Is the right hon. Gentleman seriously preaching the Dukes plan—the T.U.C. speech suggesting compensation be given to the men in Burma if they stay out there a little longer? It was a speech by Charles Dukes at the Trade-Union Congress which has been the subject of much correspondence in the various journals in the Far East.

MR. CHURCHILL: I thought I was preaching my own plan.

MR. WALKDEN: This is rather important. Is the right hon. Gentleman aware that what he is now preaching has been condemned bell, book and candle by the men in Burma and that they have vigorously attacked it in correspondence to Members on both sides of this House?

20

MR. CHURCHILL: However that may be, I am saying what I think is in the interest of the State.

MR. WALKDEN: The right hon. Gentleman should ask the men in Burma then?

MR. CHURCHILL: With considerable responsibility and after much heart searching, I am making a positive contribution to this Debate. It can be knocked about from all quarters, but I hope to see at any rate a foundation for thought and discussion on a matter in which we cannot afford to rest in a half paralysed deadlock. Supposing every man were given double pay for every day he was kept beyond his proper priority, that would be a small burden on the State compared with the enormous waste such as is going on now. Certainly a great effort should be made to solve this problem. If it makes possible a far larger rate of releases, the general rejoicing will sweep away many invidious reflections.

We are told that very large numbers of men here at home must be kept under arms because the men abroad would think it unfair that they should have the advantage of gaining employment before them. But nothing we can do will prevent men at home, who have the opportunity of moving about this country when on leave and furlough, from having an advantage in finding employment over men who are still kept beyond the oceans. Why should this difficulty be based only upon the uniformed men at home? Over 1,500,000 munition workers have been released from their war-time jobs. Only 50,000 of these, I understand, are to be used for the intake. They are being absorbed, I trust, rapidly in peace-time industry. Are not these munition workers having an advantage over men kept abroad and over the men kept in uniform at home? Are not they getting the first pick of the jobs in peace-time industry? Whatever we do, there must be heart-burnings, but these heart-burnings are more likely to be eased by paying substantial compensation to the sufferers than by inflicting suffering on larger numbers.

I am well aware that in paragraph 5 of his recent paper the Minister of Labour and National Service has stated that once the release of a group has become due, the men in that group are let go at once and not kept with the Colours until the men abroad have been found transportation and have been brought to this country. That was a very reasonable concession, but it departs from the principle of absolutely equal treatment as between men abroad and men at home. Men in the same group may get out several months earlier merely because they are serving at home. We have been driven from the position of absolute abstract justice with reason and good sense, and surely, having departed from the principle with good reason and with good results, we should not exclude from our minds a further advance.

Now I come to the women. I have never admitted that the principles of the Bevin scheme of priority of release in accordance with age and length of service need necessarily be applied to the women in the three fighting Services. Whatever men in group A might feel about other men with less service being released before them, or the order of priority being broken to their relative disadvantage, they do not feel the same about women. The women do not compete with the men in the same way or to the same degree. Besides, the innate chivalry of British soldiers will not dwell long upon nice calculations of relative age and length of service as between men and women. If it can be proved that a woman is necessary for some indispensable task connected with our commitments or our demobilisation, let her be kept until the due time for her release arrives. More especially is this true if it can be shown that in any particular instance a woman is replacing a man higher up the scale who can be released as a result of her retention.

But I am not speaking of this class. I am speaking of the very large numbers of young women in the three Services who have been kept doing nothing, fooling around with every kind of futile, fanciful task, to their own annoyance and at wasteful expense to the State. Every woman who is not irreplaceable in her present Service job, except by a man of higher category, should be released on giving a month's notice.

I earnestly hope that the Government will give unprejudiced attention to the suggestions I have ventured to make. They are put forward in no spirit of controversy but in the general interest. If we do not get this country going again pretty soon, if we do not get the great wheels turning, we may lose for ever our rightful place in the post-war economic world and we may involve our finances in dire and irretrievable confusion. It is no party matter, but one in which the House as a whole should make its opinion felt in a way that will override all hesitations and obstacles which are found in the path. In order to bring us all together, I will end this practical discourse in a philosophic vein. The inherent vice of capitalism is the unequal sharing of blessings. The inherent virtue of Socialism is the equal sharing of miseries. In the present case, where an overwhelming majority of Service men and women would gain the blessings, can we not unite on the broad democratic principle of "The greatest good of the greatest number" ?

THE ALAMEIN DINNER

A SPEECH IN THE ALBERT HALL
23 OCTOBER 1945

THIS is indeed a memorable occasion, for it is the first of the Eighth Army Alamein Dinners held since the War was won, and I hope it will be the precursor of a long line of annual celebrations. The Battle of Alamein takes its place with the most famous victories in British history. It was the turning point in British military fortunes during the World War. Up till Alamein we survived. After Alamein we conquered. It coincided also with the turn of the tide on the immense Russian Front and was the herald of the great Anglo-American invasion of North-West Africa.

When I arrived in Cairo at the beginning of August, 1942, I found a grave and critical situation. I found also a British and Imperial Army that did not know why it had been forced to retreat 400 miles with the loss of 80,000 men. It was an Army in no wise daunted, but an Army bewildered and enraged. My visit synchronised with the arrival of very powerful reinforcements, including the very latest weapons and tanks, which had been set in motion some months before. It was only after most careful consideration, aided by the advice of General Brooke and Field Marshal Smuts, that I proposed to the Cabinet the changes of command which were necessary. General Alexander became the Commander-in-Chief in the Middle East, with a definite Directive to concentrate all his efforts against Rommel and, after the death in action of General Gott, the illustrious Field Marshal who has just spoken, took the command of the Eighth Army into his strong and skilful hands. The appointment of these two great officers, whose names at the time were little known outside professional circles, will be acclaimed by history. Neither of these two men was ever defeated or long checked in the intense and bloody fighting which was before us all in so many different lands in the thirty-three months which lay before us and our goal. "Alex" and "Monty" are now household words. They are beloved by the peoples of the Empire, as they were by their soldiers, and their fame will long be cherished by their fellow countrymen and honoured by the free nations of the world.

It is of Monty, as I have been for some time allowed to call him, that I speak especially to-night. The advances of the Eighth Army under his command will ever be a glittering episode in the martial annals of Britain and, not only of Britain but, as the Field Marshal has said, of the mighty array of Commonwealth and Empire which gathered around this small island and found its representation in all the desert battles. Field Marshal Montgomery is one of the greatest living masters of the art of war. Like Stonewall Jackson, he was a professor and teacher of the military science before he became an actor on the world stage. It has been my fortune and great pleasure often to be with him at important moments in the long march from Mersa Matruh to the Rhine. Either on the eve of great battles, or while the struggle was actually in progress, always I have found the same buoyant, vigorous, efficient personality with every aspect of the vast operation in his mind, and every unit of mighty armies in his grip.

He is now discharging a task of enormous responsibility and difficulty in the administration of shattered and ruined Germany and we look to him to help those misguided and now terribly smitten people through the sombre winter which is approaching. I cannot doubt that after that he has further first-rate contributions to make to the future structure of the British Army. I therefore feel it an honour that he should have proposed my health and that he should have wished to associate me here with the Eighth Army and its glorious victory.

Long may old comradeship continue between those who fought side by side at Alamein. May it also continue among all who fought in the desert and by their unflinching courage and unwearying vitality and fidelity raised the reputation of the British Armies.

FOREIGN POLICY
[MOTION FOR THE ADJOURNMENT]

A SPEECH TO THE HOUSE OF COMMONS
7 NOVEMBER 1945

---

27 October—President Truman, speaking at Navy Day celebration in New York City, says that "the United States will not recognise any government imposed upon any nation by the force of a foreign power and that the present differences among the Allies are not hopeless or irreconcilable". He adds that the United States must hold the atomic bomb as a sacred trust and urges world co-operation as a means of outlawing atomic destruction.

1 November—Lord Winster, Minister of Civil Aviation, announces Government's intention to nationalise air transport.

1 November— Dr. Dalton, Chancellor of the Exchequer, announces plan to nationalise Cable & Wireless, Ltd.

[7 November 1945

THE departure of the Prime Minister for the United States in all the present circumstances is so important, that we thought it right there should be a Debate in this House beforehand. Although we are divided in domestic affairs by a considerable and widening gulf, we earnestly desire that in our foreign relations, we shall still speak as the great united British Nation, the British Commonwealth and Empire, which strove through all the perils and havoc of the war, unconquered and unconquerable. It is our wish, on this side of the House, so far as we can give effect to it, and as long as we can give effect to it, that the Prime Minister shall represent abroad, not only the Socialist majority in the present, and we trust, transient House of Commons, but all parties in the State. What I am anxious to submit to the House this afternoon has no other object than that.

From the conversations I have had with the Prime Minister and the Foreign Secretary, I have formed the opinion that His Majesty's Government would think it inopportune to-day for our Debate to range over the whole European scene, or to deviate either into the tangled problems of particular European countries, or into the troubles of the Middle East, for example, Greece, Syria, Palestine, Egypt. It would seem wise to concentrate, therefore, as much as possible, on the eve of a mission of this character, upon the supreme matter of our relations with the United States, and, in particular, as it seems to me, upon the momentous declaration to the world made by President Truman in his Navy Day address in New York on Saturday, October 27th.

It would not, however, be possible to speak on this subject of the United States without referring to the other great partner in our victory over the terrible foe. To proceed otherwise would be to derange the balance which must always be preserved, if the harmony and poise of world affairs is to be maintained. I must, therefore, begin by expressing what I am sure is in everybody's heart, namely, the deep sense of gratitude we owe to the noble Russian people and valiant Soviet Armies, who, when they were attacked by Hitler, poured out their blood and suffered immeasurable torments until absolute victory was gained. Therefore, I say that it is the profound desire of this House—and the House speaks in the name of the British nation—that these feelings of comradeship and friendship, which have developed between the British and Russian peoples, should be not only preserved but rapidly expanded. Here I wish to say how glad we all are to know and feel that Generalissimo Stalin is still strongly holding the helm and steering his tremendous ship. Personally, I cannot feel anything but the most lively admiration for this truly great man, the father of his country, the ruler of its destinies in times of peace, and the victorious defender of its life in time of war.

Even if—as alas, is possible—we should develop strong differences on many aspects of policy, political, social, even, as we think, moral, with the Soviet Government, no state of mind must be allowed to occur in this country which ruptures or withers those great associations between our two peoples which were our glory and our safety, in the late frightful convulsion. I am already trespassing a little beyond those limits within which I have agreed with the Government it would be useful that this Debate should lie, but I feel it necessary to pay this tribute to Soviet Russia with all her tragic load of suffering, all her awful losses and devastation, all her grand simple enduring effort. Any idea of Britain pursuing an anti-Russian policy, or making elaborate combinations to the detriment of Russia, is utterly opposed to British thought and conscience. Nothing but a long period of very marked injuries and antagonisms, which we all hope may be averted, could develop any such mood again in this land.

I must tell the House, speaking with my own knowledge, that the world outlook is, in several respects, to-day less promising than it seemed after the German capitulation of 1918, or after the Treaty of Versailles in 1919. I remember well the period immediately after the last war, when I was a Minister in high office and very close to the Prime Minister of the day. Then, there were much higher hopes of the world's future than there are now. Many things, no doubt, have been done better this time, though we have not yet felt the effects of them, but certainly there is to-day none of that confidence among men that they or their children will never see another world war, which there undoubtedly was in 1919. In 1919 there was the same sense of hope and belief as there is now that we were moving into a new world and that easements and ameliorations awaited the masses of our people. But added to that, there was the buoyant and comforting conviction that all the wars were ended. Personally, I did not share that conviction even at that enthusiastic moment, but one felt it all round one in a degree that is lacking to-day.

It is our first duty to supply the solid grounds on which this hope may arise again and live. I think the speech of the President of the United States on October 27th is the dominant factor in the present world situation. This was the speech of the head of a State and nation, which has proved its ability to maintain armies of millions, in constant victorious battle in both hemispheres at the same time. If I read him and understand him correctly, President Truman said, in effect, that the United States would maintain its vast military power and potentialities, and would join with any like-minded nations, not only to resist but to prevent aggression no matter from what quarter it came, or in what form it presented itself. Further, he made it plain that in regions which have come under the control of the Allies, unfair tyrannical Governments not in accordance with the broad principles of democracy as we understand them, would not receive recognition from the Government of the United States. Finally, he made it clear that the United States must prepare to abandon oldfashioned isolation and accept the duty of joining with other friendly, and well-disposed nations, to prevent, and to carry out those high purposes, if necessary, by the use of force carried to its extreme limits.

It is, of course, true that all these propositions and purposes have been set forth in the Declaration of the United Nations at San Francisco in May. None the less, this reaffirmation by the President of the United States on October 27th is of transcendant importance. If such a statement had been made in the Summer of 1914, the Kaiser would never have launched an aggresive war over a Balkan incident. All would have come to a great parley, between the most powerful Governments of those days. In the face of such a declaration, the world war of 1914 would not have occurred. Such a declaration in 1919, would have led to a real Treaty of Peace and a real armed League of Nations. Such a declaration at any time between the two wars, would have prevented the second. It would have made the League of Nations, or a world League strong enough to prevent that re-arming of Germany which has led all of us through so much tribulation and danger, and Germany herself to punishment and ruin which may well shock the soul of man. Therefore, I feel it is our duty to-day in the most definite manner, to welcome and salute the noble declaration made by the President of the United States and to make it plain that upon the principles set forth in the 12 Articles, which follow so closely upon those of the Atlantic Charter, we stand by the United States with a conviction which overrides all other considerations. I cannot bring myself to visualise, in its frightful character, another world war, but none of us knows what would happen if such a thing occurred. It is a sombre thought that, so long as the new world organisation is so loosely formed, such possibilities and their consequences are practically beyond human control.

There is a general opinion which I have noticed, that it would be a serious disaster if the particular minor planet which we inhabit blew itself to pieces, or if all human life were extinguished upon its surface, apart that is to say, from fierce beings, armed with obsolescent firearms, dwelling in the caverns of the Stone Age. There is a general feeling that that would be a regrettable event. Perhaps, however, we flatter ourselves. Perhaps we are biased: but everyone realises how far scientific knowledge has outstripped human virtue. We all hope that men are better, wiser, more merciful than they were 10,000 years ago. There is certainly a great atmosphere of comprehension. There is a growing factor which one may call world public opinion, most powerful, most persuasive, most valuable. We understand our unhappy lot, even if we have no power to control it.

Those same deep, uncontrollable anxieties which some of us felt in the years before the war recur, but we have also a hope that we had not got then. That hope is the strength and resolve of the United States to play a leading part in world affairs. There is this mighty State and nation, which offers power and sacrifice in order to bring mankind out of the dark valley through which we have been travelling. The valley is indeed dark, and the dangers most menacing, but we know that not so far away are the broad uplands of assured peace. Can we reach them? We must reach them. This is our sole duty.

I am sure we should now make it clear to the United States that we will march at their side in the cause that President Truman has devised, that we add our strength to their strength, and that their stern sober effort shall be matched by our own. After all, if everything else fails—which we must not assume—here is the best chance of survival. Personally, I feel that it is more than survival. It may even be safety, and, with safety, a vast expansion of prosperity. Having regard to all these facts of which many of us here are aware at the present time, we may confidently believe that with the British Empire and Commonwealth standing at the side of the United States, we shall together, be strong enough to prevent another world catastrophe. As long as our peoples act in absolute faith and honour to each other, and to all other nations, they need fear none and they need fear nothing. The British and American peoples come together naturally, and without the need of policy or design. That is because they speak the same language, were brought up on the same common law, and have similar institutions and an equal love of individual liberty. There is often no need for policy or statecraft to make British and Americans agree together at an international council table. They can hardly help agreeing on three out of four things. They look at things in the same way. No policies, no pacts, no secret understandings are needed between them. On many of the main issues affecting our conduct and our existence, the English-speaking peoples of the world are in general agreement.

It would be a mistake to suppose that increasingly close and friendly relations between Great Britain and the United States imply an adverse outlook towards any other Power. Our friendship may be special, but it is not exclusive. On the contrary, every problem dealing with other Powers is simplified by Anglo-American agreement and harmony. That is a fact which I do not think the Foreign Secretary, or any one who took part in the recent Conference, would doubt. It is not as if it were necessary to work out some arrangement between British and Americans at a conference. In nearly every case where there is not some special difficulty between them, they take the same view of the same set of circumstances, and the fact that it is so, makes it all the more hopeful that other Powers gathered at the Conference will be drawn into the circle of agreement which must precede action.

It is on this basis I come to the atomic bomb. According to our present understanding with the United States, neither country is entitled to disclose its secrets to a third country without the approval of the other. A great deal has already been disclosed by the United States in agreement with us. An elaborate document giving an immense amount of information on the scientific and theoretical aspects was published by the Americans several weeks ago. A great deal of information is also common property all over the world. We are told by those who advocate immediate public disclosure, that the Soviet Government are already possessed of the scientific knowledge, and that they will be able to make atomic bombs in a very short time. This, I may point out, is somewhat inconsistent with the argument that they have a grievance, and also with the argument, for what it is worth, that we and the United States have at this moment, any great gift to bestow, such as would induce a complete melting of hearts and create some entirely new relationship.

What the United States do not wish to disclose is the practical production method which they have developed, at enormous expense and on a gigantic scale. This would not be an affair of scientists or diplomatists handing over envelopes containing formulæ. If effective, any such disclosure would have to take the form of a considerable number of Soviet specialists, engineers and scientists visiting the United States arsenals, for that is what the manufacturing centres of the atomic bomb really are. They would have to visit them, and they would have to dwell there amid the plant, so that it could all be explained to them at length and at leisure. These specialists would then return to their own country, carrying with them the blue-prints and all the information which they had obtained together, no doubt, with any further improvements which might have occurred to them. I trust that we are not going to put pressure on the United States to adopt such a course. I am sure that if the circumstances were reversed, and we or the Americans asked for similar access to the Russian arsenals, it would not be granted. During the war we imparted many secrets to the Russians especially in connection with Radar, but we were not conscious of any adequate reciprocity. Even in the heat of the war both countries acted under considerable reserve.

Therefore, I hope that Great Britain, Canada and the United States will adhere to the policy proclaimed by President Truman, and will treat their knowledge and processes as a sacred trust to be guarded for the benefit of all nations and as a deterrent against aggressive war. I myself, as a British subject, cannot feel the slightest anxiety that these great powers should at the present moment be in the hands of the United States. I am sure they will not use them in any aggressive sense, or in the indulgence of territorial or commercial appetites. They, like Great Britain, have no need or desire for territorial gains. Personally, I feel it must be in most men's minds to-day that it is a matter for rejoicing that these powers of manufacture are in such good hands. The possession of these powers will help the United States and our Allies to build up the structure of world security. It may be the necessary lever which is required to build up that great structure of world security.

How long, we may ask, is it likely that this advantage will rest with the United States? In the Debate on the Address I hazarded the estimate that it would be three or four years. According to the best information I have been able to obtain, I see no reason to alter that estimate, and certainly none to diminish it. But even when that period is over, whatever it may prove to be, the progress made by the United States' scientists and, I trust, by our own, both in experiment and manufacture, may well leave us and them with the prime power and responsibility for the use of these dire super-human weapons. I also agree with President Truman when he says that those who argue that, because of the atomic bomb, there is no need for armies, navies and air forces, are at present 100 per cent wrong. I should be glad to hear, in whatever terms His Majesty's Ministers care to express themselves, that this is also the view of His Majesty's Government.

I cannot leave this subject without referring to another aspect which is forced upon me by speeches made in a recent Debate on the Adjournment. It was said that unless all knowledge of atomic energy, whether of theory or production, were shared among all the nations of the world, some of the British and American scientists would act independently, by which, I suppose, is meant that they would betray to foreign countries whatever secrets remained. In that case, I hope the law would be used against those men with the utmost rigour. Whatever may be decided on these matters should surely be decided by Parliaments and responsible governments, and not by scientists, however eminent and however ardent they may be. Mr. Gladstone said that expert knowledge is limited knowledge. On many occasions in the past we have seen attempts to rule the world by experts of one

kind and another. There have been theocratic governments, military governments and aristocratic governments.
It is now suggested that we should have scientistic—not
scientific—governments. It is the duty of scientists, like
all other people, to serve the State and not to rule it
because they are scientists. If they want to rule the State
they must get elected to Parliament or win distinction in
the Upper House and so gain access to some of the
various administrations which are formed from time to
time. Most people in the English-speaking world will,
I believe, think it much better that great decisions should
rest with governments lawfully elected on democratic
lines. I associate myself with the majority in that opinion.

The hon. and gallant Gentleman the Member for the
King's Norton Division of Birmingham [Captain Black-
burn] showed the other night that some breach of trust
had already occurred, when he referred to the secret
agreement signed by President Roosevelt and myself at
Quebec in 1943, and endeavoured to give some account
of it. Let me say that, so far as I am concerned, I have
no objection to the publication of any document or any
agreement which I have signed on this subject with the
late President. Surely, however, this is a matter for both
the British and United States governments to settle
together in full agreement. Neither of them has the right
to publish without the consent of the other, and it would
be very wrong for anyone to try to force their hands or
press them unduly.

CAPTAIN BLACKBURN [Birmingham, King's Norton]:
May I point out that I did not make the suggestion
that I knew of any secret agreement or that a leakage
had occurred. I said that it was apparent from the Smyth
Report, to which the right hon. Gentleman has referred,
and from the White Paper and other circumstances, that
some such agreement must, in fact, have been entered
into.

MR. CHURCHILL: I took great pains to read carefully
what the hon. and gallant Gentleman said in his very
eloquent and able speech, and I think the references
which I have made to-day, and which also were carefully
considered, will be found appropriate and not unjust. I
am not making any attack. I only say that it occurred to
me to be quite clear from what he said that there has been

somewhere a breach of confidence, which he published and brought to the notice of the House in the exercise of his responsibilities as a Member of Parliament. This, of course, was immediately telegraphed to the United States, and at the Press Conference the next day President Truman was questioned about it. A truncated report appeared in some of the newspapers here, with the answers which he gave, but not setting forth the exact question which elicited the answer. I have taken pains to verify the actual text of the answers which President Truman gave at his Press Conference on October 31st. He was asked by correspondents the following question:

"Mr. President, it was said in the House of Commons yesterday that President Roosevelt and former Prime Minister Churchill reached a secret agreement at Quebec on the peacetime use of the atom bomb. Do you——"

The President interposed:

"I do not think that is true."

Those were the exact words, where he interposed.

"As nearly as I can find out, on the atom energy release programme, Great Britain, Canada and the United States are in equal partnership on its development, and Mr. Attlee is coming over here to discuss that phase of the situation with the President of the United States.

QUESTION: Well, Mr. President, are these three countries in equal possession of the knowledge of how we produce the bomb?

THE PRESIDENT: They are.

QUESTION: Great Britain knows as much about how we produced that as we do?

THE PRESIDENT: They do."

It seems to me that that is a satisfactory statement of the whole position, and it affords an exceedingly good basis upon which the Prime Minister may begin any discussion he may wish to have with the President. Subject to anything that the Foreign Secretary may say, I strongly advise the House for the present to leave the question where it now lies.

May I in conclusion submit to the House a few simple points which, it seems to me, should gain its approval? First, we should fortify in every way our special and friendly connections with the United States, aiming always at a fraternal association for the purpose of common protection and world peace. Secondly, this association should in no way have a point against any other country, great or small, in the world, but should, on the contrary, be used to draw the leading victorious Powers ever more closely together on equal terms and in all good faith and good will. Thirdly, we should not abandon our special relationship with the United States and Canada about the atomic bomb, and we should aid the United States to guard this weapon as a sacred trust for the maintenance of peace. Fourthly, we should seek constantly to promote and strengthen the world organisation of the United Nations, so that, in due course, it may eventually be fitted to become the safe and trusted repository of these great agents. Fifthly, and this, I take it, is already agreed, we should make atomic bombs, and have them here, even if manufactured elsewhere, in suitable safe storage with the least possible delay. Finally, let me say on behalf of the whole House that we wish the Prime Minister the utmost success in his forthcoming highly important visit to Washington.

BRUSSELS UNIVERSITY

A SPEECH ON RECEIVING DEGREE
15 NOVEMBER 1945

MONSIEUR LE PRESIDENT, Monsieur le Recteur, Ladies and Gentlemen.

It is a real pleasure for me to visit this great seat of learning and an honour, which I deeply appreciate, to receive, on the occasion of my visit, the degree of Doctor in the Faculty of Law. If there is one word which men associate with the name of Brussels University it is Freedom. Founded in an atmosphere of newly-won freedom for the purpose of defending freedom of thought against all encroachments, the University can proudly claim to have fulfilled its mission.

It was right that it should close its doors during the German occupation; for there was no place for it in a Nazified Europe. Only when the armies of our deadly enemy had been swept away from Belgian soil could professors and students meet again to resume their normal tasks.

This did not mean that they were idle while the University was closed. Many of them entered the ranks of the resistance movement. Some of the University's choicest sons have suffered death at the hands of Hitler's executioners or in his loathsome concentration camps. Their example will, I am sure, shine like a beacon for those who follow the path they once trod.

You said, in the course of your address, for which I thank you, Monsieur le Recteur, that one of the principles for which this University stands was "the free examination of thought and ideas". How little then is it be wondered at that this institution should have been one of the first targets of the German invader in Belgium. For while the Nazis affected to despise thought and criticism, actually they feared and hated it even more than the physical weapons of their adversaries. How often used Hitler to sneer at the virtues of objectivity and toleration! How zealously did his army of brownshirts set about stamping them out wherever they were to be found in Germany itself during the early days of his régime! That people, always so docile in the face of a tyrant, watched one puny bastion of freedom after another go down before the Nazi onslaught without stirring a finger to protect them.

Yet when the Nazis overran the occupied countries, they found to their cost that here freedom was built on firmer foundations. They used every kind of method to achieve their ends. More subtle than the Kaiser's Huns they sought at first to conceal their brutal aims behind a screen of correct behaviour and specious promises. It was a gilded cage into which they tried to entice the unwary.

The concessions which they at first demanded seemed even reasonable. Some there were in the occupied countries who in the early days found themselves caught behind the glittering bars. Let us be thankful that there were institutions like Brussels, like Leyden, like Prague, where the traditions of liberty were so firmly rooted that no thoughts of compromise could be entertained. The wave of totalitarianism beat against them in vain. The example they set was soon followed by the rest of their fellow-countrymen. Many who had been dismayed by the German victories took fresh courage: many who had been for a moment deceived by the enemy's specious promises, recovered themselves and became men again. The movements of active resistance were born and played a worthy part in their countries' liberation. So the evil dream passed and the chance to renew their lives in an atmosphere of freedom was restored to the sorely-stricken countries of Europe.

Yet the champions of freedom can never afford to sleep. Intolerance and persecution are no sooner overcome than they return in new shapes. Institutions like Brussels University, which have so manfully withstood the assaults of Nazidom, have special importance in a Europe which is emerging from its long sickness. This is my message to those whom I am so happy to call my new associates. Always be on guard against tyranny whatever shape it may assume. Remember the cause of Freedom for which heroes died. Thus, and thus alone, will you be worthy sons and daughters of the honoured University to which you belong.

LOUVAIN UNIVERSITY

A SPEECH ON RECEIVING HONORARY DEGREE
AT THE BRITISH EMBASSY, BRUSSELS
15 NOVEMBER 1945

MONSEIGNEUR,

The Catholic University of Louvain has a long and noble history; for there the Christian virtues have been taught ever since the fifteenth century. Among the names of its Rectors, your own will be remembered in its annals as one of the most distinguished of all. Therefore, I am greatly honoured by the decision of this seat of learning to confer on me the degree of Doctor of Law. It is a source of regret to me that the shortness of my stay in Belgium has prevented me from receiving this honour in the University itself, and I must thank you and your colleagues for your courtesy in coming here for the purpose of holding this ceremony.

I have just returned from your sister University of Brussels where a similar honour has been conferred upon me, and where I had occasion to congratulate professors and students for their worthy attitude during the German occupation of your country. I know well that when the members of its Council reached their resolve to close their doors sooner than yield to the demands of the Nazi oppressors, they were fortified by the knowledge that they could count on a hospitable welcome for their students at Louvain. More fortunate for the moment than they, thanks to the powerful protection of the Vatican, you were able to set their minds at rest on the one score which might have caused them anxiety—the future of their charges. Thus, forgetting old rivalries, the Universities of Belgium—for Liége and Ghent did the same—presented a united front to the Germans, thereby laying the foundations for that future resistance which was to prove so effective an element in victory.

When, as was inevitable, the Nazis turned their attention to Louvain and demanded from you, Monseigneur, the lists of your students with a view to conscripting them for slave labour in their war factories, they met with a firm refusal. Threats were of no avail: nor when they imprisoned you in a common gaol, did you flinch for a moment. Let me assure you that when the news of actions such as yours reached the shores of Britain from the occupied countries, they provided no small encouragement to us in our struggle, for they showed us that in Europe there were still men and women who had faith in our ultimate victory and who were prepared to risk imprisonment and death in the same cause for which we ourselves were fighting.

Thirty years ago all the world heard of the destruction of the Library of Louvain University. A wanton deed, a horrid scene, lit—as Mr. Asquith called it—by the "flames of barbarian vengeance". Much was done by American generosity to repair the losses after that war. Now this time you again fell a victim to the same ruthless foe. Many of your treasured possessions have again been burnt or destroyed. The lustre which the University has won must be your consolation. I beg you to convey my sincere regrets to all teachers and students that I have been prevented from expressing my thanks and good wishes to them in Louvain itself. I wish you all success in your work of reconstruction and in the larger purposes that lie before you.

A SPEECH TO
THE JOINT MEETING OF THE SENATE AND
CHAMBER, BRUSSELS

16 NOVEMBER

---

16 *November—Tudeh Party in Azerbaijan rebels against Persian Government.*

[16 *November* 1945

THE ties between Great Britain and Belgium found their culmination in the great struggle from 1914-1918. It was hoped that the wars were over. Yet we have witnessed an even more destructive world-wide struggle. Need we have done so? I have no doubt whatever that firm guidance and united action on the part of the Victorious Powers would have prevented this last catastrophe. President Roosevelt one day asked what this War should be called. My answer was, "The Unnecessary War". If the United States had taken an active part in the League of Nations, and if the League of Nations had been prepared to use concerted force, even had it only been European force, to prevent the re-armament of Germany, there was no need for further serious bloodshed. If the Allies had resisted Hitler strongly in his early stages, even up to his seizure of the Rhineland in 1936, he would have been forced to recoil, and a chance would have been given to the sane elements in German life, which were very powerful especially in the High Command, to free Germany of the maniacal Government and system into the grip of which she was falling.

Do not forget that twice the German people, by a majority, voted against Hitler, but the Allies and the League of Nations acted with such feebleness and lack of clair-voyance, that each of Hitler's encroachments became a triumph for him over all moderate and restraining forces until, finally, we resigned ourselves without further protest to the vast process of German re-armament and war pre-

41

paration which ended in a renewed outbreak of destructive war. Let us profit at least by this terrible lesson. In vain did I attempt to teach it before the war.

The tragedy of Europe shocks mankind. It darkens the pages of human history. It will excite the amazement and horror of future generations. Here in these beautiful, fertile and temperate lands, where so many of the noblest races of mankind, the heirs of Roman civilisation, the champions of Christian chivalry, have developed their character, their arts, and their literature, we have twice in our own lifetime seen all rent asunder and torn to pieces in frightful convulsions which have left their mark in blackened devastation throughout many ancient States and famous cities. And had not Europe's children of earlier times come back across the Atlantic Ocean with strong and rescuing arms, all the peoples of Europe might have fallen into the long night of Nazi totalitarian despotism.

In this work of rescue our British island, which has repeatedly in the last 400 years headed victorious Coalitions against European tyrants, has also now played a decisive part. Upon Britain fell the proud but awful responsibility of keeping the Flag of Freedom flying in the Old World till the forces of the New World could arrive. But now the tornado has passed away. The thunder of the cannons has ceased, the terror from the skies is over, the oppressors are cast out and broken, and we find ourselves breathless but still alive, exhausted but free. The future stands before us, to make or mar. Two supreme tasks confront us. We have to revive the prosperity of Europe: and European civilisation must rise again from the chaos and carnage into which it has been plunged: and at the same time we have to devise those measures of world security which will prevent disaster descending upon us again.

In both these tasks, Belgium and the Belgian people must play an honourable part. The restoration and rebuilding of Europe, both physical and moral, is animated and guided by the kindred themes of Liberty and Democracy. These words are on every lip. They have cheered us and helped to unify us in the struggle. They inspire our rejoicings in the hour of victory. Now that the fighting is over, it is necessary to define these glorious war cries with more fullness and precision.

You will pardon me if I come a little closer to the
conception of free democracy based upon the people's will
and expressing itself through representative assemblies
under generally accepted constitutional forms. There are
certain simple, practical tests by which the virtue and
reality of any political democracy may be measured. Does
the Government in any country rest upon a free, constitutional basis, assuring the people the right to vote according
to their will? Is there the right of free expression of opinion,
free support, free opposition, free advocacy, and free
criticism of the Government of the day? Are there Courts
of Justice free from interference by the Executive or from
threats of mob violence, and free from all association with
particular political parties? Will these Courts administer
open and well established laws associated in the human
mind with the broad principles of decency and justice?
Will there be fair play for the poor as well as for the rich,
and for private persons as well as for Government officials?
Will the rights of the individual, subject to his duties to
the State, be maintained, asserted, and exalted? In short,
do the Government own the people, or do the people own
the Government?Here are some of the more obvious tests
by which the political health and soundness of any community may be ascertained.

Above all, there must be tolerance, the recognition of the
charm of variety, and the respect for the rights of minorities.
There was a time when the Age of Faith endeavoured to
prevent the Age of Reason, and another time when the
Age of Freedom endeavoured to destroy the Age of Faith.
Tolerance was one of the chief features of the great
liberalising movements which were the glory of the latter
part of the nineteenth century, by which states of society
were reached where the most fervent devotion to religion
subsisted side by side with the fullest exercise of free
thought. We may well recur to those bygone days, from
whose standards of enlightenment, compassion and hopeful
progress, the terrible twentieth century has fallen so far.

Now let us think of our other supreme task, the building
of a world-instrument of security, in which all peoples,
great and small, have a vital interest, and assuredly none
more than those who dwell in the famous "cockpit of
Europe". I do not take the view which was fashionable
some time ago that the day of small States is ended, and

that the modern world can only adapt itself to great Empires. I trust that the new world-instrument of the United Nations, upon which so many of our hopes are centred, will be strong enough and comprehensive enough to afford security and justice to large and small States alike. For this purpose however the help and guidance of the greatest Powers, as they now stand forth in the world, cannot be set aside. The more closely these Great Powers are bound together in bonds of faith and friendship, the more effective will be the safeguards against war and the higher the security of all other States and nations.

It is evident of course that the affairs of Great Britain and the British Commonwealth and Empire are becoming ever more closely interwoven with those of the United States, and that an underlying unity of thought and conviction increasingly pervades the English-speaking world. There can be nothing but advantage to the whole world from such a vast and benevolent synthesis. But we also in Britain have our Twenty Years' Treaty with Soviet Russia which in no way conflicts with other associations, but is none the less cherished by us as one of the sure anchors of world peace. We hope that in due course the natural unity and alliance between Great Britain and France may find reaffirmation in a new treaty. Then there are our well-known ancient links with Belgium and other countries, which in past years have stood such formidable trials.

Special associations within the circle of the United Nations, such as those of which I have been speaking, or the great unity of the British Empire, or the association which prevails throughout the Americas, far from weakening the structure of the supreme body, should all be capable of being fused together in such a way as to make it indivisible and invincible. I see no reason why, under the guardianship of a world organisation, there should not arise the United States of Europe, which will unify this Continent in a manner never known since the fall of the Roman Empire, and within which all its peoples may dwell together in prosperity, in justice, and in peace.

CONSERVATIVE PARTY
CENTRAL COUNCIL MEETING

A SPEECH AT FRIENDS HOUSE, EUSTON ROAD
28 NOVEMBER 1945

---

21 *November—Russian troops halt Persian troops sent to suppress rebellion.*

21 *November—Opening of the International Military Tribunal at Nuremberg.*

[28 *November* 1945

YOU give a generous welcome to one who has led you through one of the greatest political defeats in the history of the Tory Party. It may perhaps be that you give me some indulgence for leading you in some other matters which have not turned out so badly.

In October 1940, at your desire I accepted the Leadership of the Conservative Party because I felt it absolutely necessary for the sustained, vigorous direction of the War to be political chief of this great, strong Party with whom I have so many ties of sentiment and conviction. With the solid, unflinching, unwavering support of the Conservative Party, with its large majority over all other Parties in the House of Commons, I was able to impart those elements of stability and authority to the Coalition Government which carried us safely through the long years of war. On my decisive dismissal from power by the electors when the victory was won, I deemed it my duty to remain at the head of the Conservative Party until better arrangements could be made. But I am sure you will all realise that I hold the Leadership you have conferred upon me, not from any motives of personal ambition—for what could I possibly want?—but only because of the strong convictions which I hold about the future of our country, and my desire to serve you as long as you may think me of any use, or I feel that I have anything worthy of your acceptance to give.

I have used such facilities as remain to me to organise an opposition Front Bench in the House of Commons of really able, competent, modern-minded men, and we have at least a score of trained and experienced politicians, including new and younger figures, all of whom are united in their resolve to carry forward the cause of the greatness of Britain, her Commonwealth and Empire, and her place in the world. Behind us the new Parliament has brought a large accession of ability by which we shall be steadily supported and reinforced as the work of the present Parliament proceeds. It is well that this should be so, because the plight into which our country has fallen on the morrow of its wonderful victory, requires the utmost persistent endeavours of all who believe in the strength, the continuity, and the grandeur of the British name.

I hope you will believe that it is with no personal bias, soreness or conceit that I declare that the vote of the nation at the General Election was one of the greatest disasters that has smitten us in our long and chequered history. We need not waste time in examining the reasons which led to that event. As I said in the House of Commons in June, 1940—that breathless moment in our existence; "If we open a quarrel between the past and the present we shall find that we have lost the future." Let us advance then into the future with the same confidence and dogged determination which all the world admired in those days when our national life and, may we not say, the freedom and glory of the world were at stake. If every measure is taken, as it should be taken, if every effort is made, as it must be made, if every act of comradeship and audacity is performed, as it will be performed, there is no reason why we should not lead our country out of its hideous lapse and error in domestic affairs, just as we in Britain did in the great world struggle, of which for a whole year we bore the brunt alone. Here, happily, we have not got to fight the terrible foreign foe, but only to regain the goodwill and revive the morale of our own fellow-countrymen who came such a melancholy cropper at a moment when the opportunities of Britain were so great and our tasks so hard.

We have no longer to face the mortal perils of foreign conquest and subjugation. There are however other dangers which lie about us on every side which, if not overcome and defeated, will cramp and press the British nation down to levels we have never contemplated, and rob us not only of our place in the world which we won by superb achievement, but also of that reasonable prosperity for all classes on which we have hitherto erected our English and British way of life. Therefore so long as you care to maintain me in my present position, I shall call upon every man and woman who values the true greatness of our country and the noble Commonwealth and Empire spread around it, to do their utmost to revive the powerful heart-beat of our race and nation, and to make headway against the morbid and reactionary Socialist sectarians who, in an unguarded moment, led our people so far astray and got their stranglehold upon Britain. The struggle, I can assure you, will be hard and long, but I am as certain as I ever was in the darkest days that, provided we do not fail or falter or flag, we shall once again have the honour of guiding the destiny of Britain.

Let me now survey some of the aspects of this new conflict, far above Party or class interests, on which we must embark. Only four months have passed since, for the first time in our history, we became hag-ridden by the Socialist doctrinaires. I had hoped that however the new Government might feel, or whatever their difficulties might be with their own extremists, they would at least have devoted themselves to the task of reviving and ultimately liberating these islands after the inevitable thraldom and sacrifices of the war. Surely this practical duty, so vital, so urgent to every home, should have had overriding priority above Party fads and slogans and over long-term visionary roads to Utopia.

We are at a point in our history where the choice which Oliver Cromwell placed before his victorious soldiers is again before us. It is the choice between "Being and Wellbeing". But as you know well from the daily and hourly experiences of your lives, we are being harassed, harried, hampered, tied down and stifled for the sake of vain, ill-thought-out and physically unattainable plans for a Socialist future. If we look across the Channel to a small country like Belgium, which I visited a few days ago, we see a Socialist Government in power

47

with Communists included in it. But what are they working for at the moment? Their whole idea is to get their country's head above water, to get the industries to work, get the ravages of war repaired, and make trade thrive and prosper. As we look across the broad Atlantic, we see the mighty evolution of the United States from war to peace proceeding in a violent, convulsive, passionate manner, which causes no doubt great commotion and disturbance, but which has already led to an enormous increase of output of all necessary things for the home market, with an immense, ever-growing overspill for foreign export.

Now these are very vital months for our island. We are cruelly burdened and smitten by the sacrifices and supreme exertions which we made in the war. We do not seek to live on the charity of other nations. Whatever is the standard of living we can maintain and develop in this island, we are resolved to achieve it by our own exertions. But what is Mr. Attlee's Government doing? I say they are hampering and delaying the practical recovery of Britain for the sake of their Party fads and bitter, cast-iron Socialist dogmas. From every quarter the same tale comes to hand. All enterprise, all initiative, is baffled and fettered. The queues are longer, the shelves are barer, the shops are emptier. The interference of Government Departments with daily life is more severe and more galling. More forms have to be filled up, more officials have to be consulted. Whole spheres of potential activity are frozen, rigid and numb, because this Government has to prove its Socialistic sincerity instead of showing how they can get the country alive and on the move again.

Let me set before you several major facts which are already affecting nearly every family in this island. First, the demobilisation of the Services is proceeding at a rate far below what any efficient administration would have achieved. Vast masses of men are being held under military discipline, kept not only from their homes but from the industries and jobs which are clamouring for them. No military reason justifies keeping over 4 millions of men under compulsory military service at the present moment. Many Service men were deluded into voting for the Socialists by the prospects held out to them of a far more speedy release. What has happened is that at least a million and a half are being kept doing nothing, or at invented tasks, by a pedantic adherence to the Bevin Plan. This Plan, of which in many respects I entirely approve, was prepared for a situation when the war with Germany would be over, and the war with Japan would continue for at least eighteen months thereafter. It is wholly inapplicable to the present and actual position.

Then there is Housing. Mr. Aneurin Bevan, who distinguished himself so much during the war by his bitter taunts at every moment of difficulty and exceptional danger, is in charge of Housing. But he cannot find time to rebuild our shattered houses. He is too busy chasing landlords and profiteers around the ruins. The building trades throughout the country are hampered and paralysed. The necessary builders are not being got out of the Services in order to begin the work. The whole vast, intricate building apparatus of private enterprise, which built 250,000 houses every year before the War, has been deliberately cast under a cloud as if it were something indecent and improper and, at any rate, to be sharply discouraged. But even the local authorities, which are Mr. Bevan's chosen instrument, are themselves hampered and baffled by needless labyrinths of controls and particular conditions.

The gloomy State vultures of nationalisation hover above our basic industries. It may well be that some of these experiments in nationalisation will have to be tried. There are great numbers of our fellow-countrymen who only learn, as indeed we all do, by the process of trial and error. It is only, I fear, by suffering that the British people will learn the best course to take. The profit-motive, we are told, must be eliminated from these basic industries. Instead there will be the loss motive which, after various permutations will emerge as a heavy and additional charge either upon the public in higher costs of fuel and travel, or, as is more probable, in heavy additional charges upon the national Exchequer.

We are told that everything must be concentrated upon the export trade. But whoever supposed that a fertile and healthy export trade could be maintained except on the overspill of a very much larger internal and domestic trade? A healthy export is the cream upon the far greater volume in the milkpail. Whoever thought of starving the home trade as a peacetime measure of stimulating exports?

Sir Stafford Cripps is under the profound delusion that he can build up an immense, profitable export trade while keeping everything at the minimum here at home. Look what he is doing to the motor car industry. It is astonishing so clever a lawyer should not have got his case up better. He is a great advocate of "Strength through Misery". He tried this theme on the public when he entered the Government in February, 1942. I did not like it. I preferred 'Strength through Victory", and that is what we got. And that is what we have got to get now.

Every effort is made by the Socialist Government to restrain, diminish and, if possible, destroy the purchasing or consuming power of the public. They assure us that if this purchasing power, which used to be considered the foundation of prosperity is not damped down and choked, we shall have a rise in prices which mean a continuance and aggravation of inflation, or, in other words, a fall in the purchasing power of money. But surely the remedy for this is not scarcity but abundance? The remedy is to fill the shops with the simple goods and utensils which every household and home in the country needs. Then we shall have a beneficial cycle instead of the dismal vicious circle in which at present we are forced to rotate.

All these things fit together. If we get the workers out of the Forces, and get the factories moving and get the goods into the shops, then the more purchasing power the better. The Socialists put the emphasis the wrong way round. They begin with restriction, they prolong the scarcity, and they found on this scarcity an argument for further restriction. Their root principle is that it is much better that everyone should have half-rations rather than that anyone should have double. But why not try to get whole rations for everyone even if some get more? If they began by production and the release of national energy, they would soon produce the volume of consumer goods which would enable the mass of the people to buy with their hard-won savings some of the things they need so much.

Over all this hangs the vast problem of our finance, external and internal. When Sir John Anderson, Chancellor of the Exchequer in the Coalition Government, over which I presided, framed the Budget for the year 1945-6, ending on March 31st, 1946, he planned to obtain for our war needs alone by taxation and by borrowing four thousand five hundred million pounds. That was on the basis of twelve months of war in its culminating intensity against both Germany and Japan. But Victory crowned our efforts far sooner than we dared to hope. When March 31st, next year is reached, there will only have been the equivalent of three months of war out of the twelve months for which the Budget was provided. Of course there are great winding-up expenses, but is it not a staggering fact that the new Chancellor of the Exchequer only expects to save by this nine months shortening of the war out of twelve about £200 million from a total of £4,500 million—about one fortnight of war expenditures? I say without any hesitation that at least eight hundred million could have been saved by sensible, vigorous administration of the finances, and of course by setting free on earlier dates some of the millions of men and women who are now kept in camouflaged unemployment apart from any military need, not by the Generals—that is a falsehood—but by the Socialist politicians.

All the gravely disquieting facts dominate, paralyse and starve the recovery to which the British people are entitled after their long struggle. Unless the Government can be compelled by public opinion and Parliamentary pressure to amend their courses, we shall be left far behind in the race for export markets, on which it is universally agreed we depend for half the food we eat and most of our raw materials.

In time of war when national survival is at stake, everyone expects restrictions, privations and hardships. In addition to bombing, many of the sufferings of the front are endured by the civil population at home. In wartime you have had a great deal of Socialism in our own time. Most people hoped that when the war was over and all our enemies were forced into unconditional surrender, there would be easement, improvement and liberation of national energy for peacetime production. But the Socialists as a definite part of their policy condemn us to endure the restrictions and rigours of war as a part of our normal life in time of peace. Sir Stafford Cripps appeals to us to endure austerity with fortitude.

51

I say without a moment's hesitation we are quite ready to endure any amount of necessary, unavoidable hardship. We do not shrink from austerity if that is the only road to salvation. But surely at the same time it lies with those who inculcate these sombre courses to prove that they themselves are, by every form of human wit and contrivance, trying their best to get the country on its legs again, to bring it through and out of this hard period, and so regain our place as a living and active community in the tremendous world that is growing up around us.

The attempt to socialise Great Britain is fraught with mortal danger. There has never been a community in the world like ours. Here in this small island we maintain forty-six millions of people, who played a greater part per head in winning the world-war than any other people, and who, before the war, had developed a standard of living and social services above that of any country in Europe and in many respects above that of the United States. These forty-six millions differ from every other community that has ever existed in the world by the fact that they are perched upon the completely artificial foundation of not providing even one half of their food, and being dependent for the purchase of the bulk of their food and raw materials on persuading foreign customers, to accept the wares and the services they offer. Vast, intricate, delicate, innumerable, are the methods of acquiring external wealth which the British nation has developed in recent generations, and the population has grown step by step upon the livelihood produced. This is no country of vast spaces and simple forms of mass production. We have important and substantial basic industries. We have an agriculture which, out of self-preservation, we are expanding to the utmost. But it is by many thousands of small individual enterprises and activities that the margin by which alone we can maintain ourselves has been procured.

Here is where the application of Socialist doctrines can destroy Great Britain far more surely than the magnetic mine, or the air-raid, or the U-boat warfare. They will choke and dry up, and they are choking and drying up, all these multitudinous processes and giving in return nothing but promises and formulas. The Socialists are planning to make the Thames flow; there is to be a grand opening ceremony; after long preparation the sluices will be opened, and the ancient river will roll forward amid loud cheers—but meanwhile they are cutting off and drying up all those countless rills by which alone the flood waters of our prosperity and life can be provided. A catastrophe is approaching this country of a different character but just as serious as occurred in 1939. Happily it is more easily to be avoided by sensible action while time remains. Will that action be taken or not? I am astounded that the principal Ministers in the Government do not see what is coming towards them.

I learn from the newspapers that we have borrowed or are to borrow about one thousand million pounds from the United States: how long is that going to keep us going? And what are the remedies or comforts which the Socialist Ministers offer? Fortitude—austerity—"tighten your belts"—"prepare yourselves to suffer, we are at the helm". For the rest, cheap and bitter abuse of every form of property, of every kind of enterprise except those which are owned by the State, and, above all, rigid, universal, overlapping controls throughout the whole of the infinitely varied impulses of our natural British life. I warned the nation before the war, and my advice was not taken. I warn them now that nothing but a genuine wholehearted effort not only to liberate but to stimulate the entire life-energies of our people will carry us through the crisis in our national economy into which we are already plunged and which will intensify with every month that passes.

Some have said to me: "Let us have a new policy for the Tory Party." The Four Year Plan, the greatest Social Reform Programme ever put forward by any British Government, has not even been passed into law, let alone into administration. Never mind, they say: "We want something fresh. Formulate, please, a new programme with novel counter-attractions of baits and bribes and promises to win back a majority from our large well-meaning electorate." At the same time and sometimes the same people, complain: "Why do we not oppose more strongly many of the Government's Bills?" I will tell you why. Because in many cases for some time to come they are in great measure our own Bills—like the vast Insurance Bill, —which we advocated and prepared in the Coalition, and which we are determined by conviction to place upon the Statute Book for the good of the British people. But legislation will not suffice at this moment in our national fortunes. The Socialists, in their pamphlet at the election, said: "Let us face the future". Surely now we have a more immediate task when all is so grim: "Let us face the present".

It is the duty of everyone to do their utmost for the country; night and day they should be thinking about it and its anxious problems. It is incredible to me that any patriotic man or woman could be guilty of apathy at a time like this. If we do our duty there is no reason to be downhearted, whether we succeed or not in saving the country from a grievous ordeal we shall have done our best. And why should we not succeed? Even under the adverse and unique conditions of the recent election we are half the nation. When the Socialist Government, in their clumsy arrogance, imposed upon us war-time controls for five more long years, they had not got a majority of the electorate behind them. Together with the Liberals and Independents who voted we represented a larger total of votes against the five-years' restriction than those who voted for it. The Socialists have no majority in the nation; even with all the adventitious aid they got at the last election, they are a minority. They have a right to govern and administer the country but they have no right to ride rough-shod over the majority of their fellow country-men.

All this which I have been gathering together and laying before you this morning—and it is but a small part of what could be said—leads me to a conclusion, which I beg you most gravely to ponder over in your hearts. I foresee with sorrow but without fear that in the next few years we shall come to fundamental quarrels in this country. It seems impossible to escape the fact that events are moving and will move towards the issue—"The People versus the Socialists". On the one hand will be the spirit of our people, organised and unorganised, the ancient, glorious, British people, who carried our name so high and our arms so far in this formidable world. On the other side will be the Socialists doctrinaires with all their pervasive propaganda, with all their bitter class hatred, with all their love of tyrannising, with all their Party machinery with all their hordes of officials and bureau-cracy. There lies the impending shock, and we must be ready to meet it as a true People's Party, gathering together all that is vital and healthy in our island life and caring for nothing except the glory, strength, and freedom of Britain.

GOVERNMENT POLICY (MOTION OF CENSURE)

A SPEECH TO THE HOUSE OF COMMONS
6 DECEMBER 1945

"That this House regrets that His Majesty's Government are neglecting their first duty, namely, to concentrate with full energy upon the most urgent and essential tasks of the re-conversion of our industries from war-time production to that of peace, the provision of houses, the speedy release of men and women from the Forces to industry, and the drastic curtailment of our swollen national expenditure; and deplores the pre-occupation of His Majesty's Ministers, impelled by Socialist theory, with the formulation of longterm schemes for nationalisation, creating uncertainty over the whole field of industrial and economic activity, in direct opposition to the best interest of the nation, which demands food, work and homes."

WE are here today on a Motion of Censure, but it is not the Opposition who have introduced acrimony into our proceedings. When we met for the first time four months ago, we refrained from conflict. I pointed out that there never had been a Parliament in which there was so great a body of work to be done in which all had an equal interest, or of legislation to be passed to which all parties were committed. Ideological differences may be deep and wide, but I certainly hoped that there would have been a very broad and continuing measure of co-operation upon practical tasks, and that these would have had priority. We therefore, did not divide upon the Address in reply to the Gracious Speech, and the Leader of the House taunted us the other day for not having done so. I went out of my way, perhaps further than I should have done, to mitigate any shock to our credit abroad which might have been caused by the Government's announcement of the nationalisation of the Bank of England, only to be derided by the Leader of the House for speaking in less alarmist terms than I had done in the heat of the election.

Throughout we have done our best, even when we did not entirely agree, to make easy and nationally united the course of foreign politics. The Prime Minister found it convenient to refer appreciatively to this in his speech to the American Congress. But when the Government insisted upon keeping on for five years by legislation all the extraordinary controls, which even in the heat of war we only renewed from year to year, and when they rejected our friendly proposal for a two-year period, they showed that they were imbued with the spirit of faction. They showed a desire to humiliate their defeated opponents, and a desire to have every economic detail of the social life of our country held in a war-time grip indefinitely and obviously for purposes far beyond those of the transition from war to peace. The Leader of the House actually complained, as no man charged with the duty of leading the House of Commons has ever done in my recollection, that we were not having enough "first-class" rows. The whole attitude of the Leader of the House, seconded by the Minister of Health—is to offend, wound, injure and provoke those over whom they have got so great a Parliamentary majority, but who nevertheless represent half the nation, and will shortly represent a large majority out of doors. The Prime Minister may not be aware of all this, though he has had a long and intimate experience of the personalities and methods of both the Ministers to whom I have referred. The Prime Minister has not sought in any way to embitter or inflame our proceedings. Perhaps he will have to hurry up and toe the line this afternoon, but he has no interest in doing so. The Prime Minister's prevailing interest must be the success of his Administration. He does not need to grind his personal axe, and will probably be content if he can keep hold of it. We are, therefore, glad he is here and safely back.

It is my first submission to the House and the country that the Government, through their leading mouthpieces in the House of Commons, and through their aggressive policy, have deliberately sought to aggravate the division which unhappily exists in our country, and that not only their policy but their methods and their manners are intended to provoke and exacerbate. That is my first submission. There is another theory which may be put forward to explain the Government's behaviour, or the behaviour of the Ministers who have acted in this way. They are under heavy pressure, behind the scenes, from their extremists to do more and go faster even than they themselves think possible. Unless they can show they are hurting, injuring, provoking their political opponents, they will not be able to placate their wild men, or control some odd elements that nestle under their wing. If that be so, they may at this moment be congratulating themselves on this Motion of Censure, and rejoicing that they have lured us into their trap. Whatever the explanation may be, it leaves the Government convicted of the offence of faction for faction's sake, at a time when they have an immense duty to perform, and when they need the help of all parties for their large spheres of activity at home and abroad.

Last night the hon. Member for Bilston [Mr. Nally] drew an affecting picture of my personal position; the noble stag was dying, the curs were at his throat; his own friends behind him were hogs; and the hon. Member spoke of the pathos and tragedy of the scene. Let me reassure him that so far as my personal feelings are concerned, I only remain in politics because I think it my duty to try to prevent the great position we won in the war being cast away by folly, and worse than folly, on the morrow of our victory. The hoots and howls of the curs—the hounds, as the hon. Member for Bilston put it—do not worry me at all. So long as I am acting from duty and conviction, I am indifferent to taunts and jeers. I think they will probably do me more good than harm. I must say that the maiden glance of the hon. Member for Bilston at the House of Commons should impress us somewhat with the unfavourable impression we produce upon him. Here are hogs, there are hounds. I trust that a longer experience of this Chamber will make him realize that both those branches of the animal kingdom have their virtues. I am not at all worried about anything that may be said about me. Nobody would attempt to take part in controversial politics and not expect to be attacked.

What I am deeply distressed about is the state of our affairs and the prospects ahead. Our economic plight is not only grave, but extremely perplexing. We have the enormous administrative task to fulfil of repatriating and demobilising the Armies, and changing over to peacetime industry. The housing shortage for the returning troops gapes upon us. Conditions are hard, the authority of the responsible trade union leaders is challenged in many disquieting ways. Abroad, our relations with the United States have become more distant, and those with Russia more obscure. We are told the Big Three are never to meet again, which I heard with great grief. As for the five Foreign Secretaries who were to prepare so many things, all that seems to have fallen through. The condition of Europe is a nightmare. Fateful and difficult decisions await us in India.

I am not blaming the present Government for all this. The greater part was inherited in the consequence of the war and in our faithful, unstinted and prolonged exertions for the common cause. But I wonder what would have been said if a Conservative or even a National Coalition Government had been in office and had no better showing to offer than what we see at present. Why should the Government choose this moment of all others in our history, or their life, to proclaim great new departures in political theory, and why should they try to stir far-reaching changes in every mode of thought and every walk in life? Why should they raise this great schism of militant Socialism in the land, and divide us with what must involve increasing bitterness and lack of mutual comprehension with every further step they take? Can we afford an internal struggle of such a character, at such a time? Could there be a worse occasion for deep-seated organic changes in the life of Britain, now when she is exhausted and overburdened in a fearful degree? Certainly it is a moment peculiarly difficult. One would have thought we might at least have been allowed to recover normal mentality, that we might let people regain their ordinary homes after these strenuous years, and that at any rate there would have been reasonable restoration of our national life, before we were weakened and torn by the bitter political and social strife into which the Government or some Members of the Government seek to plunge us.

Certainly it was a very difficult and harassing inheritance for the new Ministry, but it was also a noble opportunity. Especially was this so after the swift defeat of Japan had cleared the way for the great steps of release and liberation and of transition from war to peace. If the Labour Party could have done this well, the country realizing all the difficulties of the task, would indeed have awarded them the meed of lasting praise. Why can they not, even now, set aside every impediment, and concentrate upon the splendid though formidable task which they have demanded and obtained from the nation the right to discharge? Alas, it is primarily a partisan and doctrinal triumph which they seek, and not that fame and honour which would come to them from a great national task rapidly, efficiently and brilliantly executed. It is upon them that the responsibility must lie for the growing division and consequent weakening of the nation. It is they who are the innovators, they who are the disturbers.

I should have thought that the first endeavour of responsible Ministers would be to secure the greatest measure of co-operation between all parties and all forms of national activity. I do not mean a coalition, but a concerted effort. It would take all our united strength to make our way out of the dangers and embarrassments by which we are surrounded and to give the masses of the people, who have done so well and endured so long, a fair chance of renewing their lives after the harsh sunderings of war. If I had obtained a substantial majority at the last election my first thought would have been to seek the co-operation of the minority, and gather together the widest and strongest measure of agreement over the largest possible area. Very different is the treatment which has been meted out to us, and which has already produced party antagonism, bitter as anything I have seen in my long life of political conflict. I charge the Government with deliberately trying to exalt their partisan and factional interests at the cost not only of the national unity but of our recovery and of our vital interest. There is the foundation and the gravamen of this Motion of Censure.

For my part, I believe profoundly that the attempt to turn Great Britain into a Socialist State will, as it develops, produce widespread political strife, misery and ruin at home and that, if this attempt involves nationalisation of all the means of production, distribution and exchange—to quote the orthodox phrase which I understand was reaffirmed at the Labour Party meeting in May—then this island will not be able to support above three-quarters of the population which now inhabits it. Not only is this the worst time for such experiments, but this country is the least fitted of all large communities to endure such a convulsion. I was pointing out the other day how intricate, delicate, complex and precarious are our methods of gaining a living in a hard competitive world. We are not like Russia with its vast oceans of land to develop. We are an old, and, since the population expanded so largely, highly artificial country, more like Venice which built an empire on piles driven into the lagoons, or like Holland whose dykes keep out the sea, or like Egypt whose life is the Nile and irrigation. Here we have 48,000,000 of people and more than half of them must be fed from afar. Surely a measure of common prudence should regulate the actions of the British Government and restrain their triumph over their fellow countrymen.

I wish now to speak of the effect of these political party and ideological antagonisms, which the Government have caused, which I fear they feel it necessary to their internal vigour to foment, upon all the vast processes of trade and manufacture by which alone we live. Let me make it clear that it is the duty of every man in this country, wage-earner or employer, to do his best for the welfare and survival of the nation from day to day, irrespective of his political views or dislike or fear of the administration. If the bitterness which Socialist politicians are injecting into party and party life were to find its counterpart or its ally in the whole relations of capital and labour throughout the land, our misfortunes would accumulate with a hideous momentum. Every effort must be made by capitalist employers, in every form of private enterprise, to do the best possible for their businesses and for the country under the conditions which prevail. They must not allow themselves to be deflected by the hostility shown to them and their class and their functions by Socialist Ministers. They must seek for the utmost possible production of which they are capable and which is permitted to them.

The Government for their part also have to face realities. If industry and enterprise are weighted down by colossal confiscatory wartime taxation it will not be able to revive. If industry and enterprise are fettered, hampered and hobbled at every step by an ever-spreading network of controls and regulations, and if every act of commerce is first to take taxation into account, and secondly, to obtain the innumerable permits required, there will be a vast loss or even arrest of energy at a time when we can least spare it. We have had all kinds of Governments in Britain, but never in this commercial trading island a Government which set itself out to stigmatise, and so far as they dare to eliminate, as if it were an abuse or even a crime, the profit motive by which the commercial affairs of the vast majority of human beings in almost every land have been regulated since the dawn of civilisation. There has never been a Government which set out to revive our prosperity on such a confidence-killing, impulse-sapping theory as that. Undoubtedly, if the warfare which the Government are carrying out against their opponents in Parliament is extended to the class and interest they dislike in industry they will, at this most critical juncture in our national existence, enforce an enormous handicap upon the whole productive, inventive and resilient element inherent in our race and culture.

I will now deal with the affairs of the four Ministers who are directly responsible for the key departments at home—the Minister responsible for demobilisation, the Minister responsible for housing, the Minister responsible for trade and the Minister responsible for our national solvency. Here my complaint touches not only failure through political prejudice, but failure through a lack of confidence and lack of management which has already slowed down the whole movement of the Government machine, except where partisan and doctrinal stimuli are at work. Surely the taproot of everything is demobilisation. Have the Government justified themselves upon this great task or not? We know well that they have changed their minds. Their original scheme, put forward with all their authority, has proved by their own admission and corrective action to be utterly out of relation to the problem. Very considerable concessions have been wrung from them by pressure which they resent, and by criticism which the Minister of Labour—who ought to be grateful—described as "mischievous and irresponsible".

What are the facts to-day? What is the first fact which stares us in the face? There are still upwards of 4,000,000 persons detained by compulsion in the Armed Forces of the Crown. At what rate is this enormous total being reduced? We have been told that a rate of 12,000 a day has now been developed and will be maintained till the end of the year. That is certainly an improvement, but why, then, are we to prepare ourselves for a contraction of this rate to less than 9,000 in the New Year? Why in the New Year, when transport ought to be more abundant and there has been a long time to make arrangements for using transport efficiently? I ask specifically that this drop from 12,000 to 9,000 at the turn of the year should be prevented. I ask specifically that that step should be taken. What are the Americans doing? My right hon. Friend the Member for Aldershot [Mr. Lyttelton], in a massive and weighty opening speech yesterday, mentioned that in the three months after the end of the Japanese war the Americans demobilised at the rate of 35,000 a day. They are now demobilising at the rate of 50,000 per day as compared with 9,000 a day to which, we are told, unless something is done about it, we are to conform in the New Year. There is no excuse for our not demobilising at the same proportionate rate as the United States. They are 2¾ times as numerous as we are, but their demobilisation is 5½ times as fast, in fact double the British rate. As my right hon. Friend said, there is really no excuse for this. The distances over which the Americans have to repatriate large masses across the Atlantic and Pacific oceans are undoubtedly far greater in man miles than those with which we are concerned, having regard to the immense body of troops in this country, and other great bodies separated from us only by the distances from Italy and Germany to this island.

No one would object, at the present time, to any man or woman being kept in the Forces who wishes to stay on, or for whom there is a job to do. But in the circumstances with which we are confronted, is it not absolute madness to keep very large numbers of people against

63

their wish, on full pay and at great expense, doing nothing, or toiling at artificially invented work? How will it help comparatively small bodies of men in the Far East who have, to some extent, to lag behind in demobilisation through failures in the Ministry of War Transport, to know that for each one of them, eight, nine or ten men in England, Italy or Germany are kept needlessly crunching the gravel of the barrack squares or gathering seaweed by the salt sea waves? What advantage can it be to us a year hence, to have kept many hundreds of thousands of men and women on the treadmill of compulsory idleness for one, two, three, four, five or even six months extra? Anyhow, a year or 18 months hence, even on the Government's programme, they will have been released. What will it have availed us to feel they have stood about all this time, making up at our expense, a senseless accumulation of man-days of uniformed unemployment?

On the other hand, how great is the need for these men and women. On every side, the cry for more labour arises, not only for key men but for the great body of soldiers, airmen and sailors who are longed for in their homes and needed in their jobs, which are often waiting for them. I am well aware there is a counter case to this. I say, let the two cases be considered one against the other, and it will be only too plain where the balance of national advantage lies. We must do what I called the other day the greatest good to the greatest number. The Government have already departed, in important respects, from the Bevin scheme. Let preference in obtaining employment—I use the word preference deliberately, because my hon. and gallant Friend the Member for the Lonsdale Division [Sir Fraser], who is so much in touch with the British Legion and other bodies, says this is what they really care about—let preference in obtaining employment and other compensations be awarded to men retained, not deliberately but because of transport shortage or transport mismanagement beyond their proper order of release. But set the great mass free and above all set the women free as soon as they can be spared. I have never admitted for a moment that the principles of the Bevin scheme have an application in regard to women. If a woman is needed to allow a man of higher category to be released, it is another matter, but, to keep women needlessly, just because of tidiness, is, at this juncture, the quintessence of super-idiocy. I rest, in this matter, on the decisive figures that in January the Americans will be demobilising 50,000 men a day and we 9,000. That figure has a vital bearing on world recovery, and on our position in world markets at this peculiarly difficult moment.

I turn to home industry. President Truman told us last week that within 60 days of the end of the war with Japan, 93 per cent of the munitions industry of the United States had already been converted from war to peace conditions. That is a prodigious fact; not only because of its static but even more because of its dynamic significance. What proportion of our munitions industry has been reconverted? It must be remembered that the end of the Japanese war meant much less to us and the end of the German war meant much more to us proportionately than to the United States. At the end of September, when America was 93 per cent converted, we were only 3 per cent. Much vital time was evidently lost, to judge by the number of men and women still employed on supplies and equipment for the Forces, and by the end of this year the Government hope to achieve 72 per cent reconversion. I recognise the improvement, and I understand the difficulties, but it certainly is an astounding fact that, even at the end of this year, we shall be employing 670,000 more workers on making obsolete weapons of war six months after the German war is over, than in the summer of 1939, when all these horrors were about to break out upon us.

I come next to housing. I am glad to see the right hon. Gentleman the Minister of Health has emerged from the recess and taken his place on the fire-step. Contrary to the advice of the great Lord Bacon in his *Essay on Public Offices*, the Minister of Health is consistently reflecting on his predecessors, and dilating on the legacy of muddle and incompetency he has inherited from Mr. Sandys and Lord Portal. No doubt it is an attempt to excuse himself in advance from the impending failure of his own administration. I do not deny that the right hon. Gentleman inherited a legacy from the past. It is a rich legacy of achievement and preparation. This legacy he

E

has squandered with a jaunty profligacy which has rarely been equalled by a Minister who has still to make a reputation. Taking all the difficulties of the years between the wars, the British housebuilding industry grew in strength and efficiency until its output, in relation to the size of the population, was greater than that of any other country in the world. This highly-developed housebuilding machine, and the network of well-equipped manufacturing industries which support it and are almost inextricably interwoven with it, are part of the right hon. Gentleman's legacy.

The policy of the Coalition Government—not a Conservative Government—was to enlist the help of all housebuilding agencies of every kind. In addition to the emergency factory-made temporary houses, and to the normal houses built by local authorities, we intended, as soon as we were free from the day-to-day burden of the war at its peak—as soon as we got the men—to mobilise the full experience, initiative and organisation of the independent free enterprise housebuilders, including the small builder, and to produce lower-priced houses both to sell and to let. The present Government, however, have decided to deny all financial assistance to this very important section of the building industry, and to restrict their scope in all directions. Everything, in fact, is being done to make it more difficult for the independent builder to produce any large number of houses, and to place him at a disadvantage in relation to the heavily subsidised local authority. Moreover, when it comes to the allocation of labour and materials, the independent house-builder is evidently to be kept at the back of the queue. Government supporters, new-comers and experienced Parliamentarians alike, had better face this blunt fact. Without liberating, using, and encouraging the private, capitalist, profit-seeking, house-building industry to the full, as well as all other agencies, the housing problem will not be solved, and the people will suffer.

The Minister of Health, having decided to stake all on the local authorities, would surely do well to give them more practical evidence of his confidence in them. At present, they are, so I am told, hamstrung and restricted at every turn by the involved procedure of licences and approvals which have to be obtained from Government

Departments, before the first brick can be laid. If free enterprise house-building is to be chilled and checked to the utmost, cannot the local authorities be given the freedom to get on with the overwhelming task which has been piled upon them? Housing was put in the very fore-front of the Labour Party's election campaign. Socialist speakers up and down the country told the electors that their party would know how to build houses at a rate undreamt of under Conservative administrations.

"If the Labour Party is returned to power, housing can be dealt with in a fortnight."

According to the *Western Daily Press* of June 23rd, this was uttered by the President of the Board of Trade. [*Interruption.*] Well, he must have said something, you know.

THE PRESIDENT OF THE BOARD OF TRADE [SIR STAFFORD CRIPPS]: The right hon. Gentleman is per-fectly right. I said something, but not that.

MR. CHURCHILL: The right hon. Gentleman is very prudent in not endeavouring to inform us of the actual words, which he undoubtedly did use, and which were of so sanguine a nature as to give the impression that he was jumping at office like a dog at a bone. "Five million houses in quick time", was the promise of the Foreign Secretary. Let us see what progress there is to report. Until the German war was over and the builders were released, no Government could have produced any substantial number of completed permanent houses. We should, however, have expected to see by now signs of permanent house-building starting up on an appreciable scale throughout the country, whereas, as every one knows, it is still a very rare event to see a permanent house in course of construction.

The Minister of Health has allowed four months of excellent building weather to slip away. Instead of helping the house-building industry to start up again, he has been what is called "shadow boxing", against his own pet bugbear. All his opponents are racketeers, profiteers, monopolists, ring makers, and no doubt it may be that in a short time we shall also be called Fascist beasts. We have not come to that yet. Instead of tackling this essentially pratical task in a responsible and objective manner, he has been swayed at the start by

67

partisan spite and prejudice and by the hope of exploiting these vices to his own personal political ambitions. Both the industry and the local authorities have been waiting for a precise statement of the Government's policy and programme. Instead, the right hon. Gentleman's repeated evasions and vague threats have created a haze of uncertainty and suspicion, destroying confidence and paralysing initiative. Not only has he deprived himself of the most experienced sections of the house-building industry but he has insulted and discouraged the great building societies, who, before the war, did so much to help people with small means to buy their own homes. All their historic work, at a time when thought was not at all advanced on social subjects, is dismissed as mere money-lending.

While the right hon. Gentleman delivers lectures about the need for low housing costs, he has allowed the Cripps temporary bungalow to creep up to a price beyond the maximum which he allows for a full-size permanent brick house. He has callously discarded the Rural Housing Act, which provided financial assistance for the reconditioning of cottages for agricultural workers. Instead, he promises at some unspecified date to build prefabricated skyscrapers over the countryside. The right hon. Gentleman threatened us the other night with the disclosure of certain scandals if we asked questions about figures—"putrefying corpses", he called them—for which his predecessors, presumably Mr. Sandys and Lord Portal, were responsible. It is his duty to produce these facts. We cannot have a Minister of Health living among a lot of putrefying corpses. Anything would be better for these ex-Ministers, I am sure, than receiving a favour from the right hon. Gentleman. I am sure they would say with the great Duke of Wellington, when he was blackmailed by a harlot, "Publish and be damned". No doubt inspired by their colleague's example, the Minister of Works and the Minister of Supply have been busily spreading doubt and dismay throughout the whole of the building materials industry. They have announced in an airy fashion that they intend to go in for the manufacture and distribution of building materials in a big way, a ruthless State competition with the existing industry of country. When this important announcement was made the building-materials manufacturers over a very wide area of production had still not been informed of the articles they were to be expected to produce, or what materials the Government themselves intended to manufacture. In these circumstances it will not be surprising if materials and components of the right kind are not ready when they come to be needed.

The Government have reaffirmed the policy which I declared in my day of tackling house-building with the vigour of a military operation. I stand by that. The first essential of a military operation is to decide upon your objective. The Government have never made up their mind on the number of houses they hope to build by given dates, or, if they have, they are ashamed to publish the figure. The Minister of Health said, indeed, in one of his expansive and informative moments, that in the first 15 months after the war he would build very many more houses than were built by the Coalition Government after the last war. He did not mention, I notice, that the Minister of Health during most of that period was his colleague in the present Government, Lord Addison, who was sacked for his performance; nor did he mention that in the 15 months following the 1918 Armistice only about 1,000 houses were built throughout the land. Of course, if that is the yardstick by which the Government are going to measure their achievements, they certainly will not be accused of aiming too high.

The main difference between the situation now and the situation in 1918 is that the late Coalition Government, profiting by the experiences of the last war, made many of the necessary preparations for restarting house-building long before hostilities ceased. Does the Prime Minister wish to pass a Vote of Censure on himself? I am speaking of the Coalition Government, of which he was a most important Member, and I think it is true to say that many of the necessary preparations were made long before hostilities ceased. The result was that when the war came to an end last summer most of the essential legislation was already passed, and great numbers of actual building sites had already been cleared or approved, and in many cases were already in course of development. The objective of the Coalition Government was to provide 300,000 permanent houses, built or building, within two years of the end of the German war. This programme was ridiculed by the Lord Privy Seal [Mr. Arthur Green-wood] before the Election. He called it "chicken food". However, now that the election is over a new name is required, and the Minister of Health presents us with the term "crystal gazing". From "chicken food" to "crystal gazing". All these tactics will be exposed by events at no distant date, and I say to-day that unless the right hon. Gentleman changes his policy and methods and moves without the slightest delay, he will be as great a curse to this country in time of peace, as he was a squalid nuisance in time of war.

The course of my remarks now reaches the President of the Board of Trade [Sir Stafford Cripps]. Everyone knows the distinguished talents which the right hon. Gentleman brings unstintedly to the services of his fellow-countrymen. No one has made more sustained exertions to contribute to the common pot and few take less out of it than he does. I have got my vegetarian too, my honoured friend Lord Cherwell. These ethereal beings certainly do produce a very high level and a very great volume of intellectual output, with the minimum of working costs in fuel. When I learned that the right hon. Gentleman opposite had been sent to the Board of Trade I thought to myself, "if he will only deal with mighty business in a matter-of-fact, practical spirit, to produce definite results in a comparatively short space of time, he may render an enormous service to us all and even get us round the corner." I have not yet abandoned my hopes, though certainly up to the present moment his career at the Board of Trade has not only been disappointing to his friends, but disastrous to us all.

The right hon. Gentleman must dismiss from his mind the idea that it is within the power or thought of any human being at the present time, in the present organi-sation of society and with the present nature of man, to regulate in detail the entire movement and process by which our 48,000,000 people can earn their daily bread. He must clear his conscience of the awful question he has to ask himself so many times a day, "In giving this or that decision, am I betraying Socialism or not"? If he would only rid himself of these obsessions and inhibitions he could still be of great value to the fortunes of Britain.

Human beings, happily for them, do not have to direct all their bodily functions themselves. They do not have to plan in advance how many heartbeats they are to have in the next 24 hours or what relation their temperature or blood pressure should bear to those heartbeats. They do not have to decide, as a part of the daily routine, what secretions are to be made by the liver or kidneys. No official quota is set for lymph or bile. Otherwise I fear the President of the Board of Trade would find he had overdrawn his account very much. Providence has relegated these problems to the subconscious mind and left the commanding sphere to human reason.

Let the President of the Board of Trade reassure himself. We can breathe without him, if he will permit us. The country will never be without its volitions and impulses if only the Government will let it start. I assert that the revival of this country is at this moment being stopped, stifled, even strangled, by the resolve of the Board of Trade, followed by other cognate Departments of the Government, to regulate everything. Why can they not realize that the impulse and volume of national productive ingenuity and progress is overwhelmingly greater and far more fertile than anything that can be produced by Government officials or party planners? If the right hon. Gentleman would only realize the limitations of beneficial Government functions, if he would not harden his heart, like Pharaoh, and would set the people free, half his problems at least would end themselves. From every side we hear the complaint that the hands of initiative and enterprise are tied, and that permits have to be obtained for everything even in the smallest detail.

The President of the Board of Trade is trying to teach all the trades in the country how they should get back their business. He is rapidly gaining half-knowledge over a vast field. He wishes to hold everything gripped and frozen until he can form a general view and reconcile that view with the orthodox tenets of his Socialist religion. Meanwhile, the days, weeks and months are slipping away. It was with a chill that I read that in the second quarter after the end of the German war, our exports had not leapt up as enormously as one had hoped, but had actually fallen below the level of the previous quarter.

I hope there is an explanation for that. With the highest ideals, with the finest intelligence and the best intentions, the right hon. Gentleman may inflict upon this country injuries which will long last and will, as they bite deeper, bring ever greater hardship to the mass of the weekly wage-earners whom he sincerely desires to help.

The right hon. Gentleman has greatly disheartened, and still more severely hampered, the productive commercial energies of our people, and his Socialistic tenets have exercised an undue bias upon him in all his work. After all, so far as we know, in the next two, three, four or five years, the Government must rely upon private enterprise for between 80 and 90 per cent of their entire production from which the Chancellor of the Exchequer draws his revenue; and an even higher proportion rules in the export field. Why, then, harry and maltreat these thousand and one delicate and complicated productive processes? What is the use of adhering to a system of 80 per cent private enterprise for the next five years, and then declaring that the profit motive is a form of moral delinquency? Fancy a Government in a position of such economic peril and stress relying for 80 per cent of the national production upon private enterprise, and then setting themselves to denounce and, if possible, destroy the mainspring of private enterprise and, one of the main tests of its efficiency generally, private profit and general consequential benefit. The right hon. Gentleman propounded an argument from a sentence of mine taken from the report of my speech some days ago:

"Whoever thought of taking the home trade for export until the home market was satisfied?"

I never uttered such a sentence as that. The right hon. Gentleman got it from *The Times*, and in these days of paper shortage all reports are telescoped. This particular jumble was made out of several sentences and bears no relation to anything I have said or to anything which had a coherent meaning. I will not weary the House with what I actually did say, because *The Times* newspaper has printed the proper text, but I stand by what I said, and it in no way contradicts any other statement I made about the vital importance of the export trade at the present time, or the exceptional and fleeting opportunities which may be opened in that field.* All these matters are very urgent.

I referred a little while ago to Mr. Truman's statement. There is another point which should not be overlooked. President Truman said that by the middle of 1946 the metal working trades of the United States would be producing two and a half times their 1939 rate—by "rate" I presume is meant "volume"—of output of consumer goods. There is not a single peacetime manufactory in Britain which will be producing 100 per cent, and many will be far short of 60 and 70 per cent at that date. All this has its bearing on our power to reoccupy or retain the markets we have long held, and by which we have paid for our vital imports. The matter is very urgent indeed. We can see what the competition is going to be from this mighty community across the ocean, in all the neutral markets and markets on which we depend for our very daily bread.

Coming to this business of planning, the President of the Board of Trade, supported by his colleagues, demands a nationalised, planned, economic, social and financial policy. No one will deny that the Government have a great part to play in modern life and international trade. I stand by my declaration of 1943, some part of which was quoted by my right hon. friend the Member for Bromley [Mr. Harold Macmillan] yesterday. But are there not some very large questions which require State plans and Cabinet decisions, of which we have not heard much? Instead of devoting their energies to questions of ownership and of day-to-day fiddling with the multitudinous activities of this island I would invite the Ministers to pay some attention to the real economic problems facing this country and to try to formulate some plan for their solution. What, for instance, is their wages policy? There are economic arguments for keeping wages down and there are social arguments for letting them rise, although one thing is certainly wrong, and that is to allow decisions to be reached haphazardly and disconnectedly, as is apparently taking place now. If the Government believe in planning, let them plan here.

Then there is the export problem. Instead of upbraiding

---

* See page 49.

the motor industry, why does not the President of the Board of Trade take the responsibility for evolving an export policy of his own and relating it to the internal trade of the industry, an internal trade sufficient to sustain it, and put his plans forward for everyone to see? The only plan that I have heard put forward was received with howls of "Tripe" * from his assembled hosts—a form of hospitality which I cannot recommend and cannot commend, and which, in any case, would be of no use to him. What do the Government plan in capital policy? From where are the resources coming for all the projects of industrial development and much else that are in the air and that are being spoken of? A Government can usually raise money and can always print it, but the labour and materials represented by the money come in a different category. Labour and the savings of the community are the key. The pre-war unemployed have been absorbed, and possibly some of the women who have been drawn into industry will stay. We shall be very lucky if we have as much as a million more at work than we had in 1938.

How ,then, do the projects which are afoot relate to our resources? How can our resources and saving power be expanded and be made more fertile in order to meet our resources? The comments of the planners upon this situation would certainly be of interest and possibly of value. We have had no information, nor even sensible statement, from Ministers on any of these matters. The beginning of our story is the release of manpower. The end of our tale is finance. When we come to the discussions on the Budget next year, it will be necessary to unfold in a searching manner what other countries undoubtedly already know, namely, our most difficult financial position. Ours is the only country which was for almost six years in the war and which fought with its utmost strength in the workshops and in the field through all that awful peril. Very early in the days of the National Government the Chancellor of the Exchequer, Sir Kingsley Wood, raised direct taxation as a wartime measure to levels never attempted by any other modern

* During speech at Dinner of Motor Manufacturers and Traders, 15 November, 1945, when he said that Gt. Britain must go without cars.

society and to levels which cannot be surpassed, because on the higher ranges of income the amount is a complete confiscation. Every other form of taxation was also raised, and the financial conduct of the war stood at a level of strictness and severity unequalled in any other country or at any time. It is quite impossible that such scales of taxation should be maintained after the dire compulsions of war have passed away.

The Chancellor of the Exchequer [Dr. Hugh Dalton], has certainly done nothing to give confidence to the taxpayer or the investor, and, if he will allow me to say so, he has shown an altogether undue and unpleasant propensity to win party cheers by grinning and gloating over harsh financial measures. He speaks as if he had an income of £5,500,000,000 a year from which he has been graciously pleased to make an independent gift to the nation in his interim Budget of a net £90,000,000 and next year, no doubt, there will be a further benefit to come. But in the main, he plans to maintain the wartime taxes as a permanent feature of our economic life. It will be vain to look for trade revival or for the return of a general measure of easement or wellbeing in the nation as a whole. First of all, the right hon. Gentleman who holds the proud position of Chancellor of the Exchequer should insist upon the return of the manpower to civil life, and strike these millions of men and women off the useless charge account of the State. Next he should aim at giving to the taxpayer large scale and massive relief, both direct and indirect, both small and large. He should force the President of the Board of Trade to stimulate internal production as well as export trade, and thus secure at all costs some output in goods and desirable commodities to absorb the hard-won savings and purchasing power of the people. Perhaps he would not get so many cheers for this as he does in his policy of soaking the rich, so far as they exist, but a year or two hence he may win a reward in the respect of those who are acquainted with his problems and in the obvious relief in the life of the broad masses of the people. No reduction of taxation can be secured apart from a great reduction of expenditure.

Is it not a shocking thing—and this is one of the elements which led us to our Motion—that out of

£5,500,000,000 provided by Parliament for the purposes of full scale war against Germany and Japan in the present financial year, only £200,000,000 should be saved when the war will have lasted for the equivalent of only three or four months out of the 12? Of course, if you keep one and a half million men drumming their heels when they should be re-creating our vanished wealth it is easy to cast away the public treasure. However—this is a very small divagation—there is one economy which has been effected, and which might well have been dispensed with, and that is the £500 which the Government have secured by selling Hitler's bust to a parcel of malignant crackpots. I think that with all the millions flowing out, we might have denied ourselves that small appropriation in aid. Of course, if trade and industry are so hampered, disturbed and alarmed that their life thrust is diminished or arrested, no matter how high the taxes are pitched, the revenue will gain no advantage, or gain an advantage in an inflated currency alone.

We shall hear tonight what the Government have settled about the American loan. I trust, indeed, that agreement has been reached, but this above all other things I would say: Such a loan would give us, at the best, a couple of years' easement in our vital and primary import needs. We should be buying two years of grace, but for what? To set our house in order and to get our life energies on the move. If the Government are to borrow from the United States, and if strict terms are imposed by the United States, all the more is there an obligation upon Ministers to deal with our affairs upon their merits and on the dead level, and to clear away all this party and doctrinal trash and rubbish in these perilous days. Otherwise we shall come to the end of these two years with uncommon swiftness, and find ourselves in a position most hateful, namely, of being dependent upon the kindness, which may or may not be forthcoming, of a foreign Power.

As Leader of the Opposition, I have a very difficult task to discharge. I cannot bear to see so much squandered that has been so hard won, without making an effort to reverse the process. The Government reproach us with making their task more difficult, but what do they expect? Can we, with our convictions, as honourable men, as a great party in the State, afford, for the sake of appearances of unity, to acquiesce in a destructive downward trend in all our affairs at home and abroad? Are we not bound in honour to give our warnings in good time about the future, and to record our censure on the present? Would we not be blame-worthy before history if we sat supine and silent, while one folly and neglect is piled on top of another, and much that we fought for together is lost or frittered away? The only excuse for silence and inaction would be despair, and despair is not to be tolerated among Britons. Moreover, I am as firmly convinced as I was in 1940, that we have our future in our own hands, that we are still "masters of our fate and captains of our soul". But reflecting on all we have overcome, and by the mercy of Providence, survived, I cannot believe that we shall find ourselves destroyed by incompetence or partisanship. In order that Great Britain may enjoy the glory she has won and deserved, I call upon all who value her name and fame to drive home, before it is too late, by a Vote of Censure, the hard truths of the time upon a quite well-meaning, but misguided and inactive Government.

ANGLO-AMERICAN LOAN AGREEMENT
(MOTION FOR APPROVAL)

A SPEECH TO THE HOUSE OF COMMONS
13 DECEMBER 1945

EVERYONE is aware of the many objections to the Agreement which is now before us. The Government have in no way concealed their disappointment. They tell us that they have not been able to procure easier terms, and I think I may say that we wholeheartedly share their disappointment. Not only is there disappointment, there is deep misgiving as to what the consequences will be and also of our ability, however hard we try, to discharge successfully the obligations now to be imposed upon us.

I shall not attempt to repeat in detail the complicated technical arguments with which those who are particularly versed in this matter have enriched the Debate. I will only repeat the salient objections which we all feel. The first affects the loan. I was astonished that the United States should think it worth while to exact the equivalent of 1.62 per cent interest from their debtor in the special circumstances in which we find ourselves. This interest charge can play a very small part in the economy of the United States. In so far as it operates at all, it must be a deterrent upon their exporting power. They will be taking British imports direct, or round-about, in payment of the interest on the debt, instead of repayment for United States exports, which they desire and which it is in their interest to have continually increased. We are told that this is a commercial transaction and that the loan can only be viewed as a commercial transaction. I rather agree with what the hon. Member for Ipswich [Mr. Stokes] said. It is a great pity that a commercial transaction should be mixed up with other non-commercial transactions, such as the agreement at Bretton Woods, upon which we have to pass a Bill, or the Commercial Policy Declaration on which there is to be agreement between the two countries to approach together along concerted lines. All the arguments for treating the loan as a commercial transaction tell against linking with it acceptance of other extraneous, and altogether separate, agreements. It is a pity that we should have allowed a commercial loan agreement to be mixed up and linked up with other transactions. I do not like the mixture.

If we have misgivings in respect of the gold standard about Bretton Woods, or in respect of Imperial Preference about the Commercial Policy Declaration, we are told, "You are getting the loan". When it comes to discussing the loan, we are told, "This is a commercial matter and cannot be presented to Congress on any other basis". If the United States had seen fit to say, "We will give a grant-in-aid", or even "a loan without interest equal to these disbursements in America paid by the British before Lend Lease was in action", then it would have been to their interest to associate with so benevolent an act, agreements and understandings on other matters. As it is, we seem to have the worst of it both ways.

Everyone has drawn attention to the proposal to make sterling convertible into dollars within so short a time as 15 months, whereas at Bretton Woods it was contemplated there should be a delay of as much as five years before we accepted convertibility as a definite legal obligation, however much we might try, in the meanwhile, to accelerate the process in fact. From what I have heard stated in this Debate without challenge on either side of the House, and especially from my right hon. Friend the Member for Aldershot [Mr. Lyttelton], this convertibility proposal within 15 months appears to be a proposition so doubtful and perilous that the best hope is that in practice it will defeat itself, and that it is in fact too bad to be true. There is a lot in this. The trees do not grow up to the sky; indeed, I have found that to be so in a long life. That is the second obvious and salient point.

Thirdly, there are most objectionable provisions of the Commercial Policy Declaration which, for instance, require us, if we are incapable of finding dollars to pay for American imports of tobacco, cotton, or other commodities, to reduce also, in equal proportions, our imports from any alternative source. This is really a proposal upon which I earnestly trust the steady gaze of the just-minded people of the United States will be attentively fixed.

Finally, I resent, with every other hon. Member, the indecent haste with which these most serious complex matters are thrust before us, and have to be settled. There have been months of secret negotiation—each day there

have been rumours about them, which have been contra-
dicted by the rumours of the day after. Now, suddenly,
we are confronted with this set of complicated, grave,
far-reaching White Papers, and we are told that we must
accept them within a few days—indeed, within a limited
number of Parliamentary hours. I make it a cause of
complaint against the Government that they have let themselves be browbeaten in this matter of time. The date of
31 December for the ratification of the Bretton Woods
Agreement has no special sanctity. It has no more sanctity
than 31 March for the ending of our financial year. I well
remember being brought up to believe that 31 March was
a day of particular sanctity and that the world would come
to an end unless things were done by 31 March. One year
it happened that we could do nothing by 31 March, but
the world went on quite happily. I say that the date of
31 December was fixed for convenience, and it could be
altered for good reasons.

I have never heard any valid or solid reason why the
Bretton Woods date could not have been revised or
extended, or why we should not have said, "These matters
must be laid before Parliament, and Parliament will require,
at any rate, a considerable time in which to consider them
in the light of maturing public opinion". Such a request
from a cherished friend and faithful ally could never, for
any reason, have been used or made the ground for
breaking off negotiations on this matter so indispensable
to the two countries.

For these reasons, upon which it would be easy to
expatiate, we on this side of the House refuse altogether
to accept any responsibility for this set of transactions. We
recognize, that it is the duty of the Government to decide.
In international matters it is always our desire to associate
ourselves, so far as possible, with them. I very much regret
that we cannot do so on this occasion. The task falls to
me, as Leader of the Conservative Party, to give advice
to my hon. Friends as to what our conduct should be in
this present bleak and difficult situation. It would be a
great pity and would weaken us for our future tasks,
which are heavy, if we all voted in different Lobbies on
a question of this kind.

SIR WALDRON SMITHERS [Orpington]: Why?

MR. CHURCHILL: My hon. Friend asks why. I would

have thought that even the simplest process of ratiocination would enable him to supply the answer to that. We therefore thought it better and wiser to abstain as a body— [*Hon. Members: "Why"?*] For this reason. We thought it better and wiser to abstain as a body, and that is the course we intend to pursue.

THE SECRETARY OF STATE FOR FOREIGN AFFAIRS [MR. BEVIN]: How can you pursue it when you are sitting still?

MR. CHURCHILL: We are discussing the movements of the mind, and not the much more bulky shiftings of the human body. [*Laughter.*] This course is thoroughly justifiable in an Opposition whose vote cannot, in any case, decide the issue. There is no reason at all why we should share the responsibility of the Government. The responsibility lies wholly upon them, and they have the power to discharge it. Whatever we did with our votes in this House, we could not affect the position. [*Interruption.*] I am not asking for any advice from below the Gangway on the opposite side of the House as to what I should say by way of guidance to my own supporters. How do I know it would not be prejudiced advice? How would I know that those smiling gentlemen would not be anxious to lure me into some trap? They should take their advice on party leader-ship to the eminent Statesmen arrayed there in an uncomfortable line. We could not stop this arrangement if we were all united in wishing to do so. We are certainly not all united in wishing to stop it—that is a fact—any more than the party opposite are all united in wishing it to go through.

On the other hand, I cannot understand why we—the Opposition, the minority—should be expected to come forward to approve and welcome a proposal which fills every party in the House with great anxiety, and which is only commended to us by the fear of an even darker alternative. It is for the Government and their great majority to bear the burden. Whatever may be said to the contrary, our relations with the United States have definitely become more distant and more difficult since the establishment—[*Hon. Members: "No".*] Hon. Members surely want to hear the case deployed, otherwise the great gifts of the Foreign Secretary will not have full scope in answering them.

MR. GALLACHER [Fife, West]: You cannot blame me. I am sitting quiet.

MR. CHURCHILL: I am very glad there are no diversionary or distortionary tendencies evident in that quarter. Whatever may be said to the contrary, our relations have deteriorated. Both the great parties in the United States are wedded to the principle of free enterprise, and are opposed to the collectivist and totalitarian conceptions which underlie and animate Socialist policy. The fact that the United States is depicted as the last remaining haunt of capitalism, in a world which appears to them at the present time to be sinking and degenerating into Socialism or worse, consciously or unconsciously affects public opinion over there, and it affects also the movement of political thought in the American Congress. This makes the United States Executive authorities more than ever careful of the form in which their proposals are brought before Congress. If they reached an agreement with us and were not able to carry it through Congress, not only their prestige but the competence of the United States Executive as a negotiating power would be affected, and whatever their good will—and it is still very great— the Executive is inclined above all to protect itself from being stultified by a vote of the Legislature on a matter of grave international policy. Therefore, they safeguard themselves by taking every precaution, and in some cases double precaution, in the text of the documents which are made public.

It is this feeling which has told against us, and not any harsh sentiment or unworthy desire for material gain on the part of our American friends. [*Hon. Members:* "*Oh*".] We claim for our country that we fought from beginning to end, sacrificing everything for the common cause, allowing no thought for the morrow to conflict with the attainment of speedy victory. The United States may also claim, in spite of that expression of sentiment from below the Gangway, to have poured out their blood and treasure as a great fountain of Allied resistance to tyranny, and, long before they were themselves attacked by Japan, they rendered us invaluable aid through the great measure of Lend Lease, that most unsordid act in the history of nations, under which they paid over £5,000 million in aiding and expanding our war effort in the common cause. Whatever complaints we make about these present proposals, whatever misgivings—and they are very serious— are aroused in our breasts, both their generosity and the championship by the United States of the cause of freedom will ever stand forth as a monument of human virtue and of future world hope.

I am very glad that no one of the slightest responsibility, speaking in this Debate, has used any language likely to reflect upon the noble deeds of the people and Government of America, to make ill-will between our two countries, or mar the splendour of the story of the past. Neither must we underrate or fail to comprehend the point of view of the Congress and people of the United States. They see themselves confronted with a burden of internal debt amounting, I am told, to 262 thousand million dollars. That is about 65 thousand million pounds. Only their own gigantic exertions working unfettered and in free enterprise, can enable them to sustain and conquer.

MISS LEE: If there is that internal debt, does it not mean that some Americans have done what most Americans detest—some Americans have made a fat profit out of the war?

MR. CHURCHILL: I am not here to deal with the details of American administration, but very heavy excess profits duties were imposed there, as here, and even if individuals in a foreign country make profits in the course of the war, that is no reason for saying that we have not benefited greatly from the help received from that country, nor for denying our tribute of gratitude and respect. They see themselves confronted with this enormous burden of debt, they see across the Atlantic political conceptions and ideologies which they regard as widely divergent from the whole of their vast wealth-getting processes. It remains for the ineffable Mr. Laski to emphasize this aspect to them on various inopportune occasions. They have no doubt read of the dazzling expectations held out to the people of this country by those who have since been victorious at the polls, expectations which are not only of a far higher standard of life, but of a far easier life, than any that has existed in Britain before. They have, perhaps, heard talk of the 40-hour week from the T.U.C. Meanwhile, they themselves, although far better circumstanced than we are, have a host of difficulties upon them, which the most strenuous exertions of the whole vast impulse of the life-thrust of their production will be needed to overcome. While we feel acutely our position, we must not lose the faculty of understanding that of other people. It is this flow of mutual comprehension which I regard as the most hopeful element in the future.

Many speak of the privations we should suffer if we did not receive this £1,000 million loan. That, in my view, is the least part. What I should regard as utterly fatal would be a prolonged rough and tumble struggle in the economic and financial sphere between the United States and the British Commonwealth of Nations and the sterling area. I am sure we should get the worst of it, and at the end would be found only another layer of economic wreckage and ashes scattered over the tortured face of Europe and of Asia.

Moreover, the United States have an immense interest in the prosperity of Great Britain and of the British Empire, and their own prosperity could not survive for many years in the midst of a ruined world or in the presence of a ruined and broken Britain. It is in the working of these practical forces that we must put our trust for the future, and I am sure that it is along such paths and through such influences that a happy outcome will eventually be reached. United, these two countries can, without the slightest injury to other nations or to themselves, almost double each other's prosperity, and united they can surely double each other's power and safety. These matters must be carefully borne in mind by everybody who has to take a decision to-night.

Here I must digress for a moment upon a matter which I have not heard mentioned, but which should certainly be taken into consideration. Many hon. Members have said the American terms are severe; they are even harsh upon a debtor who has reduced himself to his unfortunate plight by his faithful, unstinted exertions in the common cause. But these considerations apply to other creditors as well as the United States. We are told we owe £1,200 million sterling to the Government of India and £400 million sterling to the Government of Egypt. No proposal has come from either of those countries similar to the great measure of Lend Lease. Everything has been charged against us, without the slightest recognition of the common cause. In the case of Egypt, she would have been ravaged and pillaged by the Italian and German armies, and would have suffered all the horrors and indignities of invasion and subjugation had it not been that we had defended her with our life's blood and our strong right arm. We are now told that we owe her £400 million sterling. Is there to be no reconsideration of that? Are we not entitled to say, "Here is our counter-charge which we set forth for having defended you from the worst of horrors"? My colleagues in the late Coalition know quite well that this is no new idea of mine. The same arguments apply to the Government of India. I specially reserved this matter in the Cabinet in 1942, when I saw with disquietude these immense debts mounting against us night after night.

I sympathise with the United States line of argument in connection with the loan. They did not wish to be the only creditor of Britain who had to scale down their wartime credit and balances. I welcome the perfectly clear implications of these agreements that it would be right and proper for Great Britain to insist upon a proper scaling down of these war charges, and that it is unreasonable for the Americans to be expected to pay large sums of money across the exchange, not with the object of getting Britain on her feet again as a going concern, which is a prime United States interest, but of enabling Britain to pay off other creditors against whom Britain has a far higher moral claim for easy treatment than she has against the United States. This, however, is all a matter which lies in our own hands and I do not pursue it further in this Debate.

For all these reasons I should deprecate most strongly any considerable number of the Members of the party I have the honour to lead casting their votes against the proposals which are now before the House. If individual Members have passionately strong conscientious views, no one can blame them for expressing those views in Debate or going into the Lobby, where they will find themselves with some odd companions; but any heavy vote by Conservative Members against the proposals would be specially injurious to our interests in America. It would be a gratuitous assumption of responsibilities which we have no need to seek and no power to bear. It would also be an utterly futile and even wanton proceeding, and a weak yielding to emotions which the long interest of the State requires should be stoically restrained. I would ask any of my supporters who may be inclined to cast their votes against these Measures to consider the possible reactions which a heavy Conservative vote against the proposals might produce across the Ocean and the altogether needless personal responsibilities which they will go out of their way deliberately to incur.

There is one other point which every one of my friends will, I hope, bear in mind, namely, that we agreed together only yesterday upon a course of abstention, and that for a number of gentlemen to vote against the proposals, unless compelled to do so by profound conscientious conviction, would be in fact unfair treatment of other Conservatives who, but for the agreement to abstain, would have felt it their duty to vote with the Government. I ask, therefore, for general abstention on the part of my friends which will leave us unburdened with any responsibility for these proposals and at the same time keep our party free from any attitude of antagonism to the other great branch of the English-speaking world. The agreement among ourselves has been to abstain, but I must make it quite clear, as did my right hon. Friend the Member for the Scottish Universities [Sir J. Anderson], that by thus freeing ourselves from responsibility for the passing of these measures, in which we have never been consulted in the slightest degree—they were only flung at our heads last week—we do not in any way weaken public faith in the word of Britain.

The financial obligations once entered into by His Majesty's Government are binding upon all parties, even upon those who have not taken any part in affirming them. We shall have to do our very best, our very utmost, in future years to bear the heavy load. If we fail, it must not be from any lack of sincerity or exertion, but simply because the weight that is being placed upon us may be far more than our exporting power can sustain. Although in 1931 we had to default upon our American debt incurred in the first World War, nevertheless the character and conduct of our people and the whole conduct of our State, is such that our name and honour still stand high in the world. Whatever criticism we may bring to bear on our own Government, it must be quite clearly understood that our refusal to share their responsibilities in no way relieves us from facing the consequences of their decisions in a spirit of good faith and to the utmost limit of our strength.

Finally, there is one point I must put on record about the Commercial Policy Declaration. At my first meeting with President Roosevelt at Argentia in 1941, I was very careful that the terms of the Atlantic Charter in no way prejudiced our rights to maintain the system of Imperial Preference. Those were not easy days. The United States were neutral. It was very hard to see how the war could be won, but even then I insisted upon that. Similarly when it came to the Mutual Aid Agreement, I received from President Roosevelt the explicit assurances which have since been published that we were no more committed by Article 7 to abandoning Imperial Preference than was the United States to abolish her tariffs. What we are committed to, and have been long committed to, in good faith and in good will, is to discuss both these matters. At the same time we are bound to take into consideration the views and wishes of the other Dominions of the Crown, and all has to be discussed at the forthcoming Conference in the light, not only of the actions and agreements of the English-speaking world, but also with regard to the general attitude of all other countries towards the removal of trade barriers and trade restrictions of all kinds.

Therefore, we have unquestionable latitude and discretion of judgment. Some have said that the United States might make what looks like a substantial diminution of tariffs already so high as to be prohibitive, and that then, although those tariffs still remain an effective barrier against our exports to America, we should be obliged to abandon or reduce our present preference. I could not agree with that view. On this side of the House we reserve the unlimited right of free judgment upon the issue as it appears, when definite, concrete proposals are before us. It is, therefore, in my view, quite untrue to say that we are at this time being committed by the Government to any abandonment of Imperial Preference and still less its elimination. Of course, if we find ourselves in the presence of proposals to effect a vast, sweeping reduction of tariffs and trade barriers and restrictions all over the world of a character to give a great exporting power to this island and to British shipping, which is a vital element in the services we render to other countries and a vital feature in our means of earning our daily bread, if we are faced with that, then, undoubtedly, we should be confronted with a new situation to which we should have to do justice. It would be a situation about which our Dominions would have strong views as well as ourselves, and, at that moment alone, and only at that moment, the decision about Imperial Preference would come before us.

Such is my view and interpretation of all that has occurred with the United States and also—the Government will correct me if I am wrong—what is now to be agreed with them by His Majesty's Government. I make no concealment of my personal view that if all this came to pass the vision before mankind to be would be brighter than we imagine. I do not see any probability of such a point being reached. It is more likely, on the other hand, that tariffs and trade restrictions of all kinds, even though reduced, will still be maintained at levels which severely hamper progress towards the ideal of the free interchange for mutual advantage of goods and services throughout the world. In that case, no one could in good faith demand of us to forgo the immense moral and material advantages which have flowed to us by the special development and fostering of inter-Imperial trade.

Having regard to all these facts, some of which are common ground between the Government and the Opposition and which constitute the British position, now made clear and manifest to the United States, I cannot see there is the slightest justification for suggesting that we are compromised and fettered in any way in respect of Imperial Preference. This applies not only to His Majesty's Government, but in a still more particular sense to the Conservative Party and to the Opposition who stand aside from the actual decisions tonight. On all these grounds, therefore, I counsel and urge my friends on this side of the House to follow unitedly the course we have agreed upon together, namely, of disclaiming all responsibility for the proposals of His Majesty's Government by abstaining from voting, but not, on any account, to incur responsibility about them by voting against them, and, finally, while respecting all solemn financial obligations of the State, to preserve the fullest freedom of action about all other matters that may be brought before us in the future.

UNIVERSITY OF MIAMI

A SPEECH ON RECEIVING DEGREE
26 FEBRUARY 1946

---

10 *January—First General Assembly of the United Nations representing 51 States meets in London.*

1 *February—Soviet Vice-Commissar for Foreign Affairs Vishinsky raises the question before the United Nations Security Council of British Troops in Greece. He charges that they are "a threat to peace".*

19 *February—Mr. Attlee states that the Government proposes to send to India a Special Mission of Cabinet Ministers consisting of Lord Pethick-Lawrence, Sir Stafford Cripps and Mr. A. V. Alexander to discuss with the leaders of Indian opinion the problems arising out of an early realisation by India of self-government.*

[*26 February* 1946

MR. PRESIDENT, Friends, Ladies and Gentlemen,

I have enjoyed my stay in your genial sunshine and it has done me a lot of good. I am grateful for all the kindness and consideration with which you have treated a servant of the Allied cause in the fearful war we have won. The accounts I read of the severity of life in England and the darkening scene at home make me and my wife naturally anxious to return there as soon as possible. I am very glad therefore to have an opportunity of expressing my thanks to Miami Beach, to Miami and to Florida and to all this shining coast for so easy and agreeable a wayside halt on the road we all have to travel.

This opportunity is afforded me in a manner most gratifying by the resolve of the University of Miami to give me a degree as Doctor of Law. I regard this as a very high compliment indeed, and that I should receive the degree in the presence of this vast and gracious concourse makes the occasion memorable in my life. I wish also, on behalf of my country, to thank the University of Miami for the wonderful help which they gave us in the late war by training cadets for the R.A.F., before the U.S. became a belligerent. Upwards of 1,200 cadets of the R.A.F. received here a very high quality of technical, navigational and meteorological training. They flew $5\frac{1}{2}$ million miles, I am told, over Florida upon instructional courses, and the majority, indeed a very large majority, gave their lives shortly afterwards for their country and our common cause. It is a consolation to learn that they left so many pleasant memories behind them among the two thousand Miami households who received them with true American hospitality and afterwards followed their fortunes and their fate as if they were the sons of the soil. Kindred hearts will beat in Britain on this account when they read of our ceremony here to-day.

I return, Mr. President, to the degree which you have just conferred upon me. I am specially glad of the presence here of Dr. Snavely, the Executive Director of the Association of American Colleges, and I thank him for all the far too flattering things which he has said about me. I am surprised that in my later life I should have become so experienced in taking degrees, when, as a school-boy I was so bad at passing examinations. In fact one might almost say that no one ever passed so few examinations and received so many degrees. From this a superficial thinker might argue that the way to get the most degrees is to fail in the most examinations. This would however, Ladies and Gentlemen, be a conclusion unedifying in the academic atmosphere in which I now preen myself, and I therefore hasten to draw another moral with which I am sure we shall all be in accord: namely, that no boy or girl should ever be disheartened by lack of success in their youth but should diligently and faithfully continue to persevere and make up for lost time. There at least is a sentiment which I am sure the Faculty and the Public, the scholars and the dunces will all be cordially united upon.

This raises the interesting question of the age at which knowledge and learning may be most fruitfully imparted and acquired. Owing to the pressure of life and everyone having to earn their living, a University education of the great majority of those who enjoy that high privilege is usually acquired before twenty. These are great years for young people. The world of thought and history and the treasures of learning are laid open to them. They have the chance of broadening their minds, elevating their view and arming their moral convictions by all the resources that free and wealthy communities can bestow. It is the glory of the United States that her graduates of universities are numbered not by the million but by the 10 million, and certainly any young man or woman who has these measureless advantages laid before them and has not the mother wit to profit by them to the full has no right to complain if he or she makes only a mediocre success of life.

Still Mr. President, I am going to put in a plea for the late starters. Not only is the saying true, "It is never too late to mend", but university education may be even better appreciated by those in the early twenties than by those in the later teens. The attention which a mature mind can bring to a study of the philosophies, humanities and the great literary monuments of the past is stronger and more intense than at an earlier age. The power of concentration, the retentiveness of the memory, the earnestness and zeal with which conclusions are sought should, in most cases, be greater in the older students. This, Ladies and Gentlemen, has a practical and supreme application at the present time. Millions of young men have had their education interrupted by the war. Their lives have been slashed across by its flaming sword. We must make sure that, in both our countries, they do not suffer needlessly for this particular form of the sacrifice which they have made.

I have been cheered and also, so far as my own country is concerned, spurred, by the tremendous efforts which are being made by all the educational bodies of the United States and by the American people generally to make up to these young men by all kinds of special arrangements and facilities what they may have lost by their services at the Front. I have read that it is proposed to provide facilities almost immediately for upwards of fifteen hundred thousand young men, most of whom are coming home from the fighting lines, and that in five years it is hoped that four millions may be provided for. This is indeed a splendid aim and effort. I suppose, Mr. President and Dr. Snaveley, that you are making appropriate arrangements on a great scale to adapt conditions of university life to these veterans, as you call them, though they are still pretty young to earn such a title, or warriors anyhow, who come back, after fighting their country's battles in the air, on the oceans and on the land from Okinawa and Iwo-Jima from Normandy, the Siegfried Line and the Rhine. Men who have fought in action and led others or, by their example, inspired others, have had an education invaluable to the formation of character and to the development of those qualities by which freedom and justice are preserved in strong nations and by the strong for weak nations. They must also be given the wider view, in outline at any rate, of the treasures which mankind has gathered in its long, chequered pilgrimage across the centuries. You do well to provide, as you are doing, on this prodigious scale for the baptism of such as are of riper years.

This is an age of machinery and specialisation but I hope, none the less—indeed all the more—that the purely vocational aspect of university study will not be allowed to dominate or monopolise all the attention of the returned Service men. Engines were made for men, not men for engines. Mr. Gladstone said many years ago that it ought to be part of a man's religion to see that his country is well governed. Knowledge of the past is the only foundation we have from which to peer into and try to measure the future. Expert knowledge, however indispensable, is no substitute for a generous and comprehending outlook upon the human story with all its sadness and with all its unquenchable hope.

May I not also advance the claims of literature and language. The great Bismarck—there were great Germans in those days—said at the close of his life, that the most important fact in the world was that the British and American peoples spoke the same language. Certainly we have a noble inheritance in literature. It would be an enormous waste and loss to us all if we did not respect, cherish, enjoy and develop this magnificent estate, which has come down to us from the past and which not only unites us as no such great communities have ever been united before, but is also a powerful instrument whereby our conception of justice, of freedom, and of fair play and good humour may make their invaluable contribution to the future progress of mankind.

"THE SINEWS OF PEACE"

A SPEECH TO WESTMINSTER COLLEGE, FULTON, MISSOURI 5 MARCH 1946

---

28 *February—Secretary of State Byrnes warns that the United States cannot allow aggression to be accomplished by coercion or pressure, or by subterfuges such as political infiltration.*

1 *March—Soviet Union announces it will begin withdrawing some of its forces from Iran on 2 March [the date agreed on in the British-Soviet-Iranian Treaty of 1442], but will keep others there "until the situation has been elucidated".*

[*5 March* 1946

I am glad to come to Westminster College this afternoon, and am complimented that you should give me a degree. The name "Westminster" is somehow familiar to me. I seem to have heard of it before. Indeed, it was at Westminster that I received a very large part of my education in politics, dialectic, rhetoric, and one or two other things. In fact we have both been educated at the same, or similar, or, at any rate, kindred establishments.

It is also an honour, perhaps almost unique, for a private visitor to be introduced to an academic audience by the President of the United States. Amid his heavy burdens, duties, and responsibilities—unsought but not recoiled from —the President has travelled a thousand miles to dignify and magnify our meeting here to-day and to give me an opportunity of addressing this kindred nation, as well as my own countrymen across the ocean, and perhaps some other countries too. The President has told you that it is his wish, as I am sure it is yours, that I should have full liberty to give my true and faithful counsel in these anxious and baffling times. I shall certainly avail myself of this freedom, and feel the more right to do so because any private ambitions I may have cherished in my younger days have been satisfied beyond my wildest dreams. Let me, however, make it clear that I have no official mission or status of any kind, and that I speak only for myself. There is nothing here but what you see.

I can therefore allow my mind, with the experience of a lifetime, to play over the problems which beset us on the morrow of our absolute victory in arms, and to try to make sure with what strength I have that what has been gained with so much sacrifice and suffering shall be preserved for the future glory and safety of mankind.

The United States stands at this time at the pinnacle of world power. It is a solemn moment for the American Democracy. For with primacy in power is also joined an awe-inspiring accountability to the future. If you look around you, you must feel not only the sense of duty done but also you must feel anxiety lest you fall below the level of achievement. Opportunity is here now, clear and shining for both our countries. To reject it or ignore it or fritter it away will bring upon us all the long reproaches of the after-time. It is necessary that constancy of mind, persistency of purpose, and the grand simplicity of decision shall guide and rule the conduct of the English-speaking peoples in peace as they did in war. We must, and I believe we shall, prove ourselves equal to this severe requirement.

When American military men approach some serious situation they are wont to write at the head of their directive the words "over-all strategic concept". There is wisdom in this, as it leads to clarity of thought. What then is the over-all strategic concept which we should inscribe to day? It is nothing less than the safety and welfare, the freedom and progress, of all the homes and families of all the men and women in all the lands. And here I speak particularly of the myriad cottage or apartment homes where the wage-earner strives amid the accidents and difficulties of life to guard his wife and children from privation and bring the family up in the fear of the Lord, or upon ethical conceptions which often play their potent part.

To give security to these countless homes, they must be shielded from the two giant marauders, war and tyranny. We all know the frightful disturbances in which the ordinary family is plunged when the curse of war swoops down upon the bread-winner and those for whom he works and contrives. The awful ruin of Europe, with all its vanished glories, and of large parts of Asia glares us in the eyes. When the designs of wicked men or the aggressive urge of mighty States dissolve over large areas the frame of civilised society, humble folk are confronted with difficulties with which they cannot cope. For them all is distorted, all is broken, even ground to pulp.

When I stand here this quiet afternoon I shudder to visualise what is actually happening to millions now and what is going to happen in this period when famine stalks the earth. None can compute what has been called "the unestimated sum of human pain". Our supreme task and duty is to guard the homes of the common people from the horrors and miseries of another war. We are all agreed on that.

Our American military colleagues, after having proclaimed their "over-all strategic concept" and computed available resources, always proceed to the next step—namely, the method. Here again there is widespread agreement. A world organisation has already been erected for the prime purpose of preventing war. UNO, the successor of the League of Nations, with the decisive addition of the United States and all that that means, is already at work. We must make sure that its work is fruitful, that it is a reality and not a sham, that it is a force for action, and not merely a frothing of words, that it is a true temple of peace in which the shields of many nations can some day be hung up, and not merely a cockpit in a Tower of Babel. Before we cast away the solid assurances of national armaments for self-preservation we must be certain that our temple is built, not upon shifting sands or quagmires, but upon the rock. Anyone can see with his eyes open that our path will be difficult and also long, but if we persevere together as we did in the two world wars—though not, alas, in the interval between them—I cannot doubt that we shall achieve our common purpose in the end.

I have, however, a definite and practical proposal to make for action. Courts and magistrates may be set up but they cannot function without sheriffs and constables. The United Nations Organisation must immediately begin to be equipped with an international armed force. In such a matter we can only go step by step, but we must begin now. I propose that each of the Powers and States should be invited to delegate a certain number of air squadrons to the service of the world organisation. These squadrons would be trained and prepared in their own countries, but would move around in rotation from one country to another. They would wear the uniform of their own countries but with different badges. They would not be required to act against their own nation, but in other respects they would be directed by the world organisation. This might be started on a modest scale and would grow as confidence grew. I wished to see this done after the first world war, and I devoutly trust it may be done forthwith.

It would nevertheless be wrong and imprudent to entrust the secret knowledge or experience of the atomic bomb, which the United States, Great Britain, and Canada now share, to the world organisation, while it is still in its infancy. It would be criminal madness to cast it adrift in this still agitated and un-united world. No one in any country has slept less well in their beds because this knowledge and the method and the raw materials to apply it, are at present largely retained in American hands. I do not believe we should all have slept so soundly had the positions been reversed and if some Communist or neo-Fascist State monopolised for the time being these dread agencies. The fear of them alone might easily have been used to enforce totalitarian systems upon the free democratic world, with consequences appalling to human imagination. God has willed that this shall not be and we have at least a breathing space to set our house in order before this peril has to be encountered: and even then, if no effort is spared, we should still possess so formidable a superiority as to impose effective deterrents upon its employment, or threat of employment, by others. Ultimately, when the essential brotherhood of man is truly embodied and expressed in a world organisation with all the necessary practical safeguards to make it effective, these powers would naturally be confided to that world organisation.

Now I come to the second danger of these two marauders which threatens the cottage, the home, and the ordinary people—namely, tyranny. We cannot be blind to the fact that the liberties enjoyed by individual citizens throughout the British Empire are not valid in a considerable number of countries, some of which are very powerful. In these States control is enforced upon the common people by various kinds of all-embracing police governments. The power of the State is exercised without restraint, either by dictators or by compact oligarchies operating through a privileged party and a political police. It is not our duty at this time when difficulties are so numerous to interfere forcibly in the internal affairs of countries which we have not conquered in war. But we must never cease to proclaim in fearless tones the great principles of freedom and the rights of man which are the joint inheritance of the English-speaking world and which through Magna Carta, the Bill of Rights, the Habeas Corpus, trial by jury, and the English common law find their most famous expression in the American Declaration of Independence.

All this means that the people of any country have the right, and should have the power by constitutional action, by free unfettered elections, with secret ballot, to choose or change the character or form of government under which they dwell; that freedom of speech and thought should reign; that courts of justice, independent of the executive, unbiased by any party, should administer laws which have received the broad assent of large majorities or are consecrated by time and custom. Here are the title deeds of freedom which should lie in every cottage home. Here is the message of the British and American peoples to mankind. Let us preach what we practise—let us practise what we preach.

I have now stated the two great dangers which menace the homes of the people: War and Tyranny. I have not yet spoken of poverty and privation which are in many cases the prevailing anxiety. But if the dangers of war and tyranny are removed, there is no doubt that science and co-operation can bring in the next few years to the world, certainly in the next few decades newly taught in the sharpening school of war, an expansion of material well-being beyond anything that has yet occurred in human experience. Now, at this sad and breathless moment, we are plunged in the hunger and distress which are the aftermath of our stupendous struggle; but this will pass and may pass quickly, and there is no reason except human folly or sub-human crime which should deny to all the nations the inauguration and enjoyment of an age of plenty. I have often used words which I learned fifty years ago from a great Irish-American orator, a friend of mine, Mr. Bourke Cockran, "There is enough for all. The earth is a generous mother; she will provide in plentiful abundance food for all her children if they will but cultivate her soil in justice and in peace." So far I feel that we are in full agreement.

Now, while still pursuing the method of realising our overall strategic concept, I come to the crux of what I have travelled here to say. Neither the sure prevention of war, nor the continuous rise of world organisation will be gained without what I have called the fraternal association of the English-speaking peoples. This means a special relationship between the British Commonwealth and Empire and the United States. This is no time for generalities, and I will venture to be precise. Fraternal association requires not only the growing friendship and mutual understanding between our two vast but kindred systems of society, but the continuance of the intimate relationship between our military advisers, leading to common study of potential dangers, the similarity of weapons and manuals of instructions, and to the interchange of officers and cadets at technical colleges. It should carry with it the continuance of the present facilities for mutual security by the joint use of all Naval and Air Force bases in the possession of either country all over the world. This would perhaps double the mobility of the American Navy and Air Force. It would greatly expand that of the British Empire Forces and it might well lead, if and as the world calms down, to important financial savings. Already we use together a large number of islands; more may well be entrusted to our joint care in the near future.

The United States has already a Permanent Defence Agreement with the Dominion of Canada, which is so devotedly attached to the British Commonwealth and Empire. This Agreement is more effective than many of those which have often been made under formal alliances. This principle should be extended to all British Commonwealths with full reciprocity. Thus, whatever happens, and thus only, shall we be secure ourselves and able to work together for the high and simple causes that are dear to us and bode no ill to any. Eventually there may come—I feel eventually there will come—the principle of common citizenship, but that we may be content to leave to destiny, whose outstretched arm many of us can already clearly see.

There is however an important question we must ask ourselves. Would a special relationship between the United

States and the British Commonwealth be inconsistent with our over-riding loyalties to the World Organisation? I reply that, on the contrary, it is probably the only means by which that organisation will achieve its full stature and strength. There are already the special United States relations with Canada which I have just mentioned, and there are the special relations between the United States and the South American Republics. We British have our twenty years Treaty of Collaboration and Mutual Assistance with Soviet Russia. I agree with Mr. Bevin, the Foreign Secretary of Great Britain, that it might well be a fifty years Treaty so far as we are concerned. We aim at nothing but mutual assistance and collaboration. The British have an alliance with Portugal unbroken since 1384, and which produced fruitful results at critical moments in the late war. None of these clash with the general interest of a world agreement, or a world organisation; on the contrary they help it. "In my father's house are many mansions." Special associations between members of the United Nations which have no aggressive point against any other country, which harbour no design incompatible with the Charter of the United Nations, far from being harmful, are beneficial and, as I believe, indispensable.

I spoke earlier of the Temple of Peace. Workmen from all countries must build that temple. If two of the workmen know each other particularly well and are old friends, if their families are inter-mingled, and if they have "faith in each other's purpose, hope in each other's future and charity towards each other's shortcomings"—to quote some good words I read here the other day—why cannot they work together at the common task as friends and partners? Why cannot they share their tools and thus increase each other's working powers? Indeed they must do so or else the temple may not be built, or, being built, it may collapse, and we shall all be proved again unteachable and have to go and try to learn again for a third time in a school of war, incomparably more rigorous than that from which we have just been released. The dark ages may return, the Stone Age may return on the gleaming wings of science, and what might now shower immeasurable material blessings upon mankind, may even bring about its total destruction. Beware, I say; time may be short. Do not let us take the course of allowing events to drift along until it is too late. If there is to be a fraternal association of the kind I have described, with all the extra strength and security which both our countries can derive from it, let us make sure that that great fact is known to the world, and that it plays its part in steadying and stabilising the foundations of peace. There is the path of wisdom. Prevention is better than cure.

A shadow has fallen upon the scenes so lately lighted by the Allied victory. Nobody knows what Soviet Russia and its Communist international organisation intends to do in the immediate future, or what are the limits, if any, to their expansive and proselytising tendencies. I have a strong admiration and regard for the valiant Russian people and for my wartime comrade, Marshal Stalin. There is deep sympathy and goodwill in Britain—and I doubt not here also—towards the peoples of all the Russias and a resolve to persevere through many differences and rebuffs in establishing lasting friendships. We understand the Russian need to be secure on her western frontiers by the removal of all possibility of German aggression. We welcome Russia to her rightful place among the leading nations of the world. We welcome her flag upon the seas. Above all, we welcome constant, frequent and growing contacts between the Russian people and our own people on both sides of the Atlantic. It is my duty however, for I am sure you would wish me to state the facts as I see them to you, to place before you certain facts about the present position in Europe.

From Stettin in the Baltic to Trieste in the Adriatic, an iron curtain has descended across the Continent. Behind that line lie all the capitals of the ancient states of Central and Eastern Europe. Warsaw, Berlin, Prague, Vienna, Budapest, Belgrade, Bucharest and Sofia, all these famous cities and the populations around them lie in what I must call the Soviet sphere, and all are subject in one form or another, not only to Soviet influence but to a very high and, in many cases, increasing measure of control from Moscow. Athens alone—Greece with its immortal glories—is free to decide its future at an election under British, American and French observation. The Russian-dominated Polish Government has been encouraged to make enormous and wrongful inroads upon Germany, and mass expulsions of millions of Germans on a scale grievous and undreamed-of are now taking place. The Communist parties, which were very small in all these Eastern States of Europe, have been raised to pre-eminence and power far beyond their numbers and are seeking everywhere to obtain totalitarian control. Police governments are prevailing in nearly every case, and so far, except in Czechoslovakia, there is no true democracy.

Turkey and Persia are both profoundly alarmed and disturbed at the claims which are being made upon them and at the pressure being exerted by the Moscow Government. An attempt is being made by the Russians in Berlin to build up a quasi-Communist party in their zone of Occupied Germany by showing special favours to groups of left-wing German leaders. At the end of the fighting last June, the American and British Armies withdrew westwards, in accordance with an earlier agreement, to a depth at some points of 150 miles upon a front of nearly four hundred miles, in order to allow our Russian allies to occupy this vast expanse of territory which the Western Democracies had conquered.

If now the Soviet Government tries, by separate action, to build up a pro-Communist Germany in their areas, this will cause new serious difficulties in the British and American zones, and will give the defeated Germans the power of putting themselves up to auction between the Soviets and the Western Democracies. Whatever conclusions may be drawn from these facts—and facts they are—this is certainly not the Liberated Europe we fought to build up. Nor is it one which contains the essentials of permanent peace.

The safety of the world requires a new unity in Europe, from which no nation should be permanently outcast. It is from the quarrels of the strong parent races in Europe that the world wars we have witnessed, or which occurred in former times, have sprung. Twice in our own lifetime we have seen the United States, against their wishes and their traditions, against arguments, the force of which it is impossible not to comprehend, drawn by irresistible forces, into these wars in time to secure the victory of the good cause, but only after frightful slaughter and devastation had occurred. Twice the United States has had to send several millions of its young men across the Atlantic to find the war; but now war can find any nation, wherever it may dwell between dusk and dawn. Surely we should work with conscious purpose for a grand pacification of Europe, within the structure of the United Nations and in accordance with its Charter. That I feel is an open cause of policy of very great importance.

In front of the iron curtain which lies across Europe are other causes for anxiety. In Italy the Communist Party is seriously hampered by having to support the Communist-trained Marshal Tito's claims to former Italian territory at the head of the Adriatic. Nevertheless the future of Italy hangs in the balance. Again one cannot imagine a regenerated Europe without a strong France. All my public life I have worked for a strong France and I never lost faith in her destiny, even in the darkest hours. I will not lose faith now. However, in a great number of countries, far from the Russian frontiers and throughout the world, Communist fifth columns are established and work in complete unity and absolute obedience to the directions they receive from the Communist centre. Except in the British Commonwealth and in the United States where Communism is in its infancy, the Communist parties or fifth columns constitute a growing challenge and peril to Christian civilisation. These are sombre facts for anyone to have to recite on the morrow of a victory gained by so much splendid comradeship in arms and in the cause of freedom and democracy; but we should be most unwise not to face them squarely while time remains.

The outlook is also anxious in the Far East and especially in Manchuria. The Agreement which was made at Yalta, to which I was a party, was extremely favourable to Soviet Russia, but it was made at a time when no one could say that the German war might not extend all through the summer and autumn of 1945 and when the Japanese war was expected to last for a further 18 months from the end of the German war. In this country you are all so well-informed about the Far East, and such devoted friends of China, that I do not need to expatiate on the situation there.

I have felt bound to portray the shadow which, alike in the west and in the east, falls upon the world. I was a high minister at the time of the Versailles Treaty and a close friend of Mr. Lloyd-George, who was the head of the British delegation at Versailles. I did not myself agree with many things that were done, but I have a very strong impression in my mind of that situation, and I find it painful to contrast it with that which prevails now. In those days there were high hopes and unbounded confidence that the wars were over, and that the League of Nations would become all-powerful. I do not see or feel that same confidence or even the same hopes in the haggard world at the present time.

On the other hand I repulse the idea that a new war is inevitable; still more that it is imminent. It is because I am sure that our fortunes are still in our own hands and that we hold the power to save the future, that I feel the duty to speak out now that I have the occasion and the opportunity to do so. I do not believe that Soviet Russia desires war. What they desire is the fruits of war and the indefinite expansion of their power and doctrines. But what we have to consider here to-day while time remains, is the permanent prevention of war and the establishment of conditions of freedom and democracy as rapidly as possible in all countries. Our difficulties and dangers will not be removed by closing our eyes to them. They will not be removed by mere waiting to see what happens; nor will they be removed by a policy of appeasement. What is needed is a settlement, and the longer this is delayed, the more difficult it will be and the greater our dangers will become.

From what I have seen of our Russian friends and Allies during the war, I am convinced that there is nothing they admire so much as strength, and there is nothing for which they have less respect than for weakness, especially military weakness. For that reason the old doctrine of a balance of power is unsound. We cannot afford, if we can help it, to work on narrow margins, offering temptations to a trial of strength. If the Western Democracies stand together in strict adherence to the principles of the United Nations Charter, their influence for furthering those principles will be immense and no one is likely to molest them. If however they become divided or falter in their duty and if these all-important years are allowed to slip away then indeed catastrophe may overwhelm us all.

Last time I saw it all coming and cried aloud to my own fellow-countrymen and to the world, but no one paid any attention. Up till the year 1933 or even 1935, Germany might have been saved from the awful fate which has overtaken her and we might all have been spared the miseries Hitler let loose upon mankind. There never was a war in all history easier to prevent by timely action than the one which has just desolated such great areas of the globe. It could have been prevented in my belief without the firing of a single shot, and Germany might be powerful, prosperous and honoured to-day; but no one would listen and one by one we were all sucked into the awful whirlpool. We surely must not let that happen again. This can only be achieved by reaching now, in 1946, a good understanding on all points with Russia under the general authority of the United Nations Organisation and by the maintenance of that good understanding through many peaceful years, by the world instrument, supported by the whole strength of the English-speaking world and all its connections. There is the solution which I respectfully offer to you in this Address to which I have given the title "The Sinews of Peace".

Let no man underrate the abiding power of the British Empire and Commonwealth. Because you see the 46 millions in our island harassed about their food supply, of which they only grow one half, even in war-time, or because we have difficulty in restarting our industries and export trade after six years of passionate war effort, do not suppose that we shall not come through these dark years of privation as we have come through the glorious years of agony, or that half a century from now, you will not see 70 or 80 millions of Britons spread about the world and united in defence of our traditions, our way of life, and of the world causes which you and we espouse. If the population of the English-speaking Commonwealths be added to that of the United States with all that such co-operation implies in the air, on the sea, all over the globe and in science and in industry, and in moral force, there will be no quivering, precarious balance of power to offer its temptation to ambition or adventure. On the contrary, there will be an overwhelming assurance of security. If we adhere faithfully to the Charter of the United Nations and walk forward in sedate and sober strength seeking no one's land or treasure, seeking to lay no arbitrary control upon the thoughts of men; if all British moral and material forces and convictions are joined with your own in fraternal association, the high-roads of the future will be clear, not only for us but for all, not only for our time, but for a century to come.

A SPEECH TO
THE GENERAL ASSEMBLY OF VIRGINIA
8 MARCH 1946

MR. SPEAKER, Members of the General Assembly of Virginia, Ladies and Gentlemen:

I was deeply moved by the glowing terms of the Joint Resolution of both branches of the Legislature inviting me here to address the General Assembly of Virginia. I take it as a high honour to be present here this morning to discharge that task. I always value being asked to address a Parliament. I have already on two occasions in the war addressed the Congress of the United States. I have addressed the Canadian Parliament. I have addressed a Joint Session of the Belgian Legislature, more recently, and there is a place of which you may have heard across the ocean called the House of Commons, to which, invited or uninvited, I have, from time to time, had things to say. I have also had invitations, couched in terms for which I am most grateful, from the State Legislatures of South Carolina, Kentucky and Mississippi. It would have given me the greatest pleasure to accept and fulfil all these. But as I have not the life and strength to repay all the kindness which is offered me, I felt that these other States would be willing to accept the primacy of the Virginia Assembly, as the most ancient, law-making body on the mainland of the western hemisphere. And thus I find myself here before you this morning in Richmond, in the historic capitol of world-famous Virginia.

I am also about to visit Williamsburg. During the war, at one of our Conferences, General Marshall arranged to take the British Chiefs of Staff for a visit to Williamsburg and I had planned to go with them, but the work I had to do made it necessary for me to remain in Washington; and so, on this visit to the United States, I had promised myself the treat of seeing Williamsburg, and my friend, General Eisenhower, who is with us to-day, undertook to pilot me around. I have great satisfaction in meeting him over here. We had a lot of business to do together during what I believe has been called, in another connection, "the late unpleasantness'" and I have formed impressions that will last me all my days of his single-hearted purpose,

106

wide and profound views on military science and his great power of making the soldiers and officers of our two countries work together under all the shocks and strains of war as if they were the soldiers of one single nation.

I hope I shall acquit myself to your satisfaction but the responsibility for what may happen is yours. Do you not think you are running some risk in inviting me to give you my faithful counsel on this occasion? You have not asked to see beforehand what I am going to say. I might easily, for instance, blurt out a lot of things, which people know in their hearts are true, but are a bit shy of saying in public, and this might cause a regular commotion and get you all into trouble. However, the people of Virginia and, above all, the people of Richmond have proved in the past that they have strong nerves and that they can face not only facts but fate with fortitude and pride. Of course my mind goes back into the past so much of which we have in common. The light of the Elizabethan age, which Shakespeare, Raleigh and Grenville adorned, casts its unfading lustre upon our scene here and in Williamsburg nearby. This was a cradle of the Great Republic in which more than 150 years afterwards the strong champions of freedom and independence were found to have been nursed. With what care did these early Fathers of our modern inspiration preserve the title deeds of freedom in Parliamentary privilege, in trial by jury, in the Habeas Corpus, in Magna Carta, and in the English Common Law! With what vigilance did Thomas Jefferson, Patrick Henry and Robert Henry Lee, and even George Washington, the Father of his country, defend these title deeds in later, unhappy but pregnant times! The theme of individual liberty and of the rights of citizens so painfully evolved across the centuries in England was upheld through every stress and confusion by Virginia and that theme lights the English-speaking world to-day. It lights our world and it is also a beacon shining through the mists and storms to many lands, where the rights of man—his honour, his happiness, his freedom—are yearned for or are so far enjoyed only precariously. I salute you here in this General Assembly as the guardians of the sacred flame.

Another century passes across our minds and we see Virginia and Richmond the centre of a tragedy which, however agonising at the time, is now for ever illuminated by drama and romance. I have visited most of your battle-fields on the peninsula, on the Happahannock in the Wilderness, and I was guided there some years ago by your distinguished historian Mr. Freeman, who is, I believe, here to-day, and whose works are a solid contribution, not only to the fame of the south but to the whole strength of the indissoluble Union. Yet it is in the words of an English General Officer that I shall express myself to you this morning. General Henderson, the author of *The Life of Stonewall Jackson* and of *The Campaign of Fredericksburg,* was a man I knew nearly 40 years ago, and this is what he wrote:—

Far and Wide, between the mountains and the sea stretches the fair Virginia for which Lee and Jackson and their soldiers,

'One equal temper of heroic hearts',

fought so well and unavailingly; . . . . yet her brows are bound with glory, the legacy of her lost children; and her spotless name, uplifted by their victories and manhood, is high among the nations. Surely she may rest content, knowing that so long as men turn to the records of history will their deeds live, giving to all time one of the noblest examples of unyielding courage and devotion the world has known.

My grandfather * was a Northerner in the state of New York, and you would not expect me to belie the cause for which he strove. We have moved on into a broader age and larger combinations. Old battles are remembered not as sources of bitterness but to celebrate the martial virtues and civic fidelity of both sides in that immortal struggle. Out of this story have also come examples of high character in which Americans have shown themselves in no wise wanting in the new trials and tribulations through which we have just passed.

To-day the American Union is the most powerful champion of national and individual freedom and it carries with it a large portion of the hopes of men. There was about General Robert E. Lee a quality of selflessness which raises him to the very highest rank of men, whether soldiers or statesmen, who have been concerned with the

---

* Mr. Leonard Jerome.

fortunes of nations. And in General Marshall and in General Eisenhower, and others of the Army and Navy of the United States whom I could mention, that character, that quality of selflessness has been a bond uniting all Allied Armies and the key to the victory which we have gained together.

It has been said that the dominant lesson of history is that mankind is unteachable. You will remember how my dear friend, the late President Roosevelt, had to argue only a few years ago, that Americans were not what is called "soft" and how he asserted that this was "The land of unending challenge"; and I myself have read in secret documents German reports which spoke before they met them of "these ridiculous American troops". Surely these European countries should not have forgotten or ignored so soon the example of tenacity, willpower and self-devotion which shines through all the records of the great war between the American States. We, too, in our British islands and in our great self-governing Empire spread about the world, have proved that our race when stirred to its depth has qualities deserving of respect.

In fact, in proportion to our numbers, our efforts, our sacrifices and our losses have not been surpassed. Moreover, it fell to us to have the honour of standing alone for a whole year against the main strength of the mighty Axis and the time for preparation which was thus gained was, as I am sure General Eisenhower will agree, a vital service to the United States and to the common cause.

But it is upon the future rather than upon the past that I wish to rest this morning. In these last years of my life there is a message of which I conceive myself to be a bearer. It is a very simple message which can be well understood by the people of both our countries. It is that we should stand together. We should stand together in malice to none, in greed for nothing but in defence of those causes which we hold dear not only for our own benefit, but because we believe they mean the honour and the happiness of long generations of men. We ought, as I said to the Congress of the United States in a dark hour in 1941, to walk together in majesty and peace. That I am sure is the wish of the overwhelming majority of the 200 million Britons and Americans who are spread about the globe. That this is our destiny, or, as most of us would put it, the Will of God, seems sure and certain. How it is to be expressed, in what way and in what hour it is to be achieved I cannot tell.

I read the other day that an English nobleman, whose name is new to me, has stated that England would have to become the 49th state of the American Union. I read yesterday that an able American editor had written that the United States ought not to be asked to re-enter the British Empire. It seems to me and I dare say it seems to you, that the path of wisdom lies somewhere between these scarecrow extremes. We must find the means and the method of working together not only in times of war and mortal anguish but in times of peace with all its bewilderments and clamour and clatter of tongues. It is in the years of peace that wars are prevented and that those foundations are laid upon which the noble structures of the future can be built. But peace will not be preserved without the virtues that make victory possible in war. Peace will not be preserved by pious sentiments expressed in terms of platitudes or by official grimaces and diplomatic correctitude, however desirable this may be from time to time. It will not be preserved by casting aside in dangerous years the panoply of warlike strength. There must be earnest thought. There must also be faithful perseverance and foresight. Greatheart must have his sword and armour to guard the pilgrims on their way. Above all, among the English-speaking peoples, there must be the union of hearts based upon conviction and common ideals. That is what I offer. That is what I seek.

ADDRESS TO AMERICAN AND BRITISH SERVICE MEMBERS

THE PENTAGON, WASHINGTON
9 MARCH 1946

GENERAL of the Army Eisenhower, Fleet Admiral Leahy, Fleet Admiral Nimitz, and General of the Air Spaatz. It is indeed a very great pleasure and honour to me that the Secretary of War and General Eisenhower should have asked me here to-day and have given me an opportunity, before going home, to meet the high officers of the United States services and to express to them on behalf of my own country and of the British services our admiration and gratitude for all they have done in this great common struggle carried to absolute victory in arms. The prevailing feature of our work together was the intimacy of association. Language is a great bridge. There are many, many ideas we have in common and also practice: but there was a spirit of loyalty, of good will, of comradeship which never has been seen in all the history of war between Allied Armies, Navies, Air Forces fighting together side by side. On General Eisenhower's staff, which I saw often and closely in Africa, in France and in Germany, it was carried to extreme perfection. And, as you know, the best people were picked for the various posts, and they gave orders and took orders without regard to which country their next neighbour or opposite number belonged to. I used the word "opposite number" by mistake, because there were no "opposite numbers"—there was absolute intermingling of staff work, and the same was true in the commands in the field. Many British and American troops served with perfect confidence under the commanders of the other country. And speaking for our own people, we always had more than fair treatment and felt absolute confidence in those to whom we confided the lives of our soldiers.

I am certain that our effective unity saved scores of thousands of lives, perhaps far more, and abridged the course of the struggle, as nothing else could have done. That must be regarded as a precious possession which we have in common and which whenever circumstances may

111

require it—I cannot think they will do so in our lifetime—will be available to strengthen any joint efforts our Governments may order in some future period. No one was more the champion and embodiment of this unity than General Eisenhower. I never had a chance to visit the Pacific but I am told the same conditions prevailed there as were established by him at SHAEF Headquarters and in the field. Of course, when people are on different ships they don't come so closely together as they do in the camps and billets. But it was one great force that overthrew the mighty powers with which we were confronted and which were dashed to ruin and helplessness by our exertions.

I have been thinking a great deal about the work of the United States services. I will speak a little more of the Army than of the others because I saw more of it. I greatly admired the manner in which the American Army was formed. I think it was a prodigy of organisation, of improvisation. There have been many occasions when a powerful state has wished to raise great armies, and with money and time and discipline and loyalty that can be accomplished. Nevertheless the rate at which the small American Army of only a few hundred thousand men, not long before the war, created the mighty force of millions of soldiers, is a wonder in military history.

I was here two or three years ago and visited with General Marshall, from whom I received a most delightful telegram just now, an Army Corps being trained in South Carolina, and we saw there the spectacle of what you may call the mass production of divisions. In great and rapid rotation they were formed, and moved on to further stages of their perfection. I saw the creation of this mighty force—this mighty Army, victorious in every theatre against the enemy in so short a time and from such a very small parent stock. This is an achievement which the soldiers of every other country will always study with admiration and with envy.

But that is not the whole story, nor even the greatest part of the story. To create great Armies is one thing; to lead them and to handle them is another. It remains to me a mystery as yet unexplained how the very small staffs which the United States kept during the years of peace were able not only to build up the Armies and Air Force units, but also to find the leaders and vast staffs capable of handling enormous masses and of moving them faster and farther than masses have ever been moved in war before.

The United States owes a debt to its officer corps. In time of peace in this country, as in my own, the military profession is very often required to pass a considerable number of years in the cool shade. One of Marlborough's veterans wrote the lines, now nearly 250 years ago,

> God and the soldier we adore
> In time of danger, not before;
> The danger passed and all things righted,
> God is forgotten and the soldier slighted.

Undoubtedly the military profession in the great Western democracies, which wholeheartedly desire peace, is one which has required great sacrifices from those who devote themselves to it. All around them goes the busy exciting world of business and politics with all its varieties, but the officers frugally, modestly, industriously, faithfully pursue their professional studies and duties, very often for long periods at a time, without the public notice. That you should have been able to preserve the art not only of creating mighty armies almost at the stroke of a wand— but of leading and guiding those armies upon a scale incomparably greater than anything that was prepared for or even dreamed of, constitutes a gift made by the Officer Corps of the United States to their nation in time of trouble, which I earnestly hope will never be forgotten here, and it certainly never will be forgotten in the island from which I come. You will, I am sure, permit me to associate with this amazing feat, the name of General Marshall, the creator of this Instrument of Victory.

I offer you gentlemen my most earnest congratulations on the manner in which, when the danger came, you were not found wanting. We talk a great deal about the future of armies and we are studying this matter across the ocean ourselves, and the relation between the officers and the other ranks. I speak not entirely as an amateur. I went through five years of professional training at the beginning of my life, in those impressionable years, and I have had the good fortune to be in all the wars that Great Britain has been engaged in in one capacity or another during my lifetime. We now have to choose very carefully the line of division between the officers and other ranks upon which authority should stand. There is only one line in my view, and that is professional attainment. The men have a right to feel that their officers know far better than they do how to bring them safely and victoriously through the terribly difficult decisions which arise in war. And for my part as far as Great Britain is concerned, I shall always urge that the tendency in the future should be to prolong the courses of instruction at the colleges rather than to abridge them and to equip our young officers with that special technical professional knowledge which soldiers have a right to expect from those who can give them orders, if necessary, to go to their deaths. It is quite clear that class or wealth or favour will not be allowed in the modern world to afford dividing lines. Professional attainment, based upon prolonged study, and collective study at colleges, rank by rank, and age by age—those are the title reeds of the commanders of the future armies, and the secret of future victories.

I venture to use these few words to you this afternoon because I have had a very varied experience in peace and war, and have met so many men who have played great parts, and I felt it a high honour to be invited to meet you again this afternoon, and to revive old acquaintances and shake hands with new ones. I thought these few observations I ventured to make might not be thought unfitting or unacceptable.

A SPEECH AT THE RECEPTION BY THE MAYOR AND CIVIC AUTHORITIES OF NEW YORK, THE WALDORF ASTORIA HOTEL, NEW YORK

15 MARCH 1946

---

11 *March—Referring to Mr. Churchill's speech at Fulton, Mr. Warbey asks in the House of Commons if the Prime Minister will confirm that the Government "entirely disapproves of the tone and temper of the speech". Mr. Attlee replies, "The Government is not called upon to express any opinion on a speech delivered in another country by a private individual."*

11 *March—"Pravda" denounces Mr. Churchill as an anti-Soviet warmonger and accuses him of trying to destroy the United Nations.*

13 *March—In an interview in "Pravda" Premier Stalin accuses Mr. Churchill, in his Fulton speech, of "calling for war against the Soviet Union", and compares Mr. Churchill with Hitler.*

15 *March—Marshal Stalin tenders resignation of his government to the Supreme Soviet. He is invited to form a new administration.*

15 *March—Iranian War Minister General Ahmedi announces that his government has made a second appeal to the United Nations Security Council in view of the continued presence of Russian troops in Persia.*

[15 *March* 1946

WHEN I spoke at Fulton ten days ago I felt it was necessary for someone in an unofficial position to speak in arresting terms about the present plight of the world. I do not wish to withdraw or modify a single word. I was invited to give my counsel freely in this free country and I am sure that the hope which I expressed for the increasing association of our two countries will come to pass, not because of any speech which may be made, but because of the tides that flow in human affairs and in the

115

course of the unfolding destiny of the world. The only question which in my opinion is open is whether the necessary harmony of thought and action between the American and British peoples will be reached in a sufficiently plain and clear manner and in good time to prevent a new world struggle or whether it will come about, as it has done before, only in the course of that struggle.

I remain convinced that this question will win a favourable answer. I do not believe that war is inevitable or imminent. I do not believe that the rulers of Russia wish for war at the present time. I am sure that if we stand together calmly and resolutely in defence of those ideals and principles embodied in the Charter of the United Nations, we shall find ourselves sustained by the overwhelming assent of the peoples of the world, and that, fortified by this ever-growing moral authority, the cause of peace and freedom will come safely through and we shall be able to go on with the noble work—in which the United States has a glorious primacy—of averting famine, of healing the awful wounds of Hitler's war and rebuilding the scarred and shattered structure of human civilisation. Let me declare, however, that the progress and freedom of all the peoples of the world under a reign of law enforced by a World Organisation, will not come to pass, nor will the age of plenty begin, without the persistent, faithful, and above all fearless exertions of the British and American systems of society.

In the last ten days the situation has greatly changed as the result of decisions which must have been taken some time ago. Instead of a calm discussion of broad and long-term tendencies we now find ourselves in the presence of swiftly moving events which no one can measure at the moment. I may be called upon to speak about the new situation when I get back home.

There are however a few things I am bound to say to-night lest a good cause should suffer by default. If any words that I have spoken have commanded attention, that is only because they find an echo in the breasts of those of every land and race who love freedom and are the foes of tyranny. I certainly will not allow anything said by others to weaken my regard and admiration for the Russian people or my earnest desire that Russia should

116

be safe and prosperous and should take an honoured place in the van of the World Organisation. Whether she will do so or not depends only on the decisions taken by the handful of able men who, under their renowned chief, hold all the 180 million Russians, and many more millions outside Russia, in their grip. We all remember what frightful losses Russia suffered in the Hitlerite invasion and how she survived and emerged triumphant from injuries greater than have ever been inflicted on any other community. There is deep and widespread sympathy throughout the English-speaking world for the people of Russia and an absolute readiness to work with them on fair and even terms to repair the ruin of the war in every country. If the Soviet Government does not take advantage of this sentiment, if on the contrary they discourage it, the responsibility will be entirely theirs.

There is for instance a very good way in which they could brush aside any speeches which they dislike. It is a way which is open to them now in the next fortnight. The British Government of which I was the head, signed a treaty with Russia and with Persia solemnly undertaking to respect the integrity and sovereignty of Persia and to evacuate that country by a certain date. This treaty was reaffirmed at Teheran by the Tri-partite Agreement signed by the Head of the Soviet Government, by the late President Roosevelt and by me. In fulfillment of this Agreement the United States and the British have already left that country. But we are told that the Soviet Government instead of leaving, are actually sending in more troops. Now this is one of those cases for which the United Nations Security Council was especially devised, and I am very glad to read in the newspapers that the Soviet representatives will attend the meeting of the Security Council which is to take place in New York on 25 March. By all means let the matter be thrashed out there and let respect be shown even by the greatest or more deeply-interested powers, to the conclusions of the Security Council. In this way the reign of world law and the international foundations of enduring peace would be immeasurably consolidated.

There is no reason why Soviet Russia should feel ill-rewarded for her efforts in the war. If her losses have been grievous, her gains have been magnificent. Her two tremendous antagonists, Germany and Japan, have been laid low. Japan was overthrown almost entirely by American arms. Russia recovered almost without striking a blow all that she lost to Japan forty years ago. In the west the Baltic states and a large part of Finland have been reincorporated in Russia. The Curzon Line is no longer questioned. Then we come to the Straits of the Dardanelles. I welcome the Russian flag on Russian ships on the high seas and oceans. I have always told our Soviet allies that Great Britain would support the revision of the Montreux Convention about the Straits. At Potsdam the Americans and British offered to Russia a joint guarantee of the complete freedom of the Straits in peace and war, whether for merchant ships or ships of war. To this guarantee Turkey would gladly have subscribed. But we were told that that was not enough. Russia must have a fortress inside the Straits, from which she could dominate Constantinople. But this is not to keep the Straits open but to give the power of closing them to a single nation. This is out of harmony with the principle urged by the United States representatives of the freedom of the great waterways of Europe, the Danube, the Rhine and other rivers, which run through many countries. At any rate, there was the offer and I have no doubt it is still open, and if Soviet Russia still persists in putting pressure on Turkey, the matter must in the first instance be pronounced upon by the United Nations Security Council. Thus early will come a very great test for the World Organisation on which so many hopes are founded.

It has been frequently observed in the last few days that there is a great measure of misunderstanding. I entirely agree with that. Could you have a greater example of misunderstanding than when we are told that the present British Government is not a free democratic government because it consists only of the representatives of a single party, whereas Poland, Rumania, Bulgaria and other countries have the representatives of several parties in their governments. But this also applies to the United States, where one party is in office and wields the executive power. All this argument overlooks the fact that democratic governments are based on free elections. The people choose freely and fairly the party they wish to have in office. They have every right to criticise that party, or the government based upon it and can change it by constitutional processes at any time they like or at frequent intervals. It can hardly be called a democratic election where the candidates of only one party are allowed to appear and where the voter has not even the secrecy of the ballot to protect him. These misunderstandings will be swept away if we get through the present difficult period safely and if the British, American and Russian peoples are allowed to mingle freely with one another and see how things are done in their respective countries. No doubt we all have much to learn from one another. I rejoice to read in the newspapers that there never were more Russian ships in New York harbour than there are to-night. I am sure you will give the Russian sailors a hearty welcome to the land of the free and the home of the brave.

Now I turn to the other part of my message—the relations between Great Britain and the United States. On these the life and freedom of the world depend. Unless they work together, in full loyalty to the Charter, the organisation of the United Nations will cease to have any reality. No one will be able to put his trust in it and the world will be left to the clash of nationalisms which have led us to two frightful wars. I have never asked for an Anglo-American military alliance or a treaty. I asked for something different and in a sense I asked for something more. I asked for fraternal association, free, voluntary, fraternal association. I have no doubt that it will come to pass, as surely as the sun will rise to-morrow. But you do not need a treaty to express the natural affinities and friendships which arise in a fraternal association. On the other hand, it would be wrong that the fact should be concealed or ignored. Nothing can prevent our nations drawing ever closer to one another and nothing can obscure the fact that, in their harmonious companionship, lies the main hope of a world instrument for maintaining peace on earth and goodwill to all men.

I thank you all profoundly for all your gracious kindness and hospitality to me during this visit I have paid to your shores. Mine is not the first voice raised within your spacious bounds in the cause of freedom and of peace. Nor will it be the last that will be encouraged by the broad tolerance of the American people. I come to you at a time when the United States stands at the highest point of majesty and power ever attained by any community since the fall of the Roman Empire. This imposes upon the American people a duty which cannot be rejected. With opportunities comes responsibility. Strength is granted to us all when we are needed to serve great causes. We in the British Commonwealth will stand at your side in powerful and faithful friendship, and in accordance with the World Charter, and together I am sure we shall succeed in lifting from the face of man the curse of war and the darker curse of tyranny. Thus will be opened ever more broadly to the anxious toiling millions the gateways of happiness and freedom.

A SPEECH ON RECEIVING THE FREEDOM
OF WESTMINSTER

7 MAY 1946

---

19 *March—Nikolai Schvernik succeeds Mikhail Kalinin as Chairman of the Supreme Soviet of U.S.S.R.*

22 *March—Treaty of Alliance and Friendship signed in London between Great Britain and Transjordan.*

31 *March—General Elections in Greece under supervision of Allied Electoral Mission. Parties of the Right and Centre receive 80 per cent of the votes.*

17 *April—Mr. Wilmot, Minister of Supply, announces that the Government intend to introduce a large measure of public ownership into the Iron and Steel industry.*

25 *April—Council of four Foreign Ministers, Britain, United States, France and Soviet Union, meet in Paris.*

29 *April—Secretary of State Byrnes proposes to the Foreign Ministers in Paris a four-power 25-year treaty to guarantee the disarmament of Germany. Britain and France agree "in principle"; Russia raises objections.*

5 *May—Referendum in France on proposed new Constitution; it is rejected by 10,488,000 votes to 9,327,000.*

7 *May—Mr. Attlee announces in the House of Commons the Government's decision to withdraw all British land, sea and air forces from Egypt.*

[*7 May* 1946

Mr. Mayor, your Excellencies, Mr. Speaker, my lords, ladies and gentlemen, it is an honour to me, which I shall always remember as long as I live, that I should become the first Freeman of Westminster, and that this should be accorded to me in terms of kindness and of compliment far beyond my merits, in the presence of a gathering so distinguished, so varied, so representative of the country as a whole and of all parties in the State. But the very quality and character of this assembly imposes upon me an extremely difficult task:

121

I have to walk the tight-rope of truth, between unseemly controversy on the one hand and vacuous platitudes on the other. You will, I am sure, be indulgent judges of how I perform this feat. Here also there is the additional complication of striking the happy mean between saying what we all think and what we all think had better be left unsaid. Mr. Mayor, if this is what is called receiving the Freedom, it will I am sure be realised that freedom is expressed not only by its assertions but its limitations. As a matter of fact, I am sure the Mayor will not mind my observing that I shall exercise very much less freedom in this part of Westminster than that which I am accustomed to enjoy in that other part of Westminster which has been the centre of my life for forty-seven years—the House of Commons; and perhaps I shall even exercise less freedom here than I did in another Westminster across the Atlantic Ocean in the State of Missouri a couple of months ago.

I was glad that you mentioned to the audience, Mr. Mayor, the uses to which this building has been put, because when I came into this hall I had a sort of feeling that I had been here before.

Let me begin my remarks by reminding you of the Westminster by-election of 1923. I have fought more contested elections than any one else, and of all of them the Westminster election was the most exciting and dramatic. Yet I shall offend no party, Conservative, Labour or Liberal, in referring to it. It was a non-party election in the true sense because at that election all parties were agreed in opposing me. It was only by 43 votes in an electorate of 22,000 that I was defeated. Happily the hostile operations of the three historic parties against me were not combined; the Big Three were not working together in perfect harmony on that occasion—so different from what we have now; and a few months after the conflict I found myself Chancellor of the Exchequer in a government formed by the party of my narrowly victorious opponent.

Such is life with its astonishing twists and turns. You never can tell what is going to happen next, nor can you tell what will be the consequences of any action you may take. The principle of the boomerang, a weapon which we owe to the genius of the Australian aboriginals, is, it would seem, increasingly operative in human affairs. Thus, Mr. Mayor, we may note how some of the actions of our Russian friends have helped to cement Anglo-American friendship and co-operation, and how the activities of the French Communist Party have given General Franco a new lease of life.

The relation of cause to effect which these incidents illustrate cannot always be judged with precision. The human story does not always unfold like an arithmetical calculation on the principle that two and two make four. Sometimes in life they make five or minus three; and sometimes the black-board topples down in the middle of the sum and leaves the class in disorder and the peda-gogue with a black eye. The element of the unexpected and the unforeseeable is what gives some of its relish to life and saves us from falling into the mechanical thraldom of the logicians. Now it is astonishing how often the calculators in this world are proved wrong. It is impressive how sternly is borne in upon us the simple truth that honest action from day to day, in accordance with the best promptings of our hearts, is the surest path even to worldly success.

Last week, Mr. Mayor, when I was in Aberdeen, I spoke about the state of the world. I said the world was very ill. But this is not surprising when you consider the frightful operations which have been performed upon its inhabitants and the vast injury to all its means of food and transport and the dissipation of so much of its psychic energies and resilience, which follow the intense and overstrained exertions which have been made by so many branches of the human family. But, here in Westminster, in the Abbey Division, which claims, not without reason, to be the heart of the British Empire and Commonwealth of Nations, here, under the shadow of Big Ben and the Abbey, I should like to speak a little about our own affairs in their relation to world affairs.

We must all be deeply conscious of the gravity of the times in which we live, and that our place in the world will perhaps be finally decided by what may happen in the next few years. It would, I am sure, be a profound shock to the great mass of the British people if they woke up one morning and found that our Empire and position in the East and Middle East had vanished overnight and if the mission we have faithfully discharged in so many lands came to an abrupt end and incontinent collapse. If such a disaster occurred we should certainly have the right to reproach before history all public men in any way responsible, at the present time or in previous years, for such a failure of duty on the morrow of our victory, the morrow of that victory, won by what seemed to many to be against desperate odds, which was nevertheless in the end complete and unconditional.

We are the only unbroken nation that fought against Hitler's tyranny in the war from start to finish. We declared war upon Germany when Hitler invaded Poland. We sought no material gains; we coveted no man's land or treasure. We, and with us the whole Empire and Commonwealth, all unprepared as we were, or partly prepared, drew the sword against the mighty antagonist at the call of honour and in defence of the rights of weaker nations, according to our plighted word, according to the fair play of the world. We did not fight only in the sacred cause of self-defence, like the Russian patriots who defended their native soil with sublime devotion and glorious success. No one attacked *us*. We fought for a higher and broader theme. We fought against tyranny, aggression and broken faith, and in order to establish that rule of law among the nations which alone can be the shield of freedom and progress.

Wherein did we fail? We did not fail when we were all alone. Neither did we fail, when mighty nations joined us, in giving all we had to what we from the beginning had proclaimed was the cause of mankind.

But let us look back a little upon the past. From Trafalgar and Waterloo to the first German War the British Navy was supreme upon the seas. Our sea power during the greater part of the nineteenth century equalled that of all other nations put together. Did we misuse that power? On the contrary, there never were so few warships afloat. History, which has been my guide and inspiration, will show to future ages that the control of the seas which the British held so long was used not for the exercise of warlike ambition but to keep the peace, to suppress the slave trade and to make the seas safe for the commerce of all nations. All our ports, even our own coastwise trade, were opened to the entry and competition of men and goods from every land. For at least two generations we were, as the American writer Walter Lippmann has reminded us, a guardian, and almost a guarantor of the Monroe doctrine upon which, as Canning's eye foresaw, the free development of South America was founded. We and the civilised world owe many blessings to the United States, but we have also in later generations made our contribution to their security and splendour.

What of our Empire? What of our Commonwealth of Nations? Taught by the hard necessary lessons of the American Revolution, we found the way, unique in history, to build and hold together a free association of self-governing dominions by voluntary ties and spontaneous forces, and these, like our vast Eastern and Colonial Empire, rose superior even to the awful stresses of 1940. There is not, and there never has been, and perhaps there never will be again, so widespread, so truly united a gathering of nations and races as was then and is to-day comprised within the circle of the ancient British Crown.

Will it continue or will it pass away; and if it passes away what coherent theme will take its place? What would fill the void, for void there would certainly be? These are the questions which we must ask ourselves. I grieve that it should be necessary to do so. We are bound to ask ourselves these questions. Not only are we bound to ask them of ourselves but of the world, and not only for our own sake but in the far broader interests of mankind.

I read last week an interesting and challenging report by an Anglo-American Commission on Palestine. This report declared that the British must remain in Palestine in pursuance of their mandate from the former League of Nations, and must remain there until the Jews and Arabs were content to live together as friends and fellow workers. It will evidently be a long time, Mr. Mayor, before the quarrel between Jacob and Esau has faded away from the life of the Middle East. Are we not entitled to ask our friends whose judgment is the same as ours to give us a helping hand?

But I will look further East. I must look to India. India is a continent as large as and more populous than Europe, and not less deeply divided by racial and religious differences than Europe. India has no more unity than

125

Europe, except that superficial unity which has been created by our rule and guidance in the last 150 years. India, protected by the British nation and parliament, has not in modern times been torn to pieces by hideous internal warfare; nor has it been invaded from over the sea. The anxieties felt by the Anglo-American Commission about Palestine arise in India on a far greater scale. It would be easy for Great Britain to cast away these cares. Some voices bid us quit Palestine; others bid us quit India. But surely not only Britain but all the world should consider deeply what the consequences would be and what other arrangements can be made to safeguard millions of men and women—and in India four hundred millions—from the cruel fate which has laid Europe with all its glories in dust and ashes and now threatens China with a protraction of her torment.

Naturally, amid the perplexities which beset so many governments, our hearts and our hopes go out to a world organisation, to the new United Nations structure and its Charter, to which all true-hearted men should give their allegiance. I pray that this may prosper. But what happens if the United Nations themselves are sundered by an awful schism and clash of ideologies, interests, policies and passions? What happens if, with all our loyal endeavours, we can build no more than a Tower of Babel? What is to happen if the United Nations, victorious in their grand conflict against Nazism and Fascism, give place, as they may do, to a vast confrontation of two parts of the world and two irreconcilably-opposed conceptions of human society?

It is right to pose these questions. It is even impossible not to pose them. But what are the answers going to be? You will, I am sure, feel that these are problems which should dominate the minds of all the men in all the lands. They should dominate their minds because failure to find the answers may lead the whole human race into a new period of misery, slaughter and abasement more agonising and more fatal than those which we have twice endured in the lifetime of most of us here.

I should not like to raise these tremendous issues which lie about us and beset us on every side, and which rightly preoccupy the thoughts not only of statesmen and leaders but of vast masses in many countries, without offering some guidance, such as I have sometimes done in bygone years.

The supreme hope and the prime endeavour is to reach a good and faithful understanding with Soviet Russia through the agency and organism of the United Nations. In this patient, persevering, resolute endeavour the English-speaking world and the western democracies of Europe must play their part and move together. Only in this way can catastrophe be averted; only in this way can the salvation of all nations and races be gained. I hope that in this world organisation there will be a strong France and a revived Italy, and that many smaller but ancient and famous states will make their weight tell in the noble task of building and maintaining an all-powerful world-governing instrument to preserve freedom and to prevent war. Of France particularly I would say that without a full revival of the true greatness and culture of France there can be little prospect of restoring Europe to its former fame. In the darkest days I have never lost faith in France, and I feel confident that she has now a splendid part to play in the peaceful establishment of progressive western civilisation and democracy, and that France, after all her troubles, may yet lead Europe into the peace and plenty of a free and happy age.

But let me conclude upon our own task. No state or nation is worthy to take part in this sacred, august duty of rebuilding the world under the protection of a world instrument whose men and women are not prepared to give their lives if need be, and to make whatever preparations are required to ensure that they and their country are not found impotent and unready in the world cause. The future, Mr. Mayor, is to be saved only by the generous and the strong. We here in Britain and in the Commonwealth and Empire must never fear or fail to take our place among them.

A SPEECH TO THE STATES-GENERAL OF THE NETHERLANDS, THE HAGUE

9 MAY 1946

---

8 *May—Mr. Churchill arrives in Amsterdam on a visit to Holland at the invitation of Queen Wilhelmina.*

[9 *May* 1946

MR. SPEAKER,

You do me great honour in inviting me to speak to the States-General to-day. I see in all this the regard which you have for my dear country and the relief which you had especially in gaining liberty against the invader. I thank you. Personally I have always worked for the cause of liberty against tyranny and for the steady advancement of the causes of the weak and poor. This is not, as you know, the first time I have had the opportunity of addressing august or famous Assemblies. I have already addressed the Congress of the United States, the Parliaments of Canada and Belgium, the General Assembly of Virginia and besides these there is always the House of Commons at home, where, from time to time, I venture still to speak a word or two. Let me in my turn present you my compliments upon the progress made in this country since the expulsion of the German invaders. Holland has regained stability and strength in Europe with great rapidity. I offer my respectful congratulations to all public men who, without regard to Party or interests, have contributed to this achievement. The stability of the Constitution of the Netherlands, centering upon the union of Crown and people, is an example to many countries. I trust that your affairs abroad will prosper equally with those at home.

In Britain we know and value the services which Holland has rendered to European freedom in ancient and in recent times. The Four Freedoms which the great President Roosevelt proclaimed have always been cherished in Holland and were carried by his forbears in their blood to the New World. Even in the days of the

128

Roman Empire the Batavian Republic had established a unique position. In the long, fierce convulsions in Europe which followed the Reformation, Holland and England were united as the foremost champions of Freedom. In those struggles after that change in the human mind which followed the Reformation long after the collapse of the Roman Empire, Holland and England were left as the foremost upholders of freedom. Our ancestors stood together on the bloody dykes, and there are few cities in the Netherlands which do not enshrine the memories of brave resolves and famous feats of arms. Bitter were the struggles of those old days and desperate were the odds you had to face. Looking across the generations I like to feel how Britain's stand in 1940 and 1941 resembled the glorious hour when William the Silent declared that rather than surrender, the Dutch would die on the last dyke. Holland gave us King William the Third, who led both our countries against the overweening tyranny of Louis XIV. And after him John Churchill was Commander-in-Chief not only of the British but of the far larger armies maintained by the Dutch Republic, when she had risen through freedom and independence to power and greatness 250 years ago.

Her Majesty the Queen and the Government of the Netherlands have made me a gift which will be for me for ever an honour and a treasure. They have presented me with the 613 letters which John Churchill wrote to the Grand Pensionary during the long 10 years of the Grand Alliance, which alliance he directed, largely formed and finally crowned with victory. I express again to this meeting of both your Houses my gratitude and that of my family for this extraordinary mark of your kindness to me.

Since the bygone struggles between Protestants and Catholics of the sixteenth and seventeenth centuries, there is at least one profound and beneficent new fact of which all should take account. The Church of Rome has ranged itself with those who defend the rights and dignity of the individual, and the cause of personal freedom throughout the world. I speak of course as one born of a Protestant and Episcopalian family, and I rejoice to see the new and ever-growing unity in lay matters, and not perhaps in lay matters only, between all the Christian churches with those liberalising forces which must ever light the onward march of man.

Let me pay my tribute to the part borne by Holland in the overthrow of Hitler's hideous tyranny. After your troops and water defences had been overwhelmed by the sudden, treacherous onslaught, which happened six years ago tomorrow, the Dutch people had no longer the means to maintain organised armies in the field, but the will power and firmness of character shown during the grim years of foreign oppression and occupation were definite factors in the ultimate downfall of Naziism, and the Resistance Movement, for which so many thousands of patriots gave their lives, played an even more important part. In Britain we understand how you must have suffered in these years of torment of soul and mind to which starvation and bombardment were lesser afflictions. All honour to those who perished for the cause. May their memory cement the unity of all true Dutchmen. I thank you on behalf of Great Britain for your work. I am glad to meet here my friend, Professor Gerbrandy, the former Prime Minister, who was in Britain with us in all the dark days and who was so vigilant and faithful a champion of the rights and interests of the Netherlands.

Speaking here to-day, where my words may carry far and wide, it is my first duty to affirm the sanctity of the rights of smaller States. In affirming these rights, I base myself upon that grand figure of Victorian Liberalism, Mr. Gladstone. Mr. Gladstone, in his third Midlothian speech, said on 27 November 1879:

> The sound and the sacred principle that Christendom is formed of a band of nations who are united to one another in the bonds of right; that they are without distinction of great and small; there is an absolute equality between them—the same sacredness defends the narrow limits of Belgium [and of course Holland] as attaches to the extended frontiers of Russia, or Germany, or France. I hold that he who by act or word brings that principle into peril or disparagement is endangering the peace and all the most fundamental interests of a Christian society.

The duty, Mr. Speaker, of the large powers of the modern world is to see that those rights of every nation are jealously and strictly protected. The purpose of the

United Nations Organisation is to give them the sanction of international law, for which Holland and Grotius are so justly famous, and also to make sure that the force of right will, in the ultimate issue, be protected by the right of force.

I will now, Mr. Speaker, if you will permit me, if I do not trespass too long upon your courtesy and goodwill, speak of nationalism. Is it an evil or is it a virtue? Where nationalism means the lust for pride and power, the craze for supreme domination by weight or force; where it is the senseless urge to be the biggest in the world, it is a danger and a vice. Where it means love of country and readiness to die for country; where it means love of tradition and culture and the gradual building up across the centuries of a social entity dignified by nationhood, then it is the first of virtues. It is indeed the foundation of a progressive and happy family of nations. Some of our shallow thinkers and false guides—and there are many to-day—do not distinguish between these two separate and opposing conceptions. They mix them together and use all arguments according as their fancy or their interest prompts them. They condemn nationalism as an old-world obsession and seek to reduce us all, both countries and individuals to one uniform pattern with nothing but material satisfactions as our goal. Or again, or sometimes with almost the same breath, they pervert the noble sentiments of patriotism to the hideous, aggressive expansion of old-world imperialism, and to the obliteration by force or by wrongful teaching of all the varieties and special cultures, all those dear thoughts of home and country without which existence, however logically planned, would be dreary and barren beyond thought or imagination.

After the end of the great conflict from 1914 to 1918 it was hoped that the wars were over. Yet we have witnessed an even more destructive world-wide struggle. Need we have done so? I have no doubt whatever that firm guidance and united action on the part of the Victorious Powers could have prevented this last catastrophe. If the United States had taken an active part in the League of Nations, and if the League of Nations had been prepared to use concerted force, even had it only been European force, in order to prevent the rearmament of Germany, there was no need for further serious bloodshed. Let us, Sir, profit at least by this terrible lesson. In vain did I try to teach it before the War.

Mr. Speaker, the tragedy of Europe shocks mankind. Well, as you said in your Address, "Europe is totally ravaged". The tragedy darkens the pages of human history. It will excite the amazement and horror of future generations. Here in these beautiful, fertile and temperate lands, where so many of the noblest parent races of mankind have developed their character, their arts and their literature, we have twice in our own lifetime seen all rent asunder and torn to pieces in frightful convulsions which have left their mark in blackened devastation through the entire continent. And had not Europe's children of earlier times come back across the Atlantic Ocean with strong and rescuing arms, all the peoples of Europe might have fallen into the long night of Nazi totalitarian despotism. Upon Britain fell the proud but awful responsibility of keeping the Flag of Freedom flying in the old world till the forces of the new world could arrive. But now the tornado has passed away. The thunder of the cannons has ceased, the terror from the skies is over, the oppressors are cast out and broken. We may be wounded and impoverished. But we are still alive and free. The future stands before us, to make or mar.

Two supreme tasks confront us. We have to revive the prosperity of Europe; and European civilisation must rise again from the chaos and carnage into which it has been plunged; and at the same time we have to devise those measures of world security which will prevent disaster descending upon us again. In both these tasks Holland has an important part to play. The restoration and rebuilding of Europe, both physical and moral, as you have pointed out in your Address, Mr. Speaker, is animated and guided by the kindred themes of Liberty and Democracy. These words are on every lip. They have cheered us and helped to unify us in the struggle. They inspire our rejoicings in the hour of victory. But now that the fighting is over, it is necessary to define these glorious war cries with a little more fullness and precision.

You will pardon me, I trust, if I come a little closer to the conception of free democracy based upon the people's will and expressing itself through representative assemblies under generally accepted constitutional forms. There are certain simple, practical tests by which the virtue and reality of any political democracy may be measured. Does the Government in any country rest upon a free, constitutional basis, assuring the people the right to vote according to their will, for whatever candidates they choose? Is there the right of free expression of opinion, free support, free opposition, free advocacy and free criticism of the Government of the day?

Are there Courts of Justice free from interference by the Executive or from threats of mob violence, and free from all association with particular political parties? Will these Courts administer public and well-established laws associated in the human mind with the broad principles of fair play and justice? Will there be fair play for the poor as well as for the rich? Will there be fair play for private persons as well as for Government officials? Will the rights of the individual, subject to his duties to the State, be maintained, asserted and exalted? In short, do the Government own the people, or do the people own the Government? There is the test. Here are some of the more obvious tests by which the political health and soundness of any community may be ascertained.

Now let us think of our other supreme task, the building of a world instrument of security, in which all peoples have a vital interest, and assuredly none more than those in these sorely-tried Low Countries, which have sometimes been called the cockpit of Europe.

The more closely the largest Powers of to-day are bound together in bonds of faith and friendship the more effective will be the safeguards against war and the higher the security of all other states and nations. It is evident of course that the affairs of Great Britain and the British Commonwealth and Empire, are becoming ever more closely interwoven with those of the United States, and that an underlying unity of thought and conviction increasingly pervades the English-speaking world. There can be nothing but advantage to the whole world from such a vast and benevolent synthesis. But we also in Britain have our Twenty Years' Treaty with Soviet Russia, which in no way conflicts with other associations, but which we hope may prove one of the sure anchors of world peace. We trust that in due course the natural unity and alliance between Great Britain and France will find reaffirmation in a new instrument. We welcome every step towards strength and freedom taken by the French people. We rejoice to see France moving forward to her old place in which if there were a void, Europe would be vitally wounded. We hope that the Western democracies of Europe may draw together in ever closer amity and ever closer association. This is a matter which should be very carefully considered and if found wise should be pressed from many angles with the utmost perseverance.

Special associations within the circle of the United Nations, such as those of which I have been speaking, or like the great unity of the British Empire and Commonwealth, or like the association which prevails throughout the Americas, North and South, far from weakening the structure of the supreme body of U.N.O., should all be capable of being fused together in such a way as to make U.N.O. indivisible and invincible; above all there must be tolerance, the recognition of the charm of variety, and the respect for the rights of minorities. There was a time when the Age of Faith endeavoured to prevent the Age of Reason, and another time when the Age of Reason endeavoured to destroy the Age of Faith. Tolerance was one of the chief features of the great liberalising movements which were the glory of the latter part of the nineteenth century, by which states of society were reached where the most fervent devotion to religion subsisted side by side with the fullest exercise of free thought. We may well recur to those bygone days, from whose standards of enlightenment, compassion and hopeful progress, the terrible twentieth century has fallen so far.

I say here as I said at Brussels last year that I see no reason why, under the guardianship of the world organisation, there should not ultimately arise the United States of Europe, both those of the East and those of the West which will unify this Continent in a manner never known since the fall of the Roman Empire, and within which all its peoples may dwell together in prosperity, in justice and in peace.

134

INDIA CABINET MISSION
STATEMENT ON THE ADJOURNMENT

A SPEECH TO THE HOUSE OF COMMONS
16 MAY 1946

---

12 *May—Britain's newest battleship, H.M.S. Vanguard, is christened by Princess Elizabeth at Greenock.*

[16 *May* 1946

I THINK the right hon. Gentleman [The Prime Minister] was right to read to the House the able but melancholy document to which we have listened, and it was appropriate that he should read it, instead of merely circulating it with the Votes. Certainly I have heard nothing for a long time which so deeply deserves the attention of Parliament and of the British nation, and the respectful attention which the House gave to every word uttered by the Prime Minister is a proof that this opinion is well founded. It would, of course, be most unwise this afternoon for any of us to attempt detailed comment upon the long and complicated proposals which have now been laid before us. I am bound to make clear without delay what is the position of the official Opposition. I, as the head of the Coalition Government and my colleagues of those days, are committed to the offer made to the people of India at the time of the Cripps mission in 1942, by which we offered Dominion Status as expressed by the Statute of Westminster, including, as it does, the latent right of secession. We offered this to the many peoples of India, subject to certain provisions.

The first of those provisions was that there should be broad, real, sincere agreement between the main Indian parties. The second was that in the Constitution we should have provision for the honourable discharge of the obligations we have contracted in India towards the minorities who, added together, are themselves a majority, and, also, for the discharge of those obligations embodied in our treaties with the Indian States. These proposals

135

were made by us at a moment when the danger of
Japanese invasion threatened India in a terrible manner,
and I, personally, was induced to agree to them by the
all-compelling war interest, as it seemed, of trying to
rally all the forces in India to the defence of their soil
against Japanese aggression and all the horrors that would
follow therefrom.

The Cripps mission failed. The answer which Mr.
Gandhi gave to the British Government at that moment
of mortal peril was "Quit India"; and he and the Congress
proceeded to raise or encourage a revolt, or widespread
disturbances, affecting, principally, the communications
on which the British and Indian Forces relied for holding
the threatened fronts. These disorders, although seriously
fomented, were suppressed with surprising ease and very
little loss of life, and the incitement to revolt found practically no response, outside the political classes, from the
great masses of the Indian people. We persevered with
the war; we toiled on; and presently the tide turned.
India was successfully defended, and it emerged from
this second world convulsion of our lifetime protected
from external violence by the arms, sea power and
diplomacy at the disposal of the British Empire, including,
of course, the valiant contribution of the Indian Forces
themselves and of the Gurkhas from Nepal. Nevertheless,
we still persisted in our offer which had been rejected
in 1942, and the late Secretary of State for India, Mr.
Amery, on June 14 last, when the Government had ceased
to be a Coalition and was a Conservative Government,
used the following words, which were quoted by my right
hon. Friend the Member for Saffron Walden [Mr. R. A.
Butler] when the proposal was made to send the Cabinet
Mission to India in February. This is what Mr. Amery
said:

As the statement makes clear, the offer of March
1942, stands in its entirety. That offer was based on
two main principles. The first is that no limit is set to
India's freedom to decide for herself her own destiny,
whether as a free member and partner in the British
Commonwealth or even without it. The second is that
this can only be achieved under a constitution or
constitutions framed by Indians to which the main
elements in India's national life are consenting parties.

By that statement we were and we are bound. Now, however, a new situation has arisen. We are confronted with the fact, reiterated in the Prime Minister's statement, that there is no agreement. The main elements in India's national life are not at the present time "consenting parties"—I am quoting the words of Mr. Amery's speech. No one will doubt the sincerity and the earnestness with which the Cabinet Ministers concerned and the Viceroy, [Lord Wavell], have laboured to bring about the solution of Indian disagreement. They have worked for that solution with the zeal that would be natural if it were to gain an empire and not to cast one away. But they have failed, and the fact that they have failed, through no fault of their own, in spite of all their efforts, devotion and ingenuity, is a fact which should, in itself, be an education in Indian matters, not only throughout this country, but throughout the world. During these negotiations it has been increasingly clear that the object sought for was not Dominion Status, with the subsequent and consequent right of secession, but direct and immediate independence. I am not sure that the results of this short circuit have been fully realised by the House. It certainly came as a surprise to me.

Thirdly, the new proposals which we have heard seem, at first sight, to shift the onus of deciding the future constitution of India from the Indian parties to His Majesty's Government, who have themselves come forward no doubt from the best of motives, with an elaborate and detailed scheme. In so far as this shifting of the onus may prove to be the case, it certainly seems to have been an unfortunate step. It goes beyond what we understood was the purpose of the Ministers' mission, the mandate which they received, which was—it was so defined by the Prime Minister, I think—to set up machinery for Indians to decide the form of government. It will, I hope, be common ground between us that we cannot enforce by British arms a British-made Constitution upon India against the wishes of any of the main elements in Indian life. That is a very important fact to establish.

There remains the discharge of our obligations to the Indian minorities and to the Indian States. We must study the document with prolonged and searching attention in order to see that these duties have been faithfully safeguarded. It would seem, at first sight, that attention should be particularly directed to the position of the Muslim community of nearly 80 million, who are the most warlike and formidable of all the races and creeds in the Indian sub-continent, and whose interests and culture are a matter of great consequence to India as a whole, and vital to the peace of India. Secondly, we must examine the provisions made for the depressed classes, or "untouchables" as they are called, who number nearly 60 million, and for whose status and future repeated assurances have been given and pledges made by many British Governments, in ancient and in more recent times.

Finally, there are the relations which the Indian States, which comprise a quarter of the population and a third of the territory of the Indian sub-continent, are to have to the Crown and to the new Government. At present, those relations are defined by solemn treaties dependent upon the paramountcy of the Crown. Apparently, this is to be abolished, in a sentence which was obscure: it may be neither one thing nor the other. It would be relegated to a kind of "no man's land", this question of paramountcy; and if that be so, it would seem—I do not attempt to probe the legal issues—that all foundation for these treaties would be swept away.

All these matters and many others will occur to hon. Members as they study the able White Paper. It will require several weeks of profound and earnest considera-tion, and certainly it would not, in my view, be desirable to bring this whole matter to Debate in the House of Commons, with all that a Debate in these circumstances might entail, in any precipitate manner. We do not even know at the present time, although we may elucidate that by question and answer, what are the legislative steps which would be required in the setting up of an interim government, or, in the event of an agreement being reached, for the creation of a new Constitution, or for the abrogation of the King's title as Emperor of India. Therefore, I say, in the name of the Opposition, that a new situation has been created, that we are bound to review it in the light of the existing facts, and that we reserve our entire freedom of action as to the future course we shall take.

EGYPT
[TREATY NEGOTIATIONS]
MOTION ON THE CIVIL ESTIMATES

A SPEECH TO THE HOUSE OF COMMONS
24 MAY 1946

ALTHOUGH we have not yet had the privilege of hearing his voice, I am sure I express the general sense of the House when I say that we are very glad to see the Foreign Secretary [Mr. Ernest Bevin] back in his place. I earnestly hope that his health has not been affected by the very hard work he has had to do and the amount of worry inseparable from the discharge of all his functions. I quite sympathise with his preoccupation. He was at Paris, and I regret very much that he was not able to give his full mind to the subject we are discussing to-day. He was announced as the head of the delegation, but it was understood that he could not go himself, and Lord Stansgate went. We have to be very careful not in any way to trespass on the conventions of the Chamber that nothing must be said dis-respectful to a Member of the other House, but I think I may go as far as to say that the substitution of Lord Stansgate for the Foreign Secretary involves the employment of an altogether lighter weight.

I come to the timetable of the recent Egyptian story. We must get the timetable right. Chronology is the secret of the matter. In 1936 a Treaty was made by which the British were to withdraw from Cairo and Alexandria to the Canal. The Egyptian Government were to build the barracks and installations in the Canal zone, and when they were built the British were to leave Cairo and Alexandria and repair to them. We should certainly have carried out that undertaking as and when it fell due, but later, long before the barracks were built or our time for removal to the Canal zone arrived, war burst on the world, and Egypt was soon threatened by an Italian invasion for which an army of nearly a quarter of a million troops had been moved steadily forward on the North African coast towards the Egyptian frontier. As we now know, it was to be included in Mussolini's

African Empire. Naturally, it was not possible for the Egyptian Government to build the barracks and installations during the war, nor could anybody expect that the British troops would voluntarily withdraw to the Canal zone in the years of war. If they had done so, Cairo would have been sacked by the Germans and the Italians, and the Delta would have been subjugated.

No one can suggest for a moment that we have not kept our word. No one can reproach the Egyptian Government with not having built the barracks. There is no ground whatever for what the Prime Minister the other night, I am sorry to say, called "suspicion" on the part of the Egyptians. The only sentiment that the Egyptians should permit themselves upon this war interlude is not suspicion but gratitude. However, the war has ended. Nearly all the Italians and Germans who ventured into Africa were destroyed or captured at a medium stage in the struggle. Egypt remained intact, enriched, securely defended. None of her troops were involved except in keeping internal order and for anti-aircraft defence. She was saved by the Armies of the British Empire from all the horrors which have racked the whole of Europe and large parts of Asia. And at the end we are assured that a large money debt is due from this country to Egypt for the supplies we purchased locally to feed the armies which were successfully defending the soil of the Delta. No, I repeat, gratitude, not suspicion, is the only sentiment becoming to the Government of Egypt.

There is however one practical step which should have been taken by us. It was mentioned to-day by my right hon. Friend the Member for Warwick and Leamington [Mr. Eden]. The withdrawal of the troops from Cairo and Alexandria ought to have been completed many months ago. It would have been a wise act of policy, and of efficient administration. It would have been entirely in the spirit, and going far beyond the letter, of the Treaty of 1936, to withdraw the British troops and to withdraw the enormous swollen staff from Cairo and from Alexandria even though the barracks in the Canal zone had not been erected by the Egyptian Government. Camps could have been put up, new telegraph communications could have been arranged, or rearranged, and the necessary forces could have been moved as a gesture of good will away from the Egyptian capital. That this was not done, is the responsibility of His Majesty's Government. I have no doubt that there were many difficulties, but that it was not done is their responsibility. The fault certainly does not lie on the 1936 Treaty, or anything in connection with the carrying out of that Treaty. The fault lies on the Treasury Bench. It may not be a very grievous fault; it may be one for which there are many explanations, but when we are told that the Egyptians have suspicions of our attitude at a time when an altogether different sentiment would be natural, then I think I am bound to point out that one way in which confidence in our desire not to interfere with their independence or sovereignty could have been sustained or stimulated would have been by a very considerable exodus—I think that is a very good local word—from Cairo and Alexandria of the enormous masses of staff officers and motor cars and so forth, which have been a prevailing feature of the streets of these cities during these years of war.

I would first examine the military aspect on which many speakers have delivered themselves. His Majesty's Government have made it clear after considering any military advice they have received, that they regard it as vitally important that the Suez Canal should be defended. When we talk about defending the Suez Canal, I presume the Government mean that it should be kept open. What reason could there be for a naval Power like Britain to fear it being kept open? If the warships or transports of another nation with a weaker navy obtained passage through the Suez Canal in time of war we should encounter them in the Indian Ocean basing ourselves either on Aden or the East African harbours. We do not suffer if the Canal is kept open. We can only suffer if it is closed. I assert that it is impossible to keep it open, unless British personnel are permanently stationed in the Canal zone. There may be doubts about our ability to keep it open in the air age, even if we have garrisons and fighter aircraft in that zone. But at any rate without that personnel there is no chance of keeping it open whatever. I do not believe that any military advice by the responsible Chiefs of Staff would challenge this assertion. If I am to be told that the Chiefs of Staff say that the canal can be

141

kept open without any permanent garrison and air forces in the Canal zone, I treat their opinions with the utmost respect, but put on record that I am utterly unconvinced. But we do not know what questions were put to the Chiefs of Staff or on what political data they were called upon to report.

In the case of the Irish ports, in the Spring of 1938, absolutely wrong political data in my opinion, were put before the Chiefs of Staff—another set of Chiefs of Staff—and they gave advice which nearly brought us to our ruin. [*Laughter*] I have heard all this mocking laughter before in the time of a former Government. I remember being once alone in the House, protesting against the cession of the Southern Irish ports. I remember the looks of incredulity, the mockery, derision and laughter I had to encounter on every side, when I said that Mr. de Valera might declare Ireland neutral. We are seeing exactly the same sort of thing happening to-day, although I am not so much alone as I used to be. I would hardly have believed it possible that such things could happen twice in a lifetime.

Let me make it perfectly clear that our position is that His Majesty's Government have no right to claim the approval of the Chiefs of the Staff for any policy without informing the House of the precise questions upon which their advice was obtained. I am astonished that people should talk continuously about the Suez Canal and say nothing about the Isthmus of Suez. Until my right hon. Friend [Mr. Eden] mentioned the matter this morning, and reminded us that this extraordinary region is the junction between three Continents, I have not heard the Isthmus mentioned, or read of it in any of the newspapers. Even if the Canal were blocked by aerial bombardment, as it might be if our fighter air force were overcome, or if a lucky shot or several lucky shots fell home, there is always the means of transhipment across the Isthmus of Suez. With our fleet and air power properly disposed, this can be assured. Under proper air protection in the Suez Canal zone, and with naval command of the Eastern Mediterranean, our troops could be disembarked at Suez and could re-embark at Red Sea ports. But if the overland route across the Isthmus is to be available, with the necessary installations and air bases, it is necessary to have British, and we hope, of course, Egyptian air and ground forces in effective control of the Canal zone. Without that failure is inevitable.

Let me now examine the other alternatives which are suggested. I have, of course, no official information on these matters. I rely upon the public organs and the general discussion that goes on in this country, and upon my own knowledge which I have acquired of these subjects in the not too distant past. It is widely said that we should establish ourselves in Palestine. The British troops who will in time of war defend the Canal, and the Isthmus of Suez, will be maintained, on this hypothesis, in camps or barracks in Southern Palestine. From there they will be able to fly in or will move in by motorised transport as soon as a state of emergency is reached. Here I have to speak of Palestine as a place of arms outside Egyptian territory, for British Forces which have to re-enter Egypt, at or before the moment of crisis. It is even said that our troops are already moving off in this direction, or that plans have been made to move them as fast as possible.

The consequence on the Palestine position of such a decision must not be overlooked. I am in entire agreement with the policy of the Government in trying to enlist American aid and co-operation in solving, or at any rate in dealing with the Jewish-Arab quarrel in Palestine. My views on this question are well known. I am for a Jewish national home in Palestine, with immigration up to the full absorptive capacity. I am also convinced that we cannot carry this out unless we have the help and active collaboration of the United States. Only by the action of our two Powers together can the objects to which we are pledged, and which the President of the United States evidently desires, be attained. I admire the Report of the Anglo-American Commission; but I think it is too much to put on Britain alone, single-handed, weakened as she is by her efforts in the war. It is too much for her alone to have to carry out this policy to which we are pledged and which the United States desire. I was most hopeful that the report of the Anglo-American Commission, and the manifest interest of the United States and the declaration of President Truman about the acceptance of

143

100,000 Jews immediately in Palestine, would lead to co-operation between the two countries.

I have no difference with His Majesty's Government on that. I agree with them entirely. But from the moment when Britain is going to use Palestine as a jumping-off ground to re-enter Egypt, and defend the Canal and the Isthmus, it seems to me that quite a different question is raised, and I fear that the hope of gaining the aid of the United States on the Palestine question, the Arab-Jew question in Palestine, will be seriously prejudiced. If they refuse, far and away the best hope of a solution being reached by the two great English-speaking Powers on the Palestine difficulty—in a manner which would be respected both by Jews and Arabs—all that vanishes and we shall find ourselves left alone in Palestine, from which we derive no advantage of any kind other than that of keeping our pledged word, and we shall have to carry on alone a wearing dispute either with the Jews or with the Arabs, or possibly with both. In any case we shall incur the increasing hostility and criticism of both these powerful forces, and, of course, of all the sideline spectators in all the various countries. It seems that by using Palestine as a jumping-off ground for the re-occupation of the Canal zone in time of an emergency we will impair the prospects of American aid, and will leave ourselves with the most thankless, profitless and unfortunate task that can be imagined. That is my first conclusion.

I turn Westward. It is also said, and here again I rely upon nothing but what I read in the different public prints, we may obtain the trusteeship of Cyrenaica, where powerful air bases can be established, so that another jumping-off ground may be established there. This also seems to me a dangerous and unwise alternative. First, we throw away our grand position of seeking nothing for ourselves except honour, nothing out of the late war, after all our prodigious exertions, except to see that our duty is done as best we can, and is thoroughly and consistently maintained. We become immediately an interested party, seeking new bases in lands which were not ours, and in which we had no treaty rights before the war began, and we shall be immediately represented—and I do not need to indicate some of the quarters from which we shall be immediately represented—as a greedy, grasping nation, playing at power politics and demanding territories formerly owned by others for the sake of our own designs upon Egypt. We may be quite sure that, if we seek to build a new strategic position in Cyrenaica, in relation to the Suez Canal and Isthmus, Russia will renew or reinforce her demand for bases in the Eastern Mediterranean. Upon this argument, we should enter under every disadvantage, and I do not believe that we should succeed in gaining our desires without paying an inordinate price. Therefore, I say that, both to the East and to the West of the Canal, these alternatives for jumping-off grounds would involve us in endless difficulty and vexation, that we shall come down from our high position as a Power not seeking any advantage from the war, that we shall encourage or condone all the appetites of other countries, and pay very dearly for any accomodation that we might obtain.

I go further and submit to the Committee, in extension of this argument, that, whether we establish our jumping-off grounds in Palestine or Cyrenaica, or both, and whatever price we pay for them, they will not be of any effective use in time of emergency for the purpose of defending the Canal or the Isthmus of Suez and keeping them open. Let us try to foresee what will happen if tension grows at any time in the future and an emergency arises. My right hon. Friend [Mr. A. Eden] very fittingly referred to this matter this morning. We shall then be in dispute with some other Great Power. That makes the emergency, and the moment will come when the military advisers will say, "We ought to re-occupy the military installations, camps and airfields in the Canal zone. We ought immediately to move in from our bases to the East or to the West of Egypt." What might be the behaviour of the Egyptian Government at such a juncture? We all know of the great sympathy there is when a small country is in so terrible a situation as that. No doubt we shall be told that there would be a treaty of alliance, but I cannot feel that, under such dire pressures, it would be of any avail. The great Power with whom we shall be in dispute would, of course, say to the Egyptian Government: "We should regard any movement into the Canal zone of British Forces as an unfriendly act." Can anyone suppose that the Egyptian Government, confronted with this

J

situation and not desiring anyhow to have British troops or Air Forces in the Canal zone, will not refuse permission for us to re-enter. And what then? They will say. "We do not agree that a state of international emergency has arisen, and we deny your right to decide upon the fact contrary to us."

Meanwhile, the days will be slipping very quickly by. If such an attitude were adopted and there were no British personnel in the Canal zone, the Egyptians, or any ill-disposed persons, would be able to put out of action all the installations, radar equipment, airfields and so on, long before we could get there and the mere threat that they would do so, and had perhaps prepared the necessary measures to do so, would render our attempt to enter futile even before it was made. Can one imagine the British Government in such a situation, when the dread issue of peace or war in a renewed world struggle may be hanging in the balance, forcing the issue, whether Egypt agreed or not? My right hon. Friend the Member for Warwick and Leamington reminded us of the difficulties of staff conversation. I have seen two great wars break out, and I know what a difficulty it was in the first, even to obtain the mobilisation of the British Fleet, which, in fact, I had to order in 1914 without the consent of the Cabinet, and only upon the personal assent of the Prime Minister [Mr. Asquith] and the Foreign Secretary [Sir Edward Grey]. This is not a question of the mobilisation of our own forces; it is a positive act, an act which will be widely regarded and denounced as an act of aggression, as an act destroying the last hopes of peace. There are always hopes of peace which it is a terrible thing to trample on and extinguish. Therefore, I say, we shall purchase our jumping-off grounds, either in Palestine or Cyrenaica, or both, only at the greatest detriment to our political position and policy among the nations. And when we have lavished our money upon them, they will prove useless in the hour of need.

The United Nations Organisation might well be called upon to prohibit the incursion of the British into Egypt. This would certainly be the case if the Egyptian Government stated that, in their view, the emergency did not warrant the action. Therefore, both alternatives, costly as they will be, will be utterly futile. Now it appears that the

Egyptian Government already say: "There must be no return until Egypt declares war."

That is what I read only yesterday in the newspapers from Cairo. We have yet to learn what answer His Majesty's Government will make to this. The other night the Prime Minister said:

"We can only carry out our obligations if we have been put in a position by the Egyptian Government to bring our Forces into action in the area without loss of time in an emergency——"

I intervened to say: "Before fighting begins."

The Prime Minister answered: "Yes, certainly." That is a very solid, serious, resolute statement and the Prime Minister further said:

"If the whole matter breaks down, there is still, of course, the 1936 Treaty."

The more I think of these alternative devices, the more I feel that the surest resting place at this time would be the 1936 Treaty and that we should rest there for the next five or six years in the hope that U.N.O., meanwhile, will grow up, and gather a great world army which will put so many of these strategic dangers, nightmares and calculations back into the limbo of the vanished past. So much for the military aspect; I hope it may be carefully considered by the House.

I now come to the diplomatic procedure. The right hon. Gentleman the Foreign Secretary has been working night and day in Paris. The position which has been adopted by the Government is that, first, they will evacuate Egypt, and, secondly, they will defend the Canal. This is a complete and total contradiction in terms. Then we are told that, in order to start on the negotiations in goodwill, we had, "reluctantly", to say—that was the Lord President's [Mr. Hubert Morrison's] remark—we will evacuate Egypt and that the second stage will be to examine how the Canal and Isthmus can be defended without British troops, and if it is clearly proved that anyone can see that anything of this kind is possible, the negotiations will break down and we shall revert to the Treaty of 1936.

I cannot imagine a more lamentable and, indeed, disingenuous procedure. We promise something as a prelude to the negotiations in order to give them a good start, but, in fact, we concede the whole point at issue, subject to conditions which cannot be obtained and, then, a little later on as the discussions proceed, we shall either have to accept some pure sham, or the negotiations will break down. Then, indeed, we shall be reproached with having excited hopes which could never be realised and with having endeavoured to procure Egypt's goodwill at the outset, when all along we knew we could not possibly give them what we had promised. That is not the way to deal with any people, least of all is it the way to deal with an Oriental people. I do not believe in tantalising diplomacy, holding out hopes which fail because of the inherent difficulties in the path of the negotiators.

The course which the Government have been pursuing seems to me to be marked with the utmost unwisdom. A perfectly sensible and straightforward course was open. The Government of Egypt had the right to raise the question of the revision of the Treaty at the tenth year. They have done so. His Majesty's Government could then have replied, "We will certainly discuss the matter with you, but you should first of all tell us exactly what it is that you propose and how the essential matters of the defence of the Canal and Isthmus of Suez are to be provided for." The Egyptian Government would next, in due course, have put forward their plan. We could then have said, "We will discuss this plan with the Dominions, and especially with those Dominions who have in two wars exerted themselves in your defence, and the graves of whose soldiers in scores of thousands lie in the desert." We ought to have approached this grave issue as a united Commonwealth and Empire.

There is another important point which the late Foreign Secretary has mentioned. We ought to have made sure that the Egyptian Government speak for the other great parties in Egypt besides the Court party which is now in power. There are the Wafd who lately had a considerable majority. What has happened now? The Egyptian Government make their proposals, and if they were all accepted that would not settle our relations with Egypt. The Wafd opposition would simply go on better. As it is, they are already denouncing this offer of the evacuation of Egypt as wholly insufficient because the question of the Sudan has not been settled in a similar manner. We ought to have approached this matter with much fuller knowledge of what the Egyptians of the leading parties would agree as a settlement, and we ought to have met in council beforehand with our Dominions and presented a united delegation to take part in the discussion. That would have been a reasonable and sensible procedure.

Let me, however, say this. Great departures of this character ought not to be influenced by threats of mob violence and by threats of attacks on British troops and installations. There have always been such threats. It is the responsibility of the Egyptian Government to keep the Treaty which we have signed with them, until another one is signed, and meanwhile to maintain order in their country. I have not the slightest doubt that they have full capacity to do so. The Government have taken an entirely wrong course while there was a perfectly right and proper course open to them, and further, if this wrong course is persisted in it will ruin our interests in the Middle East, destroy our communications with our possessions and fellow Dominions in the Indian and Pacific Oceans, and will in the Foreign Secretary's own expressive phrase, "Sever the lifeline of the British Empire".

In our brief Debate on the Adjournment Motion a fortnight ago, I said that the Dominions had not been consulted. I said they had been told. I asked the Prime Minister this question pointedly, and when I shook my head at his reply, he rejoined amid a roar of cheers that I was not there. It appears, however, that I was right. The Prime Minister has withdrawn from the position which he took up. He has not only withdrawn but he has apologised —a manly and, I may also add, the only thing to do. We now know that instead of an agreement with the Dominions upon this policy of Egypt, and abandoning the defence of the Suez canal, as I have declared, all that the Governments of the Dominions have agreed, is that we should shoulder the responsibility alone. Is it our responsibility alone? Have we any moral right to assume the entire burden of dealing with the fate of our communications through the Mediterranean, and of the defence of the Canal and the Isthmus of Suez? It seems to me that this is a very dangerous right for us to claim, and a very onerous responsibility to assume. After all, in the 1914-1918 war and in this last war—the defence of these large interests has been very largely entrusted to the Australians, New Zealanders and

149

South Africans. Without their aid we would not have succeeded in protecting Egypt. It is a strange thing to call upon brave soldiers to travel thousands of miles across the ocean to fight for great strategic objectives, all well-defined and fully declared, and then to turn round immediately afterwards, and discredit altogether those strategic objectives—or apparently do so—for which so many men, at our request and under our leadership, have come so far to give their lives. Apart from the interests of Britain, apart from the danger to Imperial communications in the Eastern Mediterranean, I say a shock has been given to the British self-governing Commonwealth, and their confidence in the guidance and leadership of the mother country, has been painfully and injuriously affected by the apparent casting away of those interests which we have hitherto declared to them were vital.

It always looks so easy to solve problems by taking the line of least resistance. Again and again in my life I have seen this course lead to the most unexpected result, and what looks like being the easy road turns out to be the hardest and most cruel. No nation is so remarkable as ours for the different moods through which it passes, moments of great dejection, moments of sublime triumph, heroism, fortitude and then exhaustion. What has been gained with enormous effort and sacrifice, prodigious and superb acts of valour, slips away almost unnoticed when the struggle is over. I earnestly hope that the Government—with whom I do not attempt to pick a quarrel, but to whom I am giving a serious warning on this matter at this moment—will realise that there is only one safe resting place for this country, and that is the firm maintenance of the Treaty of 1936.

FOREIGN AFFAIRS

A SPEECH TO THE HOUSE OF COMMONS
5 JUNE 1946

THE year that has passed since the end of the German war has been darkened by a virtual breakdown or stalemate in the concert and collaboration of the three Great Powers, as well as by a painful decline in British influence and prestige. It would be wrong to cast the blame of these misfortunes upon the Foreign Secretary, to whose sombre patient speech we listened yesterday. We feel sure he has done his best to resist the sad and dangerous tendencies with which we are oppressed before the world, and he has stood forth as the representative of much that is wise and courageous in the British character. No criticism which I may make on particular aspects of his administration is intended to obscure the outstanding services which he has rendered in this period of disappointment and perplexity.

The problems of the aftermath, the moral and physical exhaustion of the victorious nations, the miserable fate of the conquered, the vast confusion of Europe and Asia, combine to make a sum total of difficulty, which, even if the Allies had preserved their wartime comradeship, would have taxed their ressources to the full. Even if we in this island had remained united, as we were in the years of peril, we should have found much to baffle our judgment, and many tasks that were beyond our strength. I am an opponent of the Socialist Party but I readily admit that they have made an important contribution to the cause of world peace. They have made this contribution by their resolute denunciation of Communism and by their refusal to allow the Communist Party to enter and permeate their ranks. The Communist Party in this island is not at present a serious danger. Everyone remembers how they urged us into the late war and how, when we were already irrevocably committed, they immediately turned about, on orders from Moscow, and after some——

MR. GALLACHER [Fife, West]: That is a lie.

HON. MEMBERS: Withdraw.

MR. CHURCHILL: I leave it to you, Mr. Speaker, I really do not mind. I thought, as I remarked on a previous occasion, that the hon. Member was well broken to the House, and not likely to make this kind of observation.

MR. GALLACHER: It is necessary occasionally.

MR. CHURCHILL: I see. I do not think that I need trouble myself very much with the hon. Member's opinion, but I quite understand that he will not like what I am going to say. I certainly will not be deterred from saying it by the prospect of any further insults from him. Everyone remembers how they immediately turned about, on orders from Moscow, and after some abject and grovelling retractions on the part of their leaders, they denounced our life struggle as a capitalist, Imperialist war. We also remember how thereafter, they did their best, their utmost—which was very little—to hamper our national defence. Nor can we forget that, as far as they were concerned, we might have sunk in 1940 and 1941 beneath the ocean and been blotted out for ever, except as Hitler's serfs, from among the nations of mankind——

MR. GALLACHER: That is not true. On a point of Order, Mr. Speaker, I challenge the Leader of the Opposition that if he goes to the Home Office he will find that the first report made on the blitz and on the means that should be taken to care for the people, was written by the hon. Member for West Fife. [*Hon. Members*: "*Speech.*"] It is a fact.

MR. SPEAKER: That is not quite a point of Order.

MR. GALLACHER: It is all wrong to say what the right hon. Gentleman has said.

MR. CHURCHILL: We might have been blotted out for ever, as far as they were concerned, and I say it will take them many years to live that down in the British Isles. But it is not at home that the Communists are important. The significance of the action of the Labour Party lies in its effects abroad. There is no doubt that it has brought strength to Great Britain at a time when other causes were weakening us, and there is no doubt that it has produced beneficial consequences on both sides of the Atlantic Ocean. The Foreign Secretary has been a leader in all this and he deserves a full share of the credit.

I shall now permit myself to make a few comments upon various aspects of our affairs in this vast and gloomy field. I must make it clear at the outset that I have no official information. Since I laid down my office at the end of July last, I have not seen any of the Foreign Office telegrams. I form my opinion from my knowledge of the past, from the newspapers, and from distinguished people from abroad who sometimes when they visit this country come to see me. His Majesty's Ministers have decided to deal with the Parliamentary Opposition on strict party lines. No doubt we have our own personal relationship arising out of the long comradeship of the war—there is always that background—but there is absolutely no official contact of any kind between the Government and the Opposition in foreign affairs, except occasional acts of courtesy like handing me a copy of an announcement of great importance half an hour before it is read——

THE PRIME MINISTER (MR. ATTLEE): It is quite true that the actual text of that announcement was only handed over a short time before the meeting, but I must point out that I did bring to the notice of the right hon. Gentleman, and also of the right hon. Gentleman the Member for Warwick and Leamington [Mr. Eden] and of the right hon. Gentleman the Member for West Bristol [Mr. O. Stanley] our intentions with regard to Egypt in the week before.

MR. CHURCHILL: I was only using this as an illustration. It is quite true, as the Prime Minister has said, that he asked me and my two colleagues to go to Downing Street about ten days before; but that was not on Egypt, that was on Palestine. He then told us of the White Paper, the report about Palestine. He was not even in a position to hand us a copy at that moment. Conversation ran on and Egypt was mentioned, it is perfectly true. It is also true, if we are to go into these matters, that a few days later I met the Prime Minister in the Lobby and we had a few words in private in my room in which he mentioned—if I may say so—the word "evacuation", and I said straight away we could not agree to that. These were not matters of important consultation. We have not been consulted in any way. [*An Hon. Member: "Why object?"*], I am not objecting at all. The French have hitherto dealt, since the war, with their foreign affairs on a national basis. The United States of America, taught by Mr. Wilson's disastrous mistake in 1919, are careful to include in their delegation leading representatives of the Republican Party; but His Majesty's Government have followed the Russian principle in foreign affairs of one-party Government. I am not complaining. I do not suggest that the practice should be altered at this late stage, when domestic divergencies grow wider and deeper month by month.

We do our utmost on this side of the House to support His Majesty's Government in the foreign sphere, and to impart as far as possible a national character to British foreign policy, but if I should be misinformed on any point in what I am going to say, and the Government have reasons for their action which they have not disclosed, the House, I hope, will make allowance for any error into which I, as a member of the general public, may fall.

Let me begin with Greece. It was not mentioned yesterday. In Greece the course of events has vindicated the policy of the National Coalition Government. This policy in the main has been followed by the present Government. For all purposes of controversy, it rests upon two documents, either of which it is very hard to challenge. The first is the report of the trade union delegation which, under Sir Walter Citrine, at my invitation visited Athens in January, 1945, and revealed the atrocities committed by the Communists in the city. The second is, of course, the report of the British, American and French Commission which supervised the elections in March, 1946. There is no doubt whatever that these elections were the fairest ever conducted in Greece, or in any Balkan State. They have proved conclusively that the Greek people did not wish to have dictatorial power in Greece seized by a Communist minority through a process of revolution, treachery, terrorism and murder, and that we were right to intervene by force of arms to prevent such a disaster.

We have never intended or desired to interfere in the affairs of Greece, except in so far as was necessary to enable the Greek people to decide freely the form and character of their own Government after the confusion of the war and of the German occupation. I thought, and I still think, that it would have been better to hold the plebiscite before the elections, and that is how it was originally planned. The Foreign Secretary told us some months ago that, while he was not opposed to monarchy in Greece if the Greek people desired it, he did not want a "party Monarchy". I am very much afraid that the reversal in procedure which he has adopted runs a risk of bringing

154

about the very thing which he wishes to avoid. Nevertheless, I hope that, should the Greek people vote for a Monarchy, the King will have the wisdom and the virtue to make it clear that he is the servant of the State, on a level above all parties and equally accessible to all parties. I hope our troops in Greece will be able to come home as soon as the plebiscite has been taken. They deserve, and I believe they will receive, the heartfelt gratitude of the Greek people.

His Majesty's Government have shown, it seems to me, a wise restraint, or, at least, a marked lack of enthusiasm, in not interfering in the internal affairs of Spain. None of us likes the Franco régime, and, personally, I like it as little as I like the present British Administration, but, between not liking a Government and trying to stir up civil war in a country, there is a very wide interval. It is said that every nation gets the government that it deserves. Obviously, this does not apply in the case of Great Britain, but I have a sort of feeling that the Spanish people had better be left alone to work out their own salvation, just as we hope to be left alone by foreigners in order to work out ours. It seemed to me very unwise of the late French Government, under Communist impulsion, to take such an aggressive line against Spain. It is a very shocking thing for the Cabinet of any State to try to solve its own political problems by beating up another country. In this case, French intervention has only had the result of giving Franco a new lease of life.

The Spaniards are a proud and morose people, and they have long memories. They have not forgotten Napoleon and the attempted French subjugation of Spain 130 years ago. Besides this, they have had a civil war which has cost them a million lives. Even the Communists in Spain will not thank foreign Governments for trying to start another civil war, and anything more silly than to tell the Spaniards that they ought to overthrow Franco, while, at the same time, assuring them that there will be no military intervention by the Allies, can hardly be imagined. Still more ill-placed is the Polish intervention before U.N.O. Everyone knows where their impulse comes from. Let us discard cant and humbug. I believe it is a fact, to put it mildly, that there is as much freedom in Spain under General Franco's reactionary régime—and actually a good deal more security and happiness for ordinary folk—than there is in Poland at the present time.

We are now confronted with a proposal that all the nations of U.N.O. should break off relations with Spain. Before I examine that project in detail, there are some general propositions now in vogue which deserve scrutiny. Let me state them in terms of precision: "All oppression from the Left is progress. All resistance from the Right is reactionary. All forward steps are good, and all backward steps are bad. When you are getting into a horrible quagmire, the only remedy is to plunge in deeper and deeper." These rules, it seems to me, from time to time require review by the intelligentsia. They require review in the light of experience and of the circumstances we see around us. I was in favour of not admitting the present Spanish Government to U.N.O. It would have given general offence in the new Assembly, upon which so much depends. But this idea of all our countries withdrawing their ambassadors, will only have the effect of preventing us worrying and admonishing General Franco with diplomatic representations and gradually smoothing the way for better times in Spain. It will also affront Spanish national pride to such an extent that there will be a general rally of Spaniards to the Government of their country, and its sovereign independance.

What is to happen when the ambassadors have been withdrawn? Our trade with Spain is very valuable. We get all sorts of things from Spain, from iron ore to oranges. We shall have to go on trading with Spain. We have an important market there, and I suppose that when we have withdrawn our Ambassadors, we shall require to have commercial counsellors, or some other arrangement, in order to remain in fruitful contact with one of the oldest and now least aggressive of the nations of Europe. I suppose there would be instituted a kind of diplomatic black market, with its agents going in through the back door, instead of through the front. We may be quite sure that 28 million people living on that great peninsula, would be in some contact with the outer world, even without the ambassadors now accredited to them. I should have thought that we had enough troubles on our hands without getting into such futile and fatuous entanglements, and I do not at all credit the Government with any such unwisdom.

156

We all hope that the conference of the Foreign Secretaries, this Big Four or Big Three—or Big Two-and-a-Half,
as the anti-British American newspapers sometimes describe
them—will soon make some progress in settling European
affairs. [*Interruption.*] I think it applied to nations, not to
individuals. I could not feel any satisfaction when I read
in the newspapers that one of the first points upon which
they had all been able to come to a unanimous decision in
Paris was to confirm the assignment of the Austrian Tyrol
to Italy. This was always held by liberal-minded folk in
many lands to be one of the worst blots on the Treaty
of Trianon which was not, in itself, a model in European
annals. It is, of course, quite true—I do not wish to conceal
anything—that Hitler and Mussolini, after the most careful
consideration of the problem, agreed to confirm and enforce
the decision. But, surely, those two miscreants are rather
out of the picture to-day. The sentence I myself contributed
to the Atlantic Charter, about no transference of territory
apart from the will of the local inhabitants, has proved, in
many cases, to be an unattainable ideal and, in any case,
did not, in my experience, apply to enemy countries. But
I know of no case in the whole of Europe, more than that
of the Austrian Tyrol, where the Atlantic Charter, and the
subsequent Charter of U.N.O., might have been extended
to the people who dwell in this small, but well-defined,
region which is now involved in the general war settlement.

Why cannot the natives of this mountainous and beautiful
land, the land of the patriot Hofer, be allowed to say a
word about their destiny on their own behalf? Why cannot
they have a fair and free plebiscite there under the supervision of the Great Powers? Let me put this question. Is
it not illogical to have one standard of ethnic criteria for
Trieste and Venezia Giulia, and another for the Southern
Tyrol? The Soviet Government are quite logical; they are
willing to override the ethnic criteria in both cases. I think
that we might try, in this case, to emulate their symmetry
of thought. There are no grounds for suggesting that any
decisions adverse to the restoration of the Southern Tyrol
to Austria were taken by the Government of which I was
the head. We made positive declarations, in agreement
with our Allies, about the independence of Austria, and by
that was meant pre-Anschluss Austria. But this is in no
way inconsistent with the addition to Anschluss Austria,

or pre-Anschluss Austria, of the Southern Tyrol, if it is the wish of the people of that country.

No quarrel remains between us and Austria. Every liberal principle which we proclaim—and the application of liberal principles is the main hope of Europe—will be impugned by the assignment of the Austrian Tyrol to Italy against the wishes of its inhabitants. I have every desire that we should live on the most friendly terms with Italy. I look forward to seeing that historic country take its place in the concert of Europe. As Ministers opposite will remember, I made the utmost exertions, as Minister of Defence, to prevent Italy from being robbed of her fleet, and I was supported by my colleagues in the War Cabinet in the loan to Russia of 13 British warships to prevent the immediate distribution of the Italian fleet, which was fighting with us, between the three great Powers. We have not been told what happens to these 13 vessels now that the Italian fleet is to be divided up among the three great Powers. It might be a graceful gesture to Russia to convert the loan into a gift. We certainly wish to welcome Russia and her navy and her merchant commerce freely to the oceans; we recognise the importance to Russia of access to warm water ports, and I should like to hear from the Government what their intentions are about these 13 vessels. I mention them now, only to show our great care for Italy, and our desire that she should draw a line between the miserable past and what I trust will be a brighter future.

We were glad to hear the important declaration of the Foreign Secretary about the port and city of Trieste. The concessions already made by Great Britain and the United States in accepting the French compromise, or *via media*, go very far, and the three leading Western democracies ought now to stand firmly together on this point. The internationlisation of the port of Trieste is, as the Foreign Secretary said, vitally important to the whole of Central Europe and, particularly, to the Danubian Basin. I welcome the firm language he has used upon that subject. From all this tangle, some salient points emerge which the House ought to recognise: the sovereignty of nations, the equal rights of States, both great and small, under world law and, in regard to borderland or disputed territory, the wishes of the people concerned to be ascertained by free and fair elections. We shall be pretty safe if we stick to those simple, broad, well-tried principles.

I turn to another quarter. I have been struck in my visits to Belgium in November and to Holland recently, with the enormous recovery made by those countries since the war, and the vigour with which all parties there are unitedly plunging into the whole process of national recovery. The close relations which are growing up between those two countries, the association of the Catholic Church with extremely advanced liberal and social policies, the general aversion from Communism, all these are evident. But what impressed me even more, was the deep affection of these countries for Great Britain. Rightly or wrongly, they have it in their hearts that Britain, by her resistance when she was all alone, saved the world and enabled their liberties to be regained. Why are we not to be close friends with the Dutch and the Belgians? Has any other nation in the world a right to object to that?

We have all watched with deep satisfaction the steady recovery and rise of France, and the strength and stability increasingly shown by her people. The wounds which France suffered in the war were frightful. They were not only physical wounds; there were times when the soul of France seemed in jeopardy. I never lost faith in the greatness of the French people or the grandeur of France, and we all rejoice to-day to see her increasingly taking her place in the forefront of the free democracies of the world. The Foreign Secretary did not make any reference to an Anglo-French treaty. Perhaps it has been wise to wait until the shape which the immediate post-war Governments of France will take has become manifest. But, of course, our relations with France do not depend on signatures attached to formal documents. Our friendship has sprung out of our comradeship, out of our former victory, out of our agony and out of our final triumph. I can only say here, as I said to the States-General at The Hague, that there can be no revival of European dignity and splendour without a strong France. I trust we shall endeavour to establish intimate and cordial relations with all our nearest neighbours on the Continent, in order that all the populations concerned can have the best standard of living possible in these hard times, and also that common regional security shall not be ignored.

Here let me deal with two expressions of prejudice which are now used in an endeavour to prevent friendly peoples coming together to mutual advantage without hostility to anyone else in the world. The first is the word *"bloc"*. To be on good, easy, sympathetic terms with your neighbours is to form a *bloc*. To form a *bloc* is a crime, according to every Communist in every land, unless it be a Communist *bloc*. So much for the word *"bloc"*. It happens also that we are closely associated with the United States. We think very much alike on great world problems on the morrow of our victory—because the British and Americans did have something to do with the victory. The Foreign Secretary often finds himself at these conferences in agreement with Mr. Byrnes, just as my right hon. Friend the Member for Warwick and Leamington [Mr. Eden] was often in agreement with Mr. Hull, and just as I was often in agreement with President Roosevelt and, after him, with President Truman. Now all this process, without which I can assure hon. Members we should not be sitting here this afternoon, is to be condemned and ruled out by the expression "ganging up". If two countries who are great friends agree on something which is right, they are "ganging up", so they must not do it. We should brush aside these terms of prejudice, which are used only to darken counsel and which replace, in certain minds, the ordinary processes of thought and human feeling. If the liberal nations of the world—the Western democracies, as they are called—are to be turned from their natural associations and true affinities by bugbear and scarecrow expressions like *"bloc"* and "ganging up", they will only have themselves to thank when once again they fall into misfortune.

The House could not but be impressed by the measured and formidable complaint which the Foreign Secretary unfolded yesterday, step by step and theatre by theatre, about the treatment which the Western Allies have been receiving from the Soviet Government. Deep and widespread sorrow has been caused in Britain by the decline of contact and goodwill between our country and Russia. There was, and there still is, an earnest desire to dwell in friendly co-operation with the Soviet Government and the Russian people. On the other hand, the Foreign Secretary received the approval of the vast majority of the people when he protested against the prolonged, systematic campaign of vilification which has been, and is being daily pumped out upon us by the Soviet propaganda machine. Apart from the Communists and the "cryptos"—that is to say, the Communists without the pluck to call themselves by their proper name—very few people were shocked by the homely language he chose to employ at the London Conference in January,* nor indeed, do the vast majority of the House of Commons dissent from the argument he unfolded in the speech with which he opened this Debate.

Nevertheless, I am sure that it is the general wish of the British and Russian peoples that they should have warm and friendly feelings towards each other. We seek nothing from them except their goodwill, and we could play our part, with other nations, in coming to their aid with such resources as we may have if their just rights or safety were assailed. We were all glad to hear the Foreign Secretary say that he was still in favour of the 50-years treaty or 20-years treaty with Russia. Personally, I attach great importance to the existing Treaty. I have never made a speech on European questions without referring to it. It may go through bad times—lots of treaties do—but it would be a great misfortune if it were incontinently discarded. But surely, talking of treaties, this Four Power 25 year treaty between America, Britain, Russia and France, which the United States have proposed to deal with Germany, is a tremendous project. The Foreign Secretary was right to say how much more valuable such a guarantee of the United States to be in the forefront of European affairs for 25 years would be to Soviet Russia for her own security, than the harnessing—"harnessing" was the word—of a number of reluctant or rebellious border or satellite States. I am very glad to know that we are to support the United States proposal, and I thought the words which the Foreign Secretary used about it were singularly well chosen.

However, there is no use in concealing the fact that the Soviet propaganda and their general attitude have made a profound impression upon this country since the war, and all kinds of people in great numbers are wondering very much whether the Soviet Government really wish to be friends with Britain or to work wholeheartedly for the speedy re-establishment of peace, freedom and plenty

---

* General Assembly of United Nations—17 January 1946.

throughout the world. Across the ocean, in Canada and the United States, the unfriendly Soviet propaganda has also been very effective in the reverse direction to what was intended. The handful of very able men who hold 180 million Soviet citizens in their grasp ought to be able to get better advice about the Western democracies. For instance, it cannot be in the interest of Russia to go on irritating the United States. There are no people in the world who are so slow to develop hostile feelings against a foreign country as the Americans, and there are no people who, once estranged, are more difficult to win back. The American eagle sits on his perch, a large, strong bird with formidable beak and claws. There he sits motionless, and M. Gromyko is sent day after day to prod him with a sharp pointed stick—now his neck, now under his wings, now his tail feathers. All the time the eagle keeps quite still. But it would be a great mistake to suppose that nothing is going on inside the breast of the eagle. I venture to give this friendly hint to my old wartime comrade, Marshal Stalin. Even here, in our patient community, Soviet propaganda has been steadily making headway backwards. I would not have believed it possible that in a year, the Soviets would have been able to do themselves so much harm, and chill so many friendships in the English-speaking world.

Let us also remember that the Soviet Government is greatly hampered in its relations with many foreign countries by the existence of Communist fifth columns. There are some States which hang in the balance, where these Communist organisms are aspiring, or conspiring, to seize the control of the Governments, although they are in a small majority in the population. Of course, if they succeed, the State is overturned and becomes harnessed as a satellite, but everywhere else the activities of Communist fifth columns only do Russia harm. In fact, they are an active process in bringing about the very thing which the Soviets most dislike, namely, a general consensus of opinion against them and their ways. I earnestly hope that when this present technique and these methods have been fully tried and found not helpful to the interests and the greatness of Soviet Russia, they will be discarded, and that a more reasonable and neighbourly spirit will prevail, in which case I am sure we would all be very ready, so far as words are concerned, to let bygones be bygones.

Then there is the Communist spy system, the exposure of which is at present confined to Canada. It has made a deep mark on Transatlantic opinion. These revelations, by no means complete, have stirred the whole Dominion of Canada. Of course, many countries have sought and seek information about the designs of other countries. But the difference between that and the Soviet system is that they do not have to hire their agents in the ordinary way. In the Communist sect it is a matter of religion to sacrifice one's native land for the sake of the Communist Utopia. People who, in ordinary life, would behave in a quite honourable manner, if they are infected with this disease of the mind will not hesitate a moment to betray their country or its secrets. There are many instances of that. It is this peculiarity which renders Soviet Communist espionage as dangerous as their propaganda is futile and often even childish. The Canadian Government and its Prime Minister, Mr. Mackenzie King, have only done their duty with courage and justice in exposing what has been brought up in the Dominion of Canada.

Far more serious than anything in the sphere of propaganda or espionage are the facts of the European situation. I have been censured for wrongly championing the Russian claims to the Curzon Line. So far as the Curzon Line is concerned, I hold strongly that this was a rightful Russian frontier, and that a free Poland should receive compensation at the expense of Germany both in the Baltic and in the West, going even to the line of the Oder and the Eastern Neisse. If I and my colleagues erred in these decisions we must be judged in relation to the circumstances of the awful conflict in which we were engaged. We are not now in the presence of the Curzon Line as the Western frontier of Soviet authority. It is no longer a question of the line of the Oder. So long as Poland is held in control the Soviet domination in one form or another, runs from Stettin in the Baltic to the outskirts of Trieste in the Adriatic, and far South of that. The Russified frontier in the North is not the Curzon Line; it is not on the Oder; it is on the Elbe. That is a tremendous fact in European history, and one which it would be the height of unwisdom to ignore. Not only has a curtain descended, from the Baltic to the Adriatic, but behind that, is a broad band of territory containing all the capitals of Eastern and Central Europe and many ancient States and nations, in which dwell nearly one-third of the population of Europe, apart from Russia. At the present moment all this is ruled or actively directed by that same group of very able men, the Commissars in the Kremlin, which already disposes with despotic power of the fortunes of their own mighty Empire. It is here in this great band or belt, if anywhere, that the seeds of a new world war are being sown.

We may be absolutely sure that the Sovietising and, in many cases, the Communising of this gigantic slice of Europe, against the wishes of the overwhelming majority of the people of many of these regions, will not be achieved in any permanent manner without giving rise to evils and conflicts which are horrible to contemplate. Meanwhile, it was clear from the speech of the Foreign Secretary that the policy of the Soviet Government seems, up to the present, to be to delay all final settlements of peace and to prevent the peoples of Western and Eastern Europe from getting together in friendly, social and economic association, as many of them would like to do. On a short-term view, time is on the side of the Soviets, because the longer a free and peaceful settlement of Europe is delayed, the more time the Russian forces and Communist organisations have at their disposal in order to liquidate whatever elements obnoxious to their ambitions venture to show themselves in these wide lands. The populations of the Baltic States are no longer recognisable as those which existed before the war. They have suffered a double liquidation, both at German hands and Russian hands. The population of Pomerania is said to be but a third of what it was before the war. There was a very interesting article in the *Manchester Guardian* on that point the other day. Every effort is being made to Communise and Russify the whole of the Soviet-occupied zone of Germany.

Poland is denied all free expression of her national will. Her worst appetites of expansion are encouraged. At the same time, she is held in strict control by a Soviet-dominated government who do not dare have a free election under the observation of representatives of the three or four Great Powers. The fate of Poland seems to be an unending tragedy, and we, who went to war, all ill-prepared, on her behalf, watch with sorrow the strange outcome of our endeavours. I deeply regret that none of the Polish troops—and I must say this—who fought with us on a score of battlefields, who poured out their blood in the common cause, are to be allowed to march in the Victory Parade. They will be in our thoughts on that day. We shall never forget their bravery and martial skill, associated with our own glories at Tobruk, at Cassino and at Arnhem. Austria and Hungary are stifled, starved and weighed down by masses of Russian troops. We agree with the Foreign Secretary in all he said on this point yesterday. I do not speak of Czechoslovakia, which is a special case. For the time being I accept President Benes's statement that it is the duty of Czechoslovakia to interpret Russia to Western Europe and Western Europe to Russia. But for the rest—I do not want to go into more detail—the position is gravely and woefully disquieting.

All this brings us to the problem of Germany. Seventy or eighty millions of Germans still exist in the centre of Europe, constituting its largest racial block. Two-fifths of the German population lie East of the "iron curtain", and three-fifths to the Westward. Together with the Americans and to some extent the French, the responsibility for the control of this vast mass of three-fifths of one of the most powerful nations in the world lies upon us. It lies upon the three Allied Western Powers. The Soviet Government are organising their own zone through the establishment in power of German Communist elements with Soviet support and control. Different methods are being adopted in the British and American zones. We have to face the fact that, as we are going on at present, two Germanys are coming into being, one organised more or less on the Russian model, or in the Russian interest, and the other on that of the Western democracies, and that the line of demarcation is not fixed with regard to any historical or economic conditions, but simply runs along the line agreed to when the whole future of the war was highly speculative, and nobody knew to what points armies would be likely to go or what would become of the struggle. It runs along the line to which, a year ago, the British and American Armies voluntarily retired—a 150 mile retreat in some cases, on a 400 mile front—after the Germans had surrendered.

Thus, the bulk of the German population and their

manufacturing resources are in Anglo-American hands and the bulk of their food grounds in Soviet hands. It would not be contrary to the decision reached at Potsdam if His Majesty's Government followed the United States in not allowing any further transference to Russia of German factories and plant under their control except in return for proportionate deliveries of food for the German people, whose livelihood and, indeed, whose lives, depend in some cases upon those factories and upon the productivity of their area. In this way alone, will the burden upon us be lessened. Either we shall get the food for the Germans for whom we are responsible, or we shall be able to take the best measures possible to enable them to earn their own living. The first thing is that the Germans should earn their own living. It would seem very foolish to deprive them of the means of doing so, and then have to take the bread out of our own children's mouths in order to keep them alive in a miserable condition.

We should be very glad, and, I am sure, the Americans also would be very glad, to reach the condition of a general peace with the German nation, however truncated or compartmented it might be, in agreement with our Russian Allies. I cannot feel, from what we read and from what we heard yesterday, that this is likely to be the position for some time, and in the meantime the only course open will be to discuss matters with the Soviets upon a realistic basis. We cannot afford, and the United States cannot afford, to let chaos and misery continue indefinitely in the zones of Germany which we occupy. I was deeply impressed by the broadcast address of Field-Marshal Smuts last week. No more than Field-Marshal Smuts have I any need to court popularity or win applause by saying fashionable things. I give my faithful counsel, as I did in bygone years, when I was always in a minority and sometimes almost alone. I must speak of Germany. Indescribable crimes have been committed by Germany under the Nazi rule. Justice must take its course, the guilty must be punished, but once that is over—and I trust it will soon be over—I fall back on the declaration of Edmund Burke, "I cannot frame an indictment against an entire people". We cannot plan or even dream of a new world or a new Europe which contains pariah nations, that is to say, nations permanently or for prolonged periods outcast from the human family. Our ultimate hopes must be founded—can only be founded—on the harmony of the human family. So far as it remains in the power of this island people to influence the course of events, we must strive over a period of years to redeem and to reincorporate the German and the Japanese peoples in a world system of free and civilised democracy. The idea of keeping scores of millions of people hanging about in a sub-human state between earth and hell, until they are worn down to a slave condition or embrace Communism, or die off from hunger, will only, if it is pursued, breed at least a moral pestilence and probably an actual war.

There are obvious limits to our powers, but so far as we have power, and in agreement with the United States great power may be exercised, we must do our best for the German people, and after the guilty have been punished for their horrible crimes we must banish revenge against an entire race from our minds. We must make sure they do not rearm, and that their industries are not capable of rapid transition to war production, but the danger to European peace and to the future of free democratic civilisation is not, at this moment, Germany—that menace belongs to the first and second acts of the world tragedy. The danger is the confusion and degeneration into which all Europe, or a very large part of it, is rapidly sinking. Moreover, we need not fear that our position will be worsened, or that its dangers will be brought more near, by the adoption of clear and firm policies.

Above all, we should not again let the years slip by while we are pushed and slide down the slippery slope. We still have a breathing space. Let us not waste it, as we did last time. The last great war could have been prevented with the utmost ease by prudent, firm and righteous action, five, four or even three years before it occurred. [*Interruption.*] No right to lay flattering unction to their souls resides upon the benches opposite in this matter. [*An Hon. Member: "Or behind you."*] I am dealing with this great matter which belongs to history, and from which no British party can draw particular credit. Other countries were concerned in that period, and I have no doubt whatever in saying that even up to 1936 it was possible, if we had utilised the full powers of the League of Nations—[*Interruption.*]—I travelled all round the country on that campaign, which amounted to what is now called "ganging up" the League of Nations against Hitler, but did not succeed.

We are not in dispute about this. We agree with His Majesty's Government that Britain cannot delay indefinitely making a peace with all those countries with whom we have been at war and with whom we have no further quarrel. They have yielded themselves unconditionally to our arms and to those of our Allies; nothing is more costly, nothing is more sterile, than vengeance. We should make a peace with Germany or with whatever parts of Germany are still in our control. We should make peace with Italy who has been our Ally for the last two years of the war. If this peace cannot be achieved by inter-Allied discussions in Paris or elsewhere, then I agree with the Foreign Secretary, and with the Government of the United States, that we should carry the matter to U.N.O., and to the 21 nations who were actively engaged in the fighting—I quote the words used from the Front Bench opposite yesterday—and make the best solution possible. But it must be a quick one.

It is in this world organisation that we must put our final hopes. If we are to be told that such a procedure as this would rend the world organisation, and that a line of division, and even of separation, might grow up between Soviet Russia and the countries she controls on the one hand, and the rest of the world on the other, then I say—and I say it with much regret, but without any hesitancy—that it would be better to face that, when all has been tried and tried in vain, than tamely to accept a continued degeneration of the whole world position. It is better to have a world united than a world divided; but it is also better to have a world divided, than a world destroyed. Nor does it follow that even in a world divided there should not be equilibrium from which a further advance to unity might be attempted as the years pass by. Anything is better than this ceaseless degeneration of the heart of Europe. Europe will die of that.

I had no direct responsibility for the peace settlement after the last war. I was in the Government, but not in the War Cabinet, nor in the main delegations which representatives of all parties comprised, and which met in Paris. Indeed, I vehemently criticised many features of the Treaties of Versailles and Trianon, and what I said is on record. But now we have no peace. President Wilson, Mr. Lloyd

George and M. Clemenceau were criticised for their long drawn out and harsh treatment of the conquered. But what is happening now? After the last war, peace was made with Germany and Austria seven months after the fighting stopped. Ten months have passed already, and no one can predict when a peace will be made, or even when relations will be established with the conquered Powers that will be in practice equivalent to peace. Rumania, Bulgaria, Austria, Hungary—they have no peace. Even Italy, which fought at our side after Mussolini's tyranny was broken, has no peace. This cannot go on.

The Foreign Secretary said he would make another effort to bring about an agreed solution of European affairs. That is, of course, for him and for His Majesty's Government to decide. I do not say he is wrong. We all hope earnestly for a successful conclusion to the approaching or, shall I say, impending, conference in Paris. We must certainly await its results. But it is surely necessary for people to begin asking themselves what course we ought to take supposing, as is not impossible, no sort of agreement is reached which would command the moral conscience and approval of the world at large. What are we to do? I am not asking the Foreign Secretary to answer that question now but, of course, his speech remains incomplete without some effective conclusion. It is no use producing a dozen points of difference with one of the greatest Powers in the world and then breaking off with a mere denial of a pessimistic state of mind.

I well understand the difficulties of His Majesty's Government, but never again will the parties of the Left be able to reproach the men of Versailles. Europe is far worse off in every respect than she was at the end of the last war. Her miseries, confusion and hatreds far exceed anything that was known in those bygone days. More than once the formidable truth has been stated that great nations are indestructible. Let us beware of delay and further degeneration. With all their virtues, democracies are changeable. After the hot fit, comes the cold. Are we to see again, as we saw the last time, the utmost severities inflicted upon the vanquished, to be followed by a period in which we let them arm anew, and in which we then seek to appease their wrath? We cannot impose our will on our Allies, but we can, at least, proclaim our own convictions. Let us proclaim them fearlessly. Let Germany live. Let Austria and Hungary be freed. Let Italy resume her place in the European system. Let Europe arise again in glory, and by her strength and unity ensure the peace of the world.

A SPEECH AT METZ

14 JULY 1946

---

18 *June—Russia vetoes an otherwise unanimous decision of the United Nations Security Council to refer to the next General Assembly Meeting the question of breaking off diplomatic relations with Spain.*

12 *July—Coal Industry Nationalisation Bill receives Royal Assent.*

12 *July—Conference of Foreign Ministers in Paris adjourns after calling 21 nation conference to settle the peace terms with Italy, Finland, Rumania, Bulgaria and Hungary.*

[14 *July* 1946

MANY memories are stirred in my mind by this visit to Metz and your joyous welcome. Sixty-three years ago my father took me on my first visit to France. It was in the summer of 1883. We drove along together through the Place de la Concorde. Being an observant child I noticed that one of the monuments was covered with wreaths and crépe and I at once asked him why. He replied, "These are monuments of the Provinces of France. Two of them, Alsace and Lorraine, have been taken from France by the Germans in the last war. The French are very unhappy about it and hope some day to get them back". I remember quite distinctly thinking to myself, "I hope they will get them back". This hope at least has not been disappointed.

Many years passed before I attended the manœuvres of the French Army in 1907. The Entente Cordiale had been established between Great Britain and France. I was already a youthful Minister of the Crown. In those days the soldiers wore blue tunics and red trousers and many of the movements were still in close order. When I saw, at the climax of the manœuvres, the great masses of French infantry storming the position, while the bands played the *Marseillaise*, I felt that by those valiant bayonets the rights of man had been gained and that by

171

them these rights and also the liberties of Europe would be faithfully guarded. That was nearly 40 years ago, but from that moment I have always worked with you not only out of friendship for France but because of the great causes for which our two countries have suffered so much and risked all. The road has been long and terrible. I am astonished to find myself here at the end of it. In all that ordeal of two generations our two countries have marched and struggled side by side and I, your guest here to-day, have never neglected anything that could preserve and fortify our united action. Therefore I speak to you not only as a friend but as a lifelong comrade. In all the frightful experiences we have undergone in our resistance to German aggression and tyranny our two countries have struggled along together to keep the flag of freedom flying and at an awful and hideous cost we have accomplished our duty. Never let us part.

I come now to the 20 years between the two Great Wars. The manpower and much of the physical and moral strength of France was exhausted by the sacrifices she had made for the victory of 1918. The world must never forget that two million Frenchmen gave their lives. With the British Empire it was a million but from a far larger population. The injury inflicted by the First Great War upon the life-energies of France was profound. Crowned with victory, lighted by glory she was drained of blood. Britain, in one of those strange reactions which have so often baffled our friends and foes alike, sank into pacifism and the U. S., with all her might and power, sought a vain refuge in isolation. These were all disasters of the first magnitude.

There never was a war more easy to prevent than this last horror through which we have passed. All that was needed was to enforce the disarmament clauses of the Treaty of Versailles and to make sure that Germany did not rearm. All that was needed was to assert the principle that solemn treaties, exacted from a beaten enemy, can only be altered by mutual agreement. In the League of Nations there was erected a noble instrument which, even without the aid of the United States, if it had been given a fair chance, could have maintained the disarmament of Germany and preserved the peace of Europe. But the Allies drifted amicably but helplessly like froth upon the ebb and flow of the tide. There is no need to apportion the blame. We have all endured the punishment, and at the end we are still alive with the future in our hands to make or mar. We have many troubles and privations to endure. There are many trials before us. But our hearts should be full of thankfulness to God that we have been preserved from the most hideous forms of destruction.

Now I come to the Second World War; not so bloody, as measured by men killed in the open field, but far more frightful and desperate. I was called upon to play some part in its events and every stage and crisis is burnt into my mind. Never have I allowed the slightest recrimination between Britain and France and never must you allow the slightest recrimination between France and Britain. History will tell its tale, for us both, of tragedy, of triumph and of honour.

It has woven our two peoples together in a manner indissoluble and inviolable. We fought each other for many centuries. And now we must help each other all we can. Shame be to any who deny this vital fact. There may be pity for those who let the ordinary worries and divergences of the daily and yearly life of nations destroy their sense of proportion and of historical continuity, but we must make sure these weaklings do not rule the future. We cannot afford to be misled or to indulge in short-term policies. Vision, courage, self-denial, faith and faithful service must animate us. And when the light does not shine clearly on our path, we must not lose heart, for I am sure—as sure as I was in 1940—that we shall steadfastly and perseveringly make our way through.

When President Roosevelt and I decided (with the support of our Governments and military men) upon the Anglo-American liberation of French North-West Africa in 1942 and in the early stages of that vast operation, General Giraud and I gave each other *rendezvous at Metz*. Well here we are. The General—he is a deputy now— and I have this in common; we shall both find a chapter in the future editions of memorable escapes. I have escaped as a prisoner-of-war and no prison has ever been able to hold him. It gives me great pleasure to salute him here in his native city where he has exercised high command and enjoys the highest esteem. When my comrade, General de Gaulle—that unconquerable French spirit—received me so splendidly in Paris in November 1944, I told him about this rendezvous at Metz and he said it must take place. I do not pretend we have never had any disagreements but we were thoroughly agreed on this. Yes, and also we have neither of us ever lost hope in the greatness of France of the conviction that victory would be won.

There are two issues which are specially appropriate to this occasion. The first is Europe. What will be the fate of Europe? Here in this continent of superior climates dwell the parent breeds of western and modern civilisation. Here is the story, descending from the ancient Roman Empire, of Christendom, of the Renaissance, and of the French Revolution. It is from the hatreds and quarrels of Europe that the catastrophes of the whole world have sprung. Shall we re-establish again the glory of Europe and thus consolidate the foundations of Peace? Why should the quarrels of Europe wreck the gigantic modern world? Twice in our lifetimes we have seen this happen. Twice in our lifetimes we have seen the brave and generous people of the U. S. spend their treasure and their blood to procure harmony in Europe and to rescue Europe from itself. Twice has the British Empire and Commonwealth of Nations plunged into the Continental struggle to prevent the overlordship of Germany. Twice has our heroic ally, Russia, poured out its blood in European battles. This time we must reach finality. Europe must arise from her ruin and spare the world a third and possibly a fatal holocaust.

We victors have set up together the United Nations Organisation to which we give our loyalty and in which we found our hopes. At the head of this stands the United States of America in all her power and virtue. But without the aid of a united Europe the great new world organisation may easily be rent asunder or evaporate in futility because of explosions which originate in Europe and may once again bring all mankind into strife and misery. Therefore the first word I give you here to-day is "Europe". May she regain her happiness and may her small, as well as her great, nations dwell together in security and peace. May there be a decent life achieved and set up for Europeans. May they all be faithful servants and guardians of the World Organisation on which the dearest hopes of tortured humanity are centred. My second word is "France". There can be no revival of Europe with its culture, its charm, its tradition and its mighty power, without a strong France. Many nations in the past have wished and tried to be strong. But never before has there been such a clear need for one country to be strong as there is now for France. When I think of the young Frenchmen growing into manhood in this shattered and bewildered world, I cannot recall any generation in any country before whose eyes duty is written more plainly or in more gleaming characters. Two hundred years ago in England the Elder and the greater Pitt addressed this invocation to his fellow-countrymen, torn, divided and confused by faction as they then were. "Be one people". That was his famous invocation. And in our island, for all its fogs and muddles, we are one people to-day, and dangers if they threaten will only bind us more firmly together. Using my privilege as your old and faithful friend, I do not hesitate to urge upon all Frenchmen, worn or worried though they may be, to unite in the task of leading Europe back in peace and freedom to broader and better days. By saving yourselves you will save Europe and by saving Europe you will save yourselves.

INDIA [CABINET MISSION]

A SPEECH TO THE HOUSE OF COMMONS
18 JULY 1946

EVERYONE is glad to see that the right hon. and learned Gentleman's [Sir Stafford Cripps's] health is restored. We were anxious about him when he was in India because naturally these long, intense, soul-stirring conferences with the Mahatma Gandhi and Mr. Nehru, accompanied by the exceptionally hot weather of the Indian summer, might well have imposed a very severe strain upon him, but we are glad to see to-day that his health is restored. He has certainly given us a very long and categorical statement of the Mission on which he has been engaged with two other Members of the Government. I shall not attempt to follow him in any proportionate length. I hope he will not think it disrespectful on my part if I do not attempt to make a reply covering the entire ground, because I thought we were all agreed that it is better to put off the general Debate upon this tremendous event in the history of India, and in our history, until we meet again in the autumn. If everyone were to do full justice to all the aspects upon which the right hon. and learned Gentleman has touched, it is perfectly certain that we should only reach our other attractive topic of bread rationing at a very late hour to-night.

We shall see more clearly, I think, in the autumn how matters stand, and we shall see the outlines, at any rate, of the decisions which have to be taken. The Government have promised a full dress Debate at a convenient moment, and the Mission recommends, by implication, the postponement of the discussion until then. When we return after the Recess, we shall have that Debate, and all I wish to do now is to put on record some of the principal divergencies which separate us, as well as recognising the points to which we are all committed.

For good or ill, we are all committed to the offer made at the time of what I may call the Cripps Mission in the spring of 1942. That offer was made at the moment when the Japanese held full naval command of the Bay of Bengal, and it seemed that India might be invaded and ravaged by a large Japanese army. I, as Prime Minister, took my full share of responsibility in those circumstances for making the offer of 1942. Those days of peril are gone. Although we received no assistance from the Congress Party in India, whose attitude throughout the war was one of non-co-operation, in spite of that, 2,000,000 or more Indians volunteered to fight for the cause of freedom. The Congress Party gave us no assistance; on the contrary, they did us the greatest injury in their power, but the disorders were easily suppressed and the danger of foreign invasion was warded off.

MR. COVE [Aberavon]: What did the Muslim League do?

MR. CHURCHILL: The Muslim League did not give active co-operation as a League, but the Punjab State alone produced upwards of 800,000 volunteers. The remarkable thing, since I am drawn into this by this interruption, is that the political parties did not at all sway the influence and actions of the Indian millions. Millions of men volunteered, without conscription, to fight, and great numbers gave their aid in war work, and the political parties, who are the only parties with whom the Government are dealing, had no means of controlling the enthusiasm and loyalty of their people.

Nevertheless, although, as I say, we got no assistance, we declared that the offer which we had made should stand. The present Government had, therefore, a right to our agreement and support in sending out the Mission of Cabinet Ministers, who have just returned after arduous experiences. The directions given to the Mission, however, went beyond, and, as I hold, needlessly beyond, those which governed the wartime Cripps Mission of 1942. The Coalition offer was, as the right hon. and learned Gentleman has just reminded us, of Dominion status, which includes, of course, the Clause in the Statute of Westminster, what we might call the escalator Clause, which affirmed the right of secession, in the last resort, from the British Commonwealth of Nations by any Dominion. The Coalition offer was also conditional upon agreement being reached between the principal parties in India, so that the offer of full Dominion status, including the right to secede, would not lead to disastrous, and possibly devastating, civil war.

L   177

His Majesty's present Government went beyond the offer of 1942. They instructed their delegates to offer full independence directly, instead of Dominion status, which left the final decision open to a fully-constituted Dominion of India, after seeing how they were getting on and how the general situation lay. So far as I can see, the result which is now put before us—and nothing in the speech of the right hon. and learned Gentleman in any way detracts from it—is the immediate independence of India and the severance of all constitutional ties uniting the former Indian Empire to the British Commonwealth of Nations. I wish to register my dissent from this extension and short-circuiting of the original offer. The responsibility for making the further advance and for pressing full and immediate independence upon India, without giving Indians a chance to get into the saddle and look around to see where their broad interests lie—the responsibility for that is the responsibility of the present Government, and I, for my part, can share no part of that responsibility. I consider that this short-circuiting or telescoping of the normal and reasonable constitutional processes upon which both parties were agreed does not give the best chance of a happy or peaceful solution of the Indian problem, and that, having regard to the elements in India to whom the Government mainly addressed themselves, it prejudges, in an adverse sense, the case of whether the vast sub-continent of India, with its population of 400,000,000, should remain, of its own free will, within the circle of the association of the British Commonwealth. The Government had the power to make this change and theirs is the responsibility for making it. That is all I am concerned to establish to-day. I am not going to trespass, if I can avoid it, upon merits. I am merely showing where we lie in the relationship to this formidable and enormous topic.

Secondly, the offer of 1942 was conditional upon agreement being reached among the principal forces and parties in the life of India. This has certainly not been achieved. The Mission proceeded themselves to shape the outlines of the settlement, and to endeavour, as far as possible, to induce all the elements concerned to agree to it as a working basis. Again, I do not challenge the right of the Government to take this action, for which,

178

no doubt, they have a large Parliamentary majority. I am only trying to make it clear that, in this respect also—the question of agreement—the Government have gone beyond any position to which I and my colleagues in the National Coalition Government were committed by the offer of 1942. I do not think that the right hon. and learned Gentleman denies that.

SIR S. CRIPPS: Will the right hon. Gentleman allow me? Surely, the right hon. Gentleman will agree that I had precisely the same job to do in 1942? I took a scheme which was got out by the Government and I tried to get both parties to agree to it. That is exactly what has happened in this case.

MR. CHURCHILL: My point was that the right hon. and learned Gentleman took out a different scheme. As a great precision man, and a man of the highest legalistic attainments, a small point like that ought not to have escaped his notice.

SIR S. CRIPPS: The right hon. Gentleman is very amusing, but not quite accurate. What he was saying was that we ought not to have imposed some settlement, but that it should be a condition that both parties agreed to it, and that, in this case, they had not agreed to it and it was something which we had imposed upon them. I was pointing out that, in 1942, under the right hon. Gentleman's Government, a scheme was got out by the Cabinet in London and was sent out, and my object was to try to get both parties to agree to a scheme which was sent out from London. The right hon. Gentleman cannot complain that what we have done now is to get two parties to agree to a scheme.

MR. CHURCHILL: In the first place, the right hon. and learned Gentleman has not got the two parties to agree; they are in the most violent disagreement, and their passion is mounting day by day. In the second place, the scheme which he took out was a different one. In the third place, when that scheme did not commend itself to those to whom he addressed himself, he took the positive action—and I do not say he was wrong from his point of view to do it—of trying to solve the Indian problem for the Indians instead of leaving it to the Indians to solve, or not to solve. He took the positive course of trying to solve it, and proposed a basis on which he hoped they would come together.

SIR S. CRIPPS: As in 1942.

MR. CHURCHILL: In 1942, the right hon. Gentleman had no authorisation to attempt to make a separate declaration apart from any view built up between Indians, as he has done now. I am not making this a complaint against the right hon. and learned Genleman; I can quite see that when they were there and nobody would agree to any-thing, the third party came in and said, "Let us have a try. Won't you agree to this?" All I say is, that it is quite different from the proposals to which we agreed.

There is a third point of great importance, namely, the faithful discharge of our obligations, contracted over so many years and affirmed by so many British Govern-ments, to the various minorities in India. I was sorry that in his speech of, I think, 15 March, the Prime Minister should have spoken in a somewhat adverse, or at least uncertain sense, about the rights of minorities, because the protection of those fundamental rights affects our duty to discharge the pledges which we have so often given. These minorities in India are very considerable. The right hon. and learned Gentleman has mentioned several of them to-day. There are, for instance, the 40 to 60 million of the depressed classes who are consternated by the lack of representation which they are to receive in the future Constituent Assembly. I have received most vehement and painful appeals from the leaders of these great communities, and I discussed them with my colleagues on this side of the House.

When one speaks of a community as large as 60 million, the word "minority" loses much of its significance. Such immense masses of human beings deserve to be treated with respect and consideration, positively and not relatively, even if there are other and still large masses who take a different view. After all, in these islands we have only 46 million, a much smaller number than the depressed classes of India. We should be sorry just to be called a minority by Europe and to have our way of life ordered for us by a mass vote of all the other countries. In fact, I think that we should very likely recur, with satisfaction, to our insular position. When the issue affecting minorities numbered by scores of millions is also one which concerns the fundamental rights of those minorities, all pledges with regard to them require most scrupulous attention by the ruling authority at the moment it hands over these masses, with their fate and their fortunes, to another system of Government. That is a point which, I trust, will not be found to be one of difference in principle, although there may be difference in emphasis.

Then there are the Muslims—who number over 80 million—and make up so large a majority of the martial races of India. There is no doubt that there is a complete lack of agreement at the present time between the two principal communities. The Mission have laboured hard, and they have dealt particularly with these two communities, allowing many other valuable and important forces, who have a right to live also, to fall back into the background. As between these two communities, the difficulties were never more acute and the gulf never more wide than at the present moment. The outlook is very grave. The acceptance by the martial races of the final settlement which we shall make before we leave India is indispensable to future peace.

Thirdly, among the elements which go to make up India, are the Indian States which, together, comprise nearly 95 million. The position of these States has been fixed by solemn treaties made with their rulers. It is proposed to abrogate those treaties and to abolish the principle of paramountcy which, at present, alone defines the relationship of these States—in some cases almost nations, in some cases models of good government in India—to whatever new Central Government is set up in India. If all the minorities are added together, they constitute much more than half the inhabitants of India. I am glad to say that, as far as I understand the position, His Majesty's Government have not abandoned the principle of the discharge of their responsibilities towards the minorities in India which aggregate at least 225 million out of 400 million. I hope we shall hear from the First Lord of the Admiralty that they have not abandoned their responsibilities in that matter.

The attitude of the Mission, and of the Government whom they represented, is expressed on this point in a single sentence of the plan which they put before the representatives of Indian life with whom they dealt. This is the sentence:

"When the constituent Assembly has completed its labours, His Majesty's Government will recommend to Parliament such action as may be necessary for the cession of sovereignty to the Indian people subject only to two provisos which are mentioned in the statement and which are not, we believe, controversial, namely, adequate provision for the protection of minorities, and willingness to conclude a treaty to cover matters arising out of the transfer of power."

This seems to me to be a somewhat light, optimistic and almost casual manner of treating responsibilities extending to an appreciable part of a human race and touching those fundamental rights—life, liberty and the pursuit of happiness—which we have regarded as the birthright of every human being. It makes it clear, however, and all I desire to do is to emphasise this by putting on record that all arrangements to be made by the Constituent Assembly, and any treaties which may subsequently be brought into existence between the Crown and Parliament of Great Britain and the new sovereign independent Government of India, must be subject to the fulfilment of the honourable discharge of our obligations. I hope we are agreeable on that. I hope we are not going to hear a contradiction from the First Lord on that. A Bill, or perhaps several Bills, will have to be presented to Parliament and will have to pass through all their stages, and that is the time when the final decision will have to be taken. Nothing must be agreed to by us at the moment of the transference of sovereignty which will be in derogation of our solemn undertaking.

I cannot conclude without referring to the question of the interim Government, in respect of which the right hon. and learned Gentleman gave us a full exposition. A great part of the Mission's work in India was devoted to the vain attempt to form a coalition cabinet acceptable alike to the Muslims and to the caste Hindus, and this Cabinet was to replace the Viceroy's Executive Council which was dismissed in order to clear the decks and make room for the new government. There was to be no change for the time being in the constitutional position. What it has led to is a temporary reversion in so far as personnel is concerned, to a government of well-tried and experienced officials. In fact, for the moment, but only for the moment, Indian affairs have gone full circle, and we are back again at the system of 40 years ago before the Morley-Minto reforms. Everyone can see that this cannot last very long. Moreover, from the reports which I have received from India, the Muslim community feel themselves deeply aggrieved by what they regard as a departure from the terms of Paragraph 8 of the statement of 16 June made by the Cabinet delegation and the Viceroy. This statement runs as follows:

"In the event of the two major parties or either of them proving unwilling to join in the setting up of a coalition government on the above lines, it is the intention of the Viceroy to proceed with the formation of an interim government which will be as representative as possible of those willing to accept the statement of 16 May."

The Muslim League agreed to enter this, and when the Hindu Congress members refused, or it broke down on this point of procedure, I understand that the Muslim League made a violent complaint. I see the force of the right hon. and learned Gentleman's argument that it is very difficult to form a coalition with only one party, or even to form a coalition and fill it up with civil servants and non-party figures. I believe that would be a difficulty. At the same time, there is the feeling among the Muslims of India that faith has been broken with them. I am not making that charge. On the contrary, I can see that it is a misunderstanding, but there is no doubt that there is a serious misunderstanding.

SIR S. CRIPPS: I would like to correct one point as regards the timing. The right hon. Gentleman said that the Muslims accepted and then Congress refused. But Congress had refused before the Muslims arrived at any decision, and they knew before they arrived at a decision, that it was useless for them to arrive at a decision because already the scheme had gone.

MR. CHURCHILL: I am not making an accusation against the Government in the matter. I am sure the right hon. and learned Gentleman does not deal with people in bad faith, and those gentlemen who were there may have been misunderstood. There has been a serious misunderstanding, but the consequences of the misunderstanding carry us forward into the future The General Secretary of the Muslim League has gone so far as to say that unless the situation is clarified, it would be suicidal for the League to enter into a Constituent Assembly. All this appears to raise the most formidable issues, because I can assure the Government—and those who have been to India know well—that the agreement of the Muslims to the new system affects the whole foundation of the problem. One cannot contemplate that British troops should be used to crush the Muslims in the interests of the caste Hindus. Whatever our responsibilities may be, whatever may be the day appointed on which we quit India, we must not make ourselves the agents of a caste Government, or a particular sectional Government in order to crush by armed force and modern weapons, another community which, although not so numerous, is numbered at 90 millions.

PALESTINE

A SPEECH TO THE HOUSE OF COMMONS
[ON THE ADJOURNMENT]
1 AUGUST 1946

---

21 *July—President Villarroel of Bolivia assassinated and his body hanged from a lamp-post in La Paz.*

22 *July—Jewish terrorists of the Irgun Zvai Leumi blow up a wing of the King David Hotel in Jerusalem, in use as British Military Headquarters and Government offices. The casualties total 91 killed and 45 injured.*

29 *July—Opening of Peace Conference of 21 nations in Paris.*

[1 *August* 1946

THE House is, naturally, obliged to the President of the Board of Trade [Sir Stafford Cripps] for the painstaking speech which he has delivered to us, and which supplements, in many points, the interesting and detailed statement delivered by the Lord President of the Council [Mr. Herbert Morrison] yesterday. We are also much obliged to my right hon. Friend the Member for West Bristol [Mr. Stanley], whose speech, I think, furnished the House with a wealth of carefully thought, judiciously selected and rightly produced facts, and represents a very large body of our opinion at the present time upon this most difficult question. In the short time which I will venture to occupy the House, I am going to touch a little on some of the grave realities which lie outside the peaceful tones of the oration of the President of the Board of Trade, and the quiet circumstances of this House, because the situation in which we are placed is a very grievous one, and one which is not improving at all. I must also go back a little into the past, because on this question we have got to look to the past.

The position which I, personally, have adopted and maintained, dates from 1919 and 1921, when as Dominions and Colonial Secretary, it fell to me to define, with the

185

approval of the then Cabinet and Parliament, the interpretation that was placed upon our obligations to the
Zionists under the Mandate for Palestine entrusted to us
by the League of Nations. This was the declaration of
1922, which I, personally, drafted for the approval of the
authorities of the day. Palestine was not to be a Jewish
National Home, but there was to be set up a Jewish
National Home in Palestine. Jewish immigration would
be allowed up to the limit of the economic absorptive
capacity—that was the phrase which I coined in those
days and which seems to remain convenient—the
Mandatory Power being, it was presumed, the final judge
of what that capacity was. During the greater part of a
quarter of a century which has passed, this policy was
carefully carried out by us. The Jewish population
multiplied, from about 80,000 to nearly 600,000. Tel-Aviv
expanded into the great city it is, a city which, I may say,
during this war and before it, welcomed and nourished
waifs and orphans flying from Nazi persecution. Many
refugees found a shelter and a sanctuary there, so that this
land, not largely productive of the means of life, became
a fountain of charity and hospitality to people in great
distress. Land reclamation and cultivation and great
electrical enterprises progressed. Trade made notable
progress, and not only did the Jewish population increase
but the Arab population, dwelling in the areas colonised
and enriched by the Jews, also increased in almost equal
numbers. The Jews multiplied six-fold and the Arabs
developed 500,000, thus showing that both races gained
a marked advantage from the Zionist policy which we
pursued and which we were developing over this period.

The right hon. and learned Gentleman, the President
of the Board of Trade, spoke of the past 25 years as being
the most unkind or unhappy Palestine has known. I
imagine that it would hardly be possible to state the
opposite of the truth more compendiously. The years
during which we have accepted the Mandate have been
the brightest that Palestine has known and were full of
hope. Of course, there was always friction, because the
Jew was, in many cases, allowed to go far beyond the
strict limits of the interpretation which was placed upon
the Mandate. Disturbances occured in 1937 and in 1938;
in 1939 Mr. Chamberlain's Government produced the

White Paper, which limited immigration on grounds other than the economic absorptive capacity of the country. That after a five-year interval, would have brought immigration to an end except by agreement with the Arab majority, which certainly would not have been obtained. This was in my view a failure to fulfil the obligations we had accepted, and I immediately protested against this departure. I found myself in full agreement with the Labour and Liberal Parties of those days.

I see that yesterday the Leader of the Liberal Party [Mr. Clement Davies] who is not here to-day, in paying a tribute to my speech on that occasion deplored the fact that I had not the courage to vote against the Government. As to the courage that is required for one to give a vote against the Government one is elected to support, we no doubt shall have many examples to-day. I did take the trouble to look up the Divisions on that occasion, and I have for greater security brought this bulky volume to the Table. I find that I did vote against the Government of the day in support of the reasoned Amendment moved by the right hon. Gentleman who is now the Lord President of the Council [Mr. Herbert Morrison] and that was the subject on which I spoke. However, I think that, on the whole, Members can always speak and not vote, though it is better to let the vote follow the speech. In this case, I conformed to the strictest tenets, and I trust that when the Leader of the Liberal Party rejoins his flock, they may acquaint him of the fact that his great responsibilities and multifarious duties have, no doubt, led him to an oversight, and a complete misstatement of a matter of fact.

I have never altered my opinion that the White Paper constituted a negation of Zionist policy which, the House must remember, was an integral and indispensable condition of the Mandate. That is the view which I hold to-day. It was violently resented by the Jews in Palestine, and by world Jewry, a large majority of whom—although there are notable exceptions—regard Zionism as a great ideal, and as the cherished hope of their race, scattered throughout the world. Then came the war. After the fall of France, and the attack upon us by Italy, when we stood utterly alone, we had great need to concentrate our troops against the enemy, and economise in our outlying garrisons and commitments. At my desire the Jewish community in Palestine was armed, encouraged to organise and, in fact, to play a part in the defence of the Holy Land, in order to liberate British units there. The horrible persecutions by the Nazis left no doubt as to which side they were on, or could be on. The possibility of a German invasion, striking through Turkey, Syria and Palestine to the Suez Canal, as well as through Persia, towards the Persian Gulf, and at what were then deemed to be our vital communications, at what was then considered to be an important element in our affairs—our Eastern Empire and possessions, as well as Australia and New Zealand —was a very real anxiety in 1941-42. At a most critical time in 1941, it was aggravated by the revolt of the pro-German Arab elements in Iraq. No doubt our Zionist policy may have led, in part, to that divergence of Arab sentiment. But the revolt was quelled, Syria was liberated, and Persia was occupied. Immense preparations and fortifications were made against German penetration of the Caucasus, and this danger complicated the whole defence of Europe from the West. But this menace was removed, at once and for ever, by the victories of Stalingrad and El Alamein.

Meanwhile, the Jewish community had developed strong, well-armed forces, and the highest military authorities reported to the Cabinet during 1941-42 that if the continued bickerings between Jews and Arabs grew into serious conflict, the Jews could not only defend themselves, but would beat the Arabs in Palestine, though that was, of course, the very opposite position from that which existed at the time of the Mandate in 1919. At that time, the Jews were a defenceless minority, and it was a great part of our duty to protect them from the hostility of the very much stronger Arab forces who emerged with so much distinction and credit from the struggle against the Turks. Thus, there are two facts to be borne in mind. First, that Zionists and the Palestine Jews were vehemently and undividedly on our side in the struggle and, secondly, that they no longer need our assistance to maintain themselves in their national home against local Arab hostility. A general attack upon them by all surrounding Arab States would be a different matter, and that would clearly be one which would have to be settled by the United Nations Organization. But the position is different from what it was when the Mandate was granted.

Meanwhile how did we treat the Arabs? We have treated them very well. The House of Hussein reigns in Iraq. Feisal was placed on the throne, his grandson is there to-day. The Emir Abdullah, whom I remember appointing at Jerusalem, in 1921, to be in charge of Transjordania, is there to-day. He has survived the shocks, strains and stresses which have altered almost every institution in the world. He has never broken his faith and loyalty to this country. Syria and the Lebanon owe their independence to the great exertions made by the British Government to make sure that the pledges made at the time when we were weak, but, nevertheless, were forced to take action by entering the country to drive out the Vichy French, were honoured. We have insisted on those pledges being made good. I cannot touch on the Arabs without paying my tribute to this splendid king, Ibn Saud, of Saudi Arabia, who in the darkest hours never failed to send messages and encouragement of his unshakable faith that we should win and gain through. I cannot admit that we have not done our utmost to treat the Arabs in a way which so great a race deserves and requires. There was no greater champion of Arab rights than the late Colonel Lawrence. He was a valued friend of mine, and of my right hon. Friend the Member for Horsham [Earl Winterton] who served with him in the Desert. With him I always kept in very close touch. When Lawrence gave me his book, *The Seven Pillars of Wisdom,* he wrote in it that I had made a happy end to this show. I will not have it that the way we treated this matter was inconsiderate to the Arabs. On the contrary, I think that they have had a very fair deal from Great Britain. With all those countries which are given to their power and control, in every way they have had a very fair deal. It was little enough, indeed, that we had asked for the Jews—a natural home in their historic Holy Land, on which they have the power and virtue to confer many blessings for enjoyment, both of Jew and Arab.

It is quite true that the claims and desires of the Zionists latterly went beyond anything which were agreed to by the Mandatory Power. This caused alarm and unrest among the Arabs, but the limits of the policy which I explained to the House have never been exceeded by any British Government, and if they are discharged they constitute the faithful fulfilment of our pledges, on which the Mandate hangs. At the General Election which followed the victorious ending of the German war, the Labour Party, which was believed to champion the Zionist cause in the terms I have defined, and not only in those terms, but going, in many cases, far beyond—to set up a Jewish State in Palestine, and so forth—this Labour Party, some of whom we see here to-day, gained a large majority in the House of Commons. During the Election, they made most strenuous pro-Zionist speeches and declarations. Many of their most important leaders were known to be ardent supporters of the Zionist cause, and their success was, naturally, regarded by the Jewish community in Palestine as a prelude to the fulfilment of the pledges which had been made to them, and indeed opening the way to further ambitions. This was certainly the least which everybody expected.

In fact, all sorts of hopes were raised among the Jews of Palestine, just as other hopes were raised elsewhere. However, when the months slipped by and no decided policy or declaration was made by the present Government, a deep and bitter resentment spread throughout the Palestine Jewish community, and violent protests were made by the Zionist supporters in the United States. The disappointment and disillusionment of the Jews at the procrastination and indecision of the British Labour Government are no excuse, as we have repeatedly affirmed here, for the dark and deadly crimes which have been committed by the fanatical extremists, and these miscreants and murderers should be rooted out, and punished with the full severity of the law. We are all agreed about that, and I was glad to hear the right hon. and learned Gentleman the President of the Board of Trade affirm the intention of the Government not to be coerced by terrorism. But the expectations which had been aroused by the Party opposite and the resultant revulsion of feeling, are facts, none the less, to be held constantly before our minds. They cannot say all these things, and then let a whole year pass away and do

190

nothing about it, and then be surprised if these pledges come home to roost in a most unpleasant manner.

Had I had the opportunity of guiding the course of events after the war was won a year ago, I should have faithfully pursued the Zionist cause as I have defined it; and I have not abandoned it to-day, although this is not a very popular moment to espouse it; but there are two things to say about it. First, I agree entirely with what the President of the Board of Trade said on this point— no one can imagine that there is room in Palestine for the great masses of Jews who wish to leave Europe, or that they could be absorbed in any period which it is now useful to contemplate. The idea that the Jewish problem could be solved or even helped by a vast dumping of the Jews of Europe into Palestine is really too silly to consume our time in the House this afternoon. I am not absolutely sure that we should be in too great a hurry to give up the idea that European Jews may live in the countries where they belong. I must say that I had no idea, when the war came to an end, of the horrible massacres which had occurred; the millions and millions that have been slaughtered. That dawned on us gradually after the struggle was over. But if all these immense millions have been killed and slaughtered, there must be a certain amount of living room for the survivors, and there must be inheritances and properties to which they can lay claim. Are we not to hope that some tolerance will be established in racial matters in Europe, and that there will be some law reigning by which, at any rate, a portion of the property of these great numbers will not be taken away from them? It is quite clear, however, that this crude idea of letting all the Jews of Europe go into Palestine has no relation either to the problem of Europe or to the problem which arises in Palestine.

MR. S. SILVERMAN: The right hon. Gentleman is not suggesting, is he, that any Jew who regarded a country in Europe as nothing but the graveyard and cemetery of all his relatives, friends and hopes should be compelled to stay there if he did not want to do so?

MR. CHURCHILL: I am against preventing Jews from doing anything which other people are allowed to do. I am against that, and I have the strongest abhorrence of the idea of anti-Semitic lines of prejudice. Secondly, I have for some years past—this is really the crux of the argument I am venturing to submit to the House—felt that an unfair burden was being thrown upon Great Britain by our having to bear the whole weight of the Zionist policy, while Arabs and Moslems, then so important to our Empire, were alarmed and estranged, and while the United States, for the Government and people of which I have the greatest regard and friendship, and other countries, sat on the sidelines and criticised our short-comings with all the freedom of perfect detachment and irresponsibility. Therefore, I had always intended to put it to our friends in America, from the very beginning of the post-war discussions, that either they should come in and help us in this Zionist problem, about which they feel so strongly, and as I think rightly, on even terms, share and share alike, or that we should resign our Mandate, as we have, of course, a perfect right to do.

Indeed, I am convinced that from the moment when we feel ourselves unable to carry out properly and honestly the Zionist policy as we have all these years defined it and accepted it, and which is the condition on which we received the Mandate for Palestine, it is our duty at any rate to offer to lay down the Mandate. We should there-fore, as soon as the war stopped, have made it clear to the United States that, unless they came in and bore their share, we would lay the whole care and burden at the feet of the United Nations organisation; and we should have fixed a date by which all our troops and forces would be withdrawn from the country. At that time we had no interest in Palestine. We have never sought or got anything out of Palestine. We have discharged a thank-less, painful, costly, laborious, inconvenient task for more than a quarter of a century with a very great measure of success. Many people have made fine speeches about the Zionist question. Many have subscribed generously in money, but it is Great Britain, and Great Britain alone, which has steadfastly carried that cause forward across a whole generation to its present actual position, and the Jews all over the world ought not to be in a hurry to forget that. If in the Jewish movement or in the Jewish Agency there are elements of murder and outrage which they cannot control, and if these strike not only at their best but at their only effective friends, they and the Zionist cause

192

must inevitably suffer from the grave and lasting reproach of the atrocious crimes which have been committed. It is perfectly clear that Jewish warfare directed against the British in Palestine will, if protracted, automatically release us from all obligations to persevere as well as destroy the inclination to make further efforts in British hearts. Indeed, there are many people who are very near that now. We must not be in a hurry to turn aside from large causes we have carried far.

There is the figure of Dr. Weizmann, that dynamic Jew whom I have known so long, the ablest and wisest leader of the cause of Zionism, his whole life devoted to the cause, his son killed in the battle for our common freedom. I ardently hope his authority will be respected by Zionists in this dark hour, and that the Government will keep in touch with him, and make every one of his compatriots feel how much he is respected here. It is perfectly clear that in that case we shall have the best opportunities of carrying this matter further forward.

I am sorry to weary the House with these reminiscences and "might have beens" but it was my intention when the war was over to place this position before our American friends in the plainest words—the plainest words, which, spoken in good will and good faith are the words to which Americans are most likely to respond. I am in full accord with every effort the Government have made to obtain American support in sharing the burden of the Zionist policy. The Anglo-American Commission was a step in the right direction; the negotiations which have taken place since are another favourable step, as was this scheme which has been read out as agreed to by the expert bodies joined on this Commission. It is far more important that there should be agreement than that there should be this or that variant of the scheme. I fully agree that the Government were right to labour with the United States. I will not try to examine the various schemes of partition or cantonisation which have been put forward, nor would I dwell on that idea, which I always championed, of a wider union—an Arab-Jew federal system of four or five States in the Middle East, which would have been one of the great Powers, with Jew and Arab combined together to share the glory and mutually protect and help each other. As

I say, almost any solution in which the United States will join us could be made to work.

All these processes of inquiry, negotiation and discussion have been the occasion, so frequently referred to in this Debate, of prolonged and very dangerous delays and if at the end of all these delays success is not attained, namely Anglo-American co-operation on equal terms to carry out a Zionist policy within the limits defined or as we may agree—if that is not attained then we are confronted with a deplorable failure in the conduct of our affairs in Palestine since the end of the second great war. It was with very great regret that I read this morning of the non-agreement of the United States, and the right hon. and learned Gentleman who has just sat down, quite bluntly and bleakly told us that there was no agreement at the present time. I hope it is not the final word. This agreement was the one great goal to which we were invited to aspire; here was the one excuse the Government could put forward for the long delays and indecisions which have involved us in so much cost and serious bloodshed. If this Anglo-American co-operation fails, as it seems so far to have failed, then I must say that the record of the Administration during this year—and a Government must be judged by results—in the handling of Palestinian affairs will stand forth as a monument of incapacity.

It may be that they have had difficulties; but Governments are judged by results. I turned up with a number of defeats during the war and I was very much criticised about it. I had several times to come down with reports of defeats, but when afterwards there were successes we were entitled to be praised. Up to this particular minute, this has been a complete failure; it has gone from bad to worse and one does not feel that there is any grip of the matter which is going to succeed. The one rightful reasonable, simple, and compulsive lever which we held and, if you will, still hold, was and is a sincere readiness to resign the mission, to lay our Mandate at the feet of the United Nations Organization and thereafter to evacuate the country with which we have no connection or tradition and where we have no sovereignty as in India and no treaty as in Egypt. Such was the position we could have adopted until a few months ago, and I am sure it would have procured a good result. The cogency of such a statement once it was believed would, I am sure, make the solution much more possible and if no solution was obtained, then our responsibilities would have been honourably discharged. Once make it clear that the British have no interests in remaining in Palestine and no wish to do so, and that they decline to carry forward single-handed this harsh, invidious burden, then you will get attention paid to what you say and what you ask and all kinds of good solutions for the Jew and Arab alike, based on the co-operation and resources of the English-speaking world, will immediately come into the field of possibility.

However, His Majesty's Government by their precipitate abandonment of their treaty rights in Egypt, and, in particular, the Suez Canal zone, are now forced to look for a strong place of arms, for a jumping-off ground in Palestine in order to protect the Canal from outside Egypt. By this unwisdom they have vitiated disinterestedness and we can now be accused of having a national strategic motive for retaining our hold on Palestine. I must regard this as a very grave disaster and an immense weakening of our position. What the Government have done in Egypt—though no doubt from very good motives—has greatly weakened our moral position in Palestine by stripping us of our disinterestedness in that country. I pointed out in the Debate on Egyptian policy a few weeks ago, that the moment we were dependent upon Palestine for a base from which to defend the Suez Canal, we should greatly hamper all possibility of obtaining American co-operation. Well, look at the position to which we have now been brought.

Take stock round the world at the present moment; after all we are entitled to survey the whole field. We declare ourselves ready to abandon the mighty Empire and Continent of India with all the work we have done in the last 200 years, territory over which we possess unimpeachable sovereignty. The Government are, apparently, ready to leave the 400 million Indians to fall into all the horrors of sanguinary civil war—civil war compared to which anything that could happen in Palestine would be microscopic; wars of elephants compared with wars of mice. Indeed we place the independence of India in hostile and feeble hands, heedless of the dark carnage and confusion which will follow. We scuttle from Egypt which we twice successfully defended from foreign massacre and pillage. We scuttle from it, we abandon the Canal zone about which our treaty rights were and still are indefeasible; but now, apparently, the one place where we are at all costs and at all inconveniences to hold on and fight it out to the death is Palestine, and we are to be at war with the Jews of Palestine, and, if necessary, with the Arabs of Palestine. For what reason? Not, all the world will say, for the faithful discharge of our long mission but because we have need, having been driven out of Egypt, to secure a satisfactory strategic base from which to pursue our Imperial aims.

I thank the House for listening. I have trespassed on their time at some length, but I wish to look forward before I conclude and not to look back. I will not go so far in criticising and in censuring without proposing positive action, with all the responsibility and the exposure to counter-attack which one incurs when one proposes definite and serious action. Here is the action—action this day. I think the Government should say that if the United States will not come and share the burden of the Zionist cause, as defined or as agreed, we should now give notice that we will return our Mandate to U.N.O. and that we will evacuate Palestine within a specified period. At the same time, we should inform Egypt that we stand by our treaty rights and will, by all means, maintain our position in the Canal zone. Those are the two positive proposals which I submit, most respectfully, to the House. In so far as the Government may have hampered themselves in any way from adopting these simple policies, they are culpable in the last degree, and the whole Empire and the Commonwealth will be the sufferers from their mismanagement.

A SPEECH AT ZURICH UNIVERSITY

19 SEPTEMBER 1946

---

8 *August—Plenary Session of the Paris Peace Conference rejects a Soviet demand for a two-thirds majority voting procedure. The British proposal for simple majority voting is upheld. Mr. Molotov describes the adoption of the British proposal as an "egregious error".*

9 *August—Secretary of State Byrnes in Paris denounces as "loose and wicked talk" charges of Soviet spokesmen that the United States and Britain have formed an anti-Russian bloc.*

13 *August—Russia demands the revision of the Montreux Treaty and joint Soviet-Turkish responsibility for the defence of the Black Sea Straits. The demand is rejected by Turkey on 22 August.*

16 *August—Serious rioting breaks out in Calcutta. After three days of violence the casualties are given as over 4,000 killed and 10,000 injured.*

18 *August—American transport plane is shot down by Jugoslav fighters near Ljublana.*

25 *August—London Passenger Transport Board declares for a "closed shop".*

26 *August—United States accepts the compulsory jurisdiction of the International Court of Justice. President Truman stipulates that the Court's jurisdiction will not apply to disputes which the United States decide are within its domestic jurisdiction.*

29 *August—United Nations Security Council accepts applications for membership from Sweden, Iceland and Afghanistan. Applications from Eire, Portugal, Albania, Transjordan and Mongolia are rejected.*

31 *August—United States Congressional Report on Russia is published. It forecasts that by 1970 Russia's available military manpower will equal that of U.S.A., Great Britain, France, Germany and Italy combined.*

5 *September—Greek plebiscite results in victory for the monarchists who poll 68.96 per cent. of votes cast.*

5 *September—The United States aircraft carrier* Franklin
D. Roosevelt, *the United States cruiser* Little Rock *and
several United States destroyers arrive at the Piræus.*

6 *September—Second instalment of American Loan is
drawn by Britain.*

9 *September—Bulgarian plebiscite results in victory for
the Republicans who poll 92.32 per cent. of votes cast.
King Simeon leaves Bulgaria.*

9 *September—London Conference on Palestine opens at
Lancaster House. Delegates from the Palestinian Arabs
and the Jewish Agency decline the invitation to attend.*

12 *September—Mr. Henry Wallace U.S. Secretary of
Commerce attacks "British Imperialism" in a speech at
Madison Square Garden.*

14 *September—President Truman withdraws his support
of the speech and requests Mr. Wallace's resignation.*

22 *September—Mr. Harriman succeeds Mr. Wallace as
Secretary of Commerce.*

[19 *September* 1946

I wish to speak to you to-day about the tragedy of
Europe. This noble continent, comprising on the whole
the fairest and the most cultivated regions of the earth,
enjoying a temperate and equable climate, is the home of
all the great parent races of the western world. It is the
fountain of Christian faith and Christian ethics. It is the
origin of most of the culture, arts, philosophy and science
both of ancient and modern times. If Europe were once
united in the sharing of its common inheritance, there would
be no limit to the happiness, to the prosperity and glory
which its three or four hundred million people would enjoy.
Yet it is from Europe that have sprung that series of
frightful nationalistic quarrels, originated by the Teutonic
nations, which we have seen even in this twentieth century
and in our own lifetime, wreck the peace and mar the
prospects of all mankind.

And what is the plight to which Europe has been
reduced? Some of the smaller States have indeed made a
good recovery, but over wide areas a vast quivering mass

of tormented, hungry, care-worn and bewildered human beings gape at the ruins of their cities and homes, and scan the dark horizons for the approach of some new peril, tyranny or terror. Among the victors there is a babel of jarring voices; among the vanquished the sullen silence of despair. That is all that Europeans, grouped in so many ancient States and nations, that is all that the Germanic Powers have got by tearing each other to pieces and spreading havoc far and wide. Indeed, but for the fact that the great Republic across the Atlantic Ocean has at length realised that the ruin or enslavement of Europe would involve their own fate as well, and has stretched out hands of succour and guidance, the Dark Ages would have returned in all their cruelty and squalor. They may still return.

Yet all the while there is a remedy which, if it were generally and spontaneously adopted, would as if by a miracle transform the whole scene, and would in a few years make all Europe, or the greater part of it, as free and as happy as Switzerland is to-day. What is this sovereign remedy? It is to re-create the European Family, or as much of it as we can, and provide it with a structure under which it can dwell in peace, in safety and in freedom. We must build a kind of United States of Europe. In this way only will hundreds of millions of toilers be able to regain the simple joys and hopes which make life worth living. The process is simple. All that is needed is the resolve of hundreds of millions of men and women to do right instead of wrong and gain as their reward blessing instead of cursing.

Much work has been done upon this task by the exertions of the Pan-European Union which owes so much to Count Coudenhove-Kalergi and which commanded the services of the famous French patriot and statesman, Aristide Briand. There is also that immense body of doctrine and procedure, which was brought into being amid high hopes after the first world war, as the League of Nations. The League of Nations did not fail because of its principles or conceptions. It failed because these principles were deserted by those States who had brought it into being. It failed because the Governments of those days feared to face the facts, and act while time remained. This disaster must not be repeated.

There is therefore much knowledge and material with which to build; and also bitter dear-bought experience.

I was very glad to read in the newspapers two days ago that my friend President Truman had expressed his interest and sympathy with this great design. There is no reason why a regional organization of Europe should in any way conflict with the world organization of the United Nations. On the contrary, I believe that the larger synthesis will only survive if it is founded upon coherent natural groupings. There is already a natural grouping in the Western Hemisphere. We British have our own Commonwealth of Nations. These do not weaken, on the contrary they strengthen, the world organization. They are in fact its main support. And why should there not be a European group which could give a sense of enlarged patriotism and common citizenship to the distracted peoples of this turbulent and mighty continent and why should it not take its rightful place with other great groupings in shaping the destinies of men? In order that this should be accomplished there must be an act of faith in which millions of families speaking many languages must consciously take part.

We all know that the two world wars through which we have passed arose out of the vain passion of a newly-united Germany to play the dominating part in the world. In this last struggle crimes and massacres have been committed for which there is no parallel since the invasions of the Mongols in the fourteenth century and no equal at any time in human history. The guilty must be punished. Germany must be deprived of the power to rearm and make another aggressive war. But when all this has been done, as it will be done, as it is being done, there must be an end to retribution. There must be what Mr. Gladstone many years ago called "a blessed act of oblivion". We must all turn our backs upon the horrors of the past. We must look to the future. We cannot afford to drag forward across the years that are to come the hatreds and revenges which have sprung from the injuries of the past. If Europe is to be saved from infinite misery, and indeed from final doom, there must be an act of faith in the European family and an act of oblivion against all the crimes and follies of the past.

Can the free peoples of Europe rise to the height of these resolves of the soul and instincts of the spirit of man?

If they can, the wrongs and injuries which have been inflicted will have been washed away on all sides by the miseries which have been endured. Is there any need for further floods of agony? Is it the only lesson of history that mankind is unteachable? Let there be justice, mercy and freedom. The peoples have only to will it, and all will achieve their hearts' desire.

I am now going to say something that will astonish you. The first step in the re-creation of the European family must be a partnership between France and Germany. In this way only can France recover the moral leadership of Europe. There can be no revival of Europe without a spiritually great France and a spiritually great Germany. The structure of the United States of Europe, if well and truly built, will be such as to make the material strength of a single state less important. Small nations will count as much as large ones and gain their honour by their contribution to the common cause. The ancient states and principalities of Germany, freely joined together for mutual convenience in a federal system, might each take their individual place among the United States of Europe. I shall not try to make a detailed programme for hundreds of millions of people who want to be happy and free, prosperous and safe, who wish to enjoy the four freedoms of which the great President Roosevelt spoke, and live in accordance with the principles embodied in the Atlantic Charter. If this is their wish, they have only to say so, and means can certainly be found, and machinery erected, to carry that wish into full fruition.

But I must give you a warning. Time may be short. At present there is a breathing-space. The cannon have ceased firing. The fighting has stopped; but the dangers have not stopped. If we are to form the United States of Europe or whatever name or form it may take, we must begin now.

In these present days we dwell strangely and precariously under the shield and protection of the atomic bomb. The atomic bomb is still only in the hands of a State and nation which we know will never use it except in the cause of right and freedom. But it may well be that in a few years this awful agency of destruction will be widespread and the catastrophe following from its use by several warring nations will not only bring to an end all that we call civilisation, but may possibly disintegrate the globe itself.

I must now sum up the propositions which are before you. Our constant aim must be to build and fortify the strength of U.N.O. Under and within that world concept we must re-create the European family in a regional structure called, it may be, the United States of Europe. The first step is to form a Council of Europe. If at first all the States of Europe are not willing or able to join the Union, we must nevertheless proceed to assemble and combine those who will and those who can. The salvation of the common people of every race and of every land from war or servitude must be established on solid foundations and must be guarded by the readiness of all men and women to die rather than submit to tyranny. In all this urgent work, France and Germany must take the lead together. Great Britain, the British Commonwealth of Nations, mighty America, and I trust Soviet Russia—for then indeed all would be well—must be the friends and sponsors of the new Europe and must champion its right to live and shine.

CONSERVATIVE PARTY CONFERENCE
AT BLACKPOOL

A SPEECH ON 5 OCTOBER 1946

---

24 *September—Marshal Stalin answers a questionnaire submitted by Mr. Alexander Werth, Moscow correspondent of the London "Sunday Times". He states that he believes absolutely in the possibility of friendly and lasting co-operation between U.S.S.R. and the Western democracies: and that he does not believe the atom bomb to be as serious a force as some politicians think.*

27 *September—General Anders is deprived of his nationality by the Polish Government.*

30 *September—Secretary of the Navy Forrestal states that the United States fleet will continue to maintain forces in the east Atlantic and the Mediterranean: to support Allied Military Governments in the discharge of their duties in occupied areas: and to protect American interests and support American policies in those areas.*

1 *October—General Franco speaking at Burgos declares that only two countries in the world know "where they are heading"—Spain and Russia.*

1 *October—The verdicts and sentences are pronounced against the Nazi Leaders on trial at Nuremberg.*

3 *October—Conservative Party Conference opens at Blackpool.*

[5 October 1946

WE have certainly had a depressing year since the General Election. I do not blame the Socialist Government—for the weather. We must also make allowances for all the difficulties which mark the aftermath of war. These difficulties would have taxed to the utmost the whole moral and physical resources of a united nation, marshalled and guided by a National Government. The Socialists broke up the national unity for the sake of their political interests, and the nation decided at the polls for a Socialist

Party Government. This was their right under our well-tried Constitution. The electors, based on universal suffrage, may do what they like. And afterwards they have to like what they do. There is a saying in England, "Experience bought is better than taught". We have bought the experience. I do not complain at all of the workings of our constitutional democratic system. If the majority of the people of Britain on the morrow of our survival and victory, felt as they did, it was right that they should have their way. In consequence a Party Government has come into office which has shown itself markedly unequal to holding our place in the world or making the best of Britain on the morrow of its prolonged, intense exertions and immortal services to mankind.

The Socialist Party have only done their duty in accepting the responsibility so unexpectedly cast upon them by the electors. If they cannot do the job, that is our misfortune, but it was their duty to try. Also it was the duty of everyone to help them to overcome the national and world problems with which they are confronted. That still remains the settled policy of His Majesty's Opposition.

As Leader of the Conservative and Unionist Party, at our annual Conference it is my duty to take a long and broad view. At present we are not, like some of our neighbours on the Continent, plunged in fundamental discussions about our Constitution. Government as well as Opposition—Socialists, Conservatives, and Liberals—are united against Communism and the Communist Party. The declared hostility of the Socialists towards Communism, although it is not at present important in this country, has exercised a significant and salutary influence abroad. There is also a considerable measure of agreement upon the main lines of foreign policy. This is especially true of our close association with the United States, whose firm and unchanging policy in Europe and abandonment of the doctrines of Isolation constitute the main bulwark of the peace of the world. We should all like also to preserve our wartime friendship with the Russian people and with the Soviet Government if they will allow us to do so, and will stop what Mr. Bevin calls "the war of nerves".

Even at home, as I stated when the new Parliament first came together, there is an immense body of social legislation upon which, apart from details, there is general agreement.

All that part which carries benefits to the cottage-home and seeks to give social security to the individual wage-earner was in fact devised, shaped, resolved and proclaimed by the National Coalition Government with its overwhelming Conservative majority. It is our most earnest desire to see our country successfully emerge from the confusion and exhaustion of war and take its part in building or rebuilding an unshakable structure and system of European and world peace. There was therefore and there still is a very great body of major issues on which the British nation is united, and if only the Socialist Government would devote themselves to national rather than Party aims, and make us feel that they are trying to find the best way out of our grievous difficulties, many benefits would come to the whole of our people and to the British Empire and Commonwealth of Nations.

We certainly do not grudge the King's Ministers their offices. It is a sign of national political health and maturity when each of the great constitutional Parties can shoulder the responsibilities of administration, when all sorts and conditions of men and women can have their turn in the high functions of State, and every dog his day. What rouses our regret and growing resentment is first, that the Socialist Ministers are so much wrapped up in their Party doctrines that they cannot give a fair chance to our national interests and prosperity. Secondly, that they pour upon us an endless drizzle of insult and abuse. To hear their speeches and to read their newspapers one would suppose that Mr. Attlee and his Socialist colleagues were the only people who had anything to do with winning the war. The Conservative Party is, according to them, a mere jumble of outworn interests and privileges which has now been swept away for ever from any share in our national life. The leader of the ten Liberals in the House of Commons re-echoes these bitter taunts. The historic theme of Liberalism—expressed by Gladstone, by John Stuart Mill—the Liberalism of John Bright and John Morley—all that great conception of a free, humane, generous and progressive civilisation is now reduced in the mind of this unfortunate person—the leader of the ten—to an animal hatred of Toryism.

But after all we are entitled to be treated with respect. We embody many of the strongest elements in the nation.

We stand for high causes. Even under the confused conditions of the General Election ten and a half million people voted for us. To-day we are half, or more than half, the country.

The Socialist Government itself did not represent a majority of the nation. Under our present electoral system they have a majority of two to one in Parliament, and as on every occasion they seem to set Party before country, they can certainly vote us down in the House of Commons and carry through their fads and fancies and, regardless of the national interests, wreak their Party spite upon the other half of their fellow-countrymen. In little more than a year they have diminished British influence abroad and very largely paralysed our revival at home. Surely after all we have gone through we have enough to bear and dangers enough to face without the obtrusion upon us of this aggressive partisanship. One would have hoped that victors of the election would rise to the level of their task, that they would have due regard for our common inheritance, that they would think for the country as a whole, and do their best for their native land. But, alas, they feel differently. They have to ram Socialist dogmas, which only a small minority of them even comprehend, down the throats of the British people in order to show what good Party men they are, no matter what it costs the ordinary working-class family in common everyday prosperity, convenience and freedom of life.

To all this they add quite exceptional ineptitude and inefficiency and many silly blunders in the conduct of our affairs. Do you seek for proofs? Look around you. Look at the taxes. Look at the unbridled expenditure which is leading us daily into inflation, with all its bitter consequences. Look at the queues as you walk about our streets. Look at the restrictions and repressions on every form of enterprise and recovery. Look at the ever-growing bureaucracy of officials quartered permanently on the public. Let us look at Food. The German U-boats in their worst endeavour never made bread-rationing necessary in war. It took a Socialist Government and Socialist planners to fasten it on us in time of peace when the seas are open and the world harvests good. At no time in the two world-wars have our people had so little bread, meat, butter, cheese and fruit to eat.

206

Look at the housing of the people. At the end of 13 months of his housing performance, Mr. Aneurin Bevan points proudly to 22,000 new permanent houses completed. Before the war between 25,000 and 30,000 permanent houses were erected in Great Britain every *month*. But now, in August, only 4,566 permanent houses were completed, that is to say only about one-sixth of the number built mainly by private enterprise without any fuss or bother every month before the war.

How shall we stigmatise the incompetence which left large numbers of buildings, camps and habitations vacant under Government control while hundreds of thousands of families yearn for any kind of roof over their heads and privacy at their hearths till something better can be provided? I have before expressed my astonishment that any man responsible for housing, like Mr. Aneurin Bevan, should not have tried to deal with his problem on the merits and make as many homes as possible in the shortest time by every means available, even if he had to lay aside during these years of emergency some of his doctrinaire malice. The amount of needless suffering, vexation and frustration his prejudices have caused cannot be measured. There is however a poetic justice in the fact that the most mischievous political mouth in wartime has also become, in peace, the most remarkable administrative failure.

Let us look at Coal. The foundation of Britain's industry, commerce and life has hitherto depended on cheap and abundant coal. Yet Mr. Shinwell boasts that the era of cheap coal is gone for ever. But the question which now concerns us is not one of cheap coal, but of an actual shortage. All the strains and pressures of the war did not prevent us from getting through the difficulties with which each winter confronted us. The Socialists assured us that the nationalisation of the coal mines would give a renewed surge of energy and time-keeping to the miners. Their work below ground—away from the light of day— is hard and exceptional and I am glad they have received an extra ration of meat. The coal position is, however, grim. The Government only just scraped through last year. We seem likely to begin this new winter with stocks about five million tons below the last year's figure. It seems certain therefore that we shall be forced to reduce the consumption of coal this winter and the only question open is whether householders will shiver or factories go on short time. As for our export of coal, which used to bring us in something like £30,000,000 a year of fertile foreign exchange, that has of course departed at the moment when we need it most. So much for the new spirit which we were assured the nationalisation of the coal mines would create among the miners.

The Socialist Minister of Agriculture recently announced —I take his own words—"very tragic and almost disastrous cuts in the supplies of animal feeding stuffs." When we learn that these cuts involve a reduction of 40 per cent of the feeding stuffs of our dairy herds and from 40 to 60 per cent of the feeding stuffs of our pigs and poultry, it is no wonder that Ministers should confess that our food will become worse than in the worst days of the war. The supply of labour for the land is precarious. Next year the acreage under corn must be largely increased. The 200,000 German prisoners of war who helped the harvesting this year will be gone, and as the Housing Rural Workers Act has been deliberately let die by the Government the shortage of houses in the country is worse even than in the towns. In fact, less than half of the agricultural workers who served in the forces are returning to the land. The long-term agricultural programme, evolved by my colleague, Mr. Hudson, in consultation with all the farming experts, has been abandoned, and nothing worthy of the name of an agricultural policy has been put in its place.

I have on other occasions set before you the immense injury which has been done to our process of recovery by the ill-considered schemes and threats of nationalisation which have cast their shadows over so many of our leading industries. The attempts to nationalise the steel industry, which was so effective in war and so buoyant in its plans for the future, is the most foolish of all the experiments in Socialism from which we have yet suffered. The wanton destruction by Sir Stafford Cripps of the Liverpool Cotton Exchange has inflicted a deep lasting injury upon the Lancashire cotton trade and upon the City of Liverpool. The nationalisation of Cables and Wireless, although agreeable to Australian Socialist conceptions, has been a dead loss to this Island, not only in foreign exchange but in facilities of communication which private enterprise had patiently built up to the national advantage. The shortage of all necessary articles for ordinary domestic consumption persists. We are complacently assured that the number of people employed on manufacture for home consumption is getting back to pre-war level, but what of the maldistribution of effort? In June we had 515,000 more people working in the metal and chemical industries than pre-war, but 456,000 less in the textile and clothing industries. Again, we had nearly 300,000 more non-industrial civil servants, but 677,000 less workers in the distributive trades. And now the British housewife, as she stands in the queue to buy her bread ration, will fumble in her pocket in vain for a silver sixpence. Under the Socialist Government *nickel* will have to be good enough for her. In future we shall still be able to say "Every cloud has a *nickel* lining".

Look where you will, we are suffering a needless decline and contraction at a time when we had the right to brighter days. I have visited many of the smaller countries on the Continent. All are making much more of themselves and of their chances than we are. Nowhere is there the drab disheartenment and frustration which the Socialist Party have fastened on Britain.

But now I turn abroad. I wish to speak of India. I am very glad you passed the Resolution about India at the Conference yesterday. You all know my views about India and how we have desired to give full Dominion Status to India, including the right embodied in the Statute of Westminster for the Indian peoples, like other Dominions, to quit the British Commonwealth of Nations altogether. The way in which the Socialist Government have handled this problem has been such as to give the vast masses of the people of India hardly any choice but to become separated from the British Crown which has so long shielded them from internal convulsions or foreign invasion. The Government of India has been placed—or I should rather say thrust—into the hands of men who have good reason to be bitterly hostile to the British connection, but who in no way represent the enormous mass of nearly 400 millions of all the races, States, and peoples of India who have dwelt so long in peace with one another. I fear that calamity impends upon this sub-Continent, which is almost as big as Europe, more populous, and even more harshly divided. It seems that in quite a short time India will become a separate, a foreign and a none too friendly country to the British

Commonwealth of Nations. Indian unity created by British rule will swiftly perish, and no one can measure the misery and bloodshed which will overtake these enormous masses of humble helpless millions, or under what new power their future and destiny will lie. All this is happening every day, every hour. The great ship is sinking in the calm sea. Those who should have devoted their utmost efforts to keep her afloat have instead opened the sea-cocks. The event will long leave its mark in history. It may well be that Burma will soon suffer the same fate. I am grieved to have to state these sombre tidings to you. Most of you will certainly live to see whether I am right or wrong. Sometimes in the past I have not been wrong. I pray that I may be wrong now.

What has been the effect of our immense act of surrender in India? On the morrow of our victory and of our services, without which human freedom would not have survived, we are divesting ourselves of the mighty and wonderful empire which had been built up in India by two hundred years of effort and sacrifice, and the number of the King's subjects is being reduced to barely a quarter of what it has been for generations. Yet at this very moment and in the presence of this unparalleled act of voluntary abdication, we are still ceaselessly abused by the Soviet wireless and by certain unfriendly elements in the United States for being a land-grabbing Imperialist power seeking expansion and aggrandisement. While Soviet Russia is expanding or seeking to expand in every direction, and has already brought many extra scores of millions of people directly or indirectly under the despotic control of the Kremlin and the rigours of Communist discipline, we, who sought nothing from this war but to do our duty and are in fact reducing ourselves to a fraction of our former size and population, are successfully held up to world censure. It is astonishing that no effective reply should be made by His Majesty's Government and that it should be left to Field Marshal Smuts, the great South African, our former valiant enemy of Boer War days, to raise his voice in vindication of British magnanimity, tolerance and good faith.

What are we to say of the handling of the Palestine problem by the Socialist Government? At the election they made lavish promises to the Zionists and their success at the polls excited passionate expectations throughout the Jewish world. These promises were no sooner made than they were discarded, and now all through this year the Government stand vacillating without any plan or policy, holding on to a mandate in which we have no vital interest, gaining the distrust and hostility both of Arab and Jew, and exposing us to worldwide reprobation for their manifest incapacity. Thus both at home and abroad the British nation and Empire have been deprived of the rewards their conduct deserves.

I have naturally considered very carefully what is my own duty in these times. It would be easy for me to retire gracefully in an odour of civic freedoms, and this plan crossed my mind frequently some months ago. I feel now however that the situation is so serious and what may have to come so grave, that I am resolved to go forward carrying the flag as long as I have the necessary strength and energy, and have your confidence. It is of the highest importance to our name and endurance as a great power and to the cohesion of our national and imperial life that there should be re-established at the earliest moment some poise and balance between the political forces in our Island, and that those who were so unexpectedly clad with overwhelming Parliamentary power should be made to realise that they are the servants, and not the masters, of the British nation. When I think of what has already happened, what is happening, and what is going to happen in the next year or two, I feel, as you feel, profoundly stirred. Our reaction must not be despair, because that is an emotion which we do not allow. It must be wrath—not despair but wrath—and wrath must translate itself not in vain expletives but in earnest action and well-conceived measures and organisation.

The Government have informed us that there will not be a General Election till the 1st of May, 1950. I have no doubt they will cling to office and exploit their Parliamentary advantage to the last possible moment. But there are many things uncertain in this world, and as soon as it is apparent, as it may soon be apparent, that the movement of the national mind and the people's will is with us, we shall be living in quite a different climate from that which we now endure. The whole tribe of highly intellectual left-wing scribblers assure us that the

Socialist Administration will rule for 20 years. All the strong forces gathered at this Conference they declare are moribund or dead. They will sing quite a different tune once they realise, and are made to realise, that they have a growing majority of the nation against them. This change can be effected in three ways. First by a continuance of wise and efficient action in the House of Commons and also in the House of Lords. Secondly, at by-elections in the country. Thirdly, and all the time, by the gathering together of those virile, vital forces in our race which keep Britain alive. Even though the present House of Commons draws out its weary term to the dregs, once we are on the move in earnest we shall feel the soil of Britain firm again under our feet.

In order to achieve a position of moral ascendancy every sacrifice and effort should be made by those to whom our country's greatness is dear. For such a purpose we must lay aside every impediment and every prejudice and marshal every scrap of strength we can. Never must we underrate the immense resources of patriotism which can be gathered for our cause, which to-day is no ordinary Party cause but carries with it, as I am sure, the life and future of Britain.

I am glad that there has been a discussion upon the name of our Party. Of course the policy for which we stand is infinitely more important than the name we bear, but we ought to make sure that the mere name is in no way a stumbling block to the great mass of voters without political affiliations who are affronted and disgusted by the Socialist mismanagement of our affairs. A new generation of electors is at hand. Great latitude in this matter has always been customary among us. At present we call ourselves, according to our liking, Unionists, Conservatives, Tories or Tory Democrats. We also have with us our faithful allies, the Liberal Nationals. But whatever name we use this party is in fact already and has been for sixty years "The Union Party", standing for the union of the Kingdom and the Empire and the union of men of good will of all classes against tyrannical and subversive elements.

We need not pay any attention to the mockery of our opponents. The Liberal Party has so mishandled its affairs and has been so mauled by the Socialists that it has very little left besides its famous name. The Labour Party have identified themselves with the fallacious, narrowing doctrines of Socialism. We can afford to disdain their taunts. Neither of these Parties is in any posture to give us advice.

The principles of our Party are not up for auction. We propose no bargain to any section of public opinion. If however there are others who, in growing numbers, are marching along the path which Duty marks out for us, no memories of past differences or outworn quarrels should be allowed to stand in the way of these natural unities which spring from a common policy and a single aim.

I do not believe in looking about for some panacea or cure-all on which we should stake our credit and fortunes trying to sell it like a patent medicine to all and sundry. It is easy to win applause by talking in an airy way about great new departures in policy, especially if all detailed proposals are avoided. We ought not to seek after some rigid, symmetrical form of doctrine, such as delights the minds of Socialists and Communists. Our own feelings and the British temperament are quite different. So are our aims. We seek a free and varied society, where there is room for many kinds of men and women to lead happy, honourable and useful lives. We are fundamentally opposed to all systems of rigid uniformity in our national life and we have grown great as a nation by indulging tolerance, rather than logic.

It certainly would be an error of the first order for us to plunge out into a programme of promises and bribes in the hopes of winning the public favour. But if you say to me: "What account are we to give of the policy of the Conservative Party? What are we to say of our theme and our cause and of the faith that is in us?" That is a question to which immediate answer can always be given.

Our main objectives are: To uphold the Christian religion and resist all attacks upon it. To defend our Monarchical and Parliamentary Constitution. To provide adequate security against external aggression and safety for our seaborne trade. To uphold law and order, and impartial justice administered by Courts free from interference or pressure on the part of the executive. To regain a sound finance and strict supervision of national income and expenditure. To defend and develop our Empire trade, without which Great Britain would perish. To promote all measures to improve the health and social conditions of the people. To support as a general rule free enterprise and initiative against State trading and nationalisation of industries.

To this I will add some further conceptions. We oppose the establishment of a Socialist State, controlling the means of production, distribution and exchange. We are asked, "What is your alternative?" Our Conservative aim is to build a property-owning democracy, both independent and interdependent. In this I include profit-sharing schemes in suitable industries and intimate consultation between employers and wage-earners. In fact we seek so far as possible to make the status of the wage-earner that of a partner rather than of an irresponsible employee. It is in the interest of the wage-earner to have many other alternatives open to him than service under one all-powerful employer called the State. He will be in a better position to bargain collectively and production will be more abundant; there will be more for all and more freedom for all when the wage-earner is able, in the large majority of cases, to choose and change his work, and to deal with a private employer who, like himself, is subject to the ordinary pressures of life and, like himself, is dependent upon his personal thrift, ingenuity and good-housekeeping. In this way alone can the traditional virtues of the British character be preserved. We do not wish the people of this ancient island reduced to a mass of State-directed proletarians, thrown hither and thither, housed here and there, by an aristocracy of privileged officials or privileged Party, sectarian or Trade Union bosses. We are opposed to the tyranny and victimisation of the closed shop. Our ideal is the consenting union of millions of free, independent families and homes to gain their livelihood and to serve true British glory and world peace.

Freedom of enterprise and freedom of service are not possible without elaborate systems of safeguards against failure, accident or misfortune. We do not seek to pull down improvidently the structures of society, but to erect balustrades upon the stairway of life, which will prevent helpless or foolish people from falling into the abyss.

Both the Conservative and Liberal Parties have made notable contributions to secure minimum standards of life and labour. I too have borne my part in this. It is 38 years ago since I introduced the first Unemployment Insurance Scheme, and 22 years ago since, as Conservative Chancellor of the Exchequer, I shaped and carried the Widows' Pensions and reduction of the Old Age Pensions from 70 to 65. We are now moving forward into another vast scheme of national insurance, which arose, even in the stress of war, from a Parliament with a great Conservative majority. It is an essential principle of Conservative, Unionist, and Tory policy—call it what you will—to defend the general public against abuses by monopolies and against restraints on trade and enterprise, whether these evils come from private corporations, from the mischievous plans of doctrinaire Governments, or from the incompetence and arbitrariness of departments of State. Finally, we declare ourselves the unsleeping opponents of all class, all official or all Party privilege, which denies the genius of our island race, whose sparks fly upwards unceasingly from the whole people, its rightful career, reward and pre-eminence alike in peace and war.

How then do we draw the lines of political battle? The British race is not actuated mainly by the hope of material gain. Otherwise we should long ago have sunk in the ocean of the past. It is stirred on almost all occasions by sentiment and instinct, rather than by programmes or worldly calculation. When this new Parliament first met, all the Socialist Members stood up and sang "The Red Flag" in their triumph. Peering ahead through the mists and mysteries of the future so far as I can; I see the division at the next election will be between those who wholeheartedly sing "The Red Flag" and those who rejoice to sing "Land of Hope and Glory". There is the noble hymn which will rally the wise, the soberminded and the good to the salvation of our native land.

THE ROOSEVELT MEMORIAL BILL

A SPEECH TO THE HOUSE OF COMMONS
11 OCTOBER 1946

I RISE to support the Second Reading of the Measure which the Prime Minister has proposed to us in felicitous terms and with so much feeling. It was my duty, eighteen months ago, to address the House on the sad occasion of President Roosevelt's death, and I am sure I did not go beyond historical fact and general conviction in describing him as the greatest American friend we have ever known, and the greatest champion of freedom who had ever brought help and comfort from the new world to the old. It is indeed fitting that a memorial should be raised to him in this island, and that old, mighty, war-scarred London should be the chosen place. I could have wished that the House had taken upon it the charges to erect this monument, as I am sure it would have been most willing to do, but the method chosen of raising money by a great number of small subscriptions has the important advantage that it permits so many people to give effect, by an individual act, to their heartfelt feelings, and it is, I think, in accordance with what President Roosevelt himself would have wished.

I am obliged to the Prime Minister for the reference which he made to the comradeship which grew between the late President and me during the war, and to the fact that this was of service to the interests of the people of our countries and to the cause for which all the Allies fought so hard and so long. This comradeship in great affairs was founded upon friendship, and roused in my heart a sentiment of sincere affection for this noble, august and charming personality. I received from him so many marks of kindness and good will that I felt buoyed up in the ordeal of the war by the fact of walking hand in hand with this outstanding chief of the American people.

The Prime Minister has spoken of Washington and Lincoln, and who can doubt that Franklin Roosevelt will take his place with them in the history, not only of the United States, but of the world? We are so much nearer to him in point of time that we cannot see his life's work in the perspective and setting which belong to the famous figures of the past, but already none can doubt his rank and stature. There are many tests by which we may try to measure the greatness of the men who have served high causes, but I shall select only one of them this morning, namely, the favourable influence exerted upon the fortunes of mankind. In this, Roosevelt's name gains pre-eminence even over those of the illustrious figures we have mentioned. Reflecting on the past, one has the feeling that the changes associated with Washington would probably have come to pass in due course by the irresistible movement and evolution of events. Nor can we doubt that slavery would have been abolished, even apart from Abraham Lincoln, in the vast spread of the humanities which lighted the nineteenth century. Of Roosevelt, however, it must be said that had he not acted when he did, in the way he did, had he not felt the generous surge of freedom in his heart, had he not resolved to give aid to Britain and to Europe in the supreme crisis through which we have passed, a hideous fate might well have overwhelmed mankind and made its whole future for centuries sink into shame and ruin. It may well be that the man whom we honour to-day not only anticipated history but altered its course, and altered it in a manner which has saved the freedom and earned the gratitude of the human race for generations to come. On this side of the House we give our cordial support to the Measure which the Prime Minister has just introduced.

FOREIGN AFFAIRS

A SPEECH TO THE HOUSE OF COMMONS
23 OCTOBER 1946

---

11 *October—Referendum in France results in the acceptance of the revised Constitution, 53.3 per cent of votes cast being in favour.*

14 *October—General Election in Australia results in victory for the Labour Party with a reduced majority.*

15 *October—Paris Peace Conference is concluded.*

16 *October—The Nazi Leaders condemned to death at Nuremberg are executed. Goering commits suicide.*

19 *October—Secretary of State Byrnes broadcasting on the results of the Peace Conference expresses "bewilderment" at the motives attributed to the United States by the Soviet delegates in Paris.*

22 *October—Two British destroyers stike mines in the Corfu Straits. 38 lives are lost.*

23 *October—The General Assembly of the United Nations opens at Flushing Meadows, New York.*

[*23 October 1946*

THE right hon. Gentleman the Foreign Secretary wished to open this Debate and I may say, merely to safeguard future practice, that it is not quite usual for a two days' Debate to be opened from the Government benches. However, I willingly agreed to the right hon. Gentleman making his statement, and we all have been greatly interested in the speech which he has made. Indeed, I think there was a very general measure of agreement in the House with everything, or nearly everything, he said. Where there may be differences, they are not differences on what he said so much as on what, for no doubt very good reasons, the right hon. Gentleman left unsaid. As to the value of what are called the "open discussions" which have been proceeding in Paris, I can only comment that they seem to be bad diplomacy, but, none the less, valuable education. As to the veto, that is a very serious matter. It is well known that Soviet Russia would not have joined the original San Francisco Conference unless they had had what they regard as the essential security of the veto. I quite agree with the right hon. Gentleman that it was never contemplated at any time that the veto should be used in the abrupt, arbitrary and almost continuous manner that we have seen it used, but that it should be reserved as a last assurance to a great Power that they would not be voted down on a matter about which they were prepared to fight. There is, certainly, a great departure from that tradition, and the Foreign Secretary will be supported on this side of the House in endeavouring to secure a modification in the uses of the veto, even if he is not a this times able to secure a very considerable restriction of its employment.

We all wish the Foreign Secretary a successful mission to the United States. No one complains of his having to be out of the country. It is his duty to go over and, indeed, I, myself, believe very much that advantage comes from that. Even in the days of the National Coalition, Ministers sometimes left the country for considerable periods, and I, having left the right hon. Gentleman the Prime Minister to carry on affairs, allowed myself all the necessary latitude in this respect. We all, as I say, wish that the right hon. Gentleman may have a successful mission in the United States, and we are confident that, in many respects, he will be upholding, not Party but national, and indeed not national, but world issues.

In the Debate yesterday the right hon. Gentleman made considerable references to Germany, and perhaps the most important part of his speech consisted of declarations of policy about Germany, and about the Anglo-American occupied zones in Germany. Agreement on this was expressed by my right hon. Friend the Member for Saffron Walden [Mr. R. A. Butler]. We are in full agreement with the modifications and the mitigations of the severity of German life under present conditions, so far as these are physically and economically possible. It is only common sense that the Germans should earn their own living, and I think it is only common sense that they should manage their own affairs, provided, and always provided, that effective disarmament is enforced and maintained over a prolonged period of years. We do not want to have the burden of teaching the Germans how to manage their own affairs, and we do not want to have the burden of earning their living for them. The remarks of the Chancellor of the Exchequer on this subject might be held by captious critics to be a criticism of the policy so far pursued by His Majesty's Government.*

However, there is just one point I should like to make on the subject of Germany managing her own affairs. The right hon. Gentleman announced that he was proceeding to nationalise the various great German industries and place them under the Commander-in-Chief. All I can tell the House is that experience shows that one may be quite sure that when the Germans have the power of managing their own affairs, they will not be attracted to a policy, whatever it may be, by the fact that it has been imposed upon them by foreigners. It was exactly what happened after the first world war when we imposed upon Germany, by force, all the blessings of a liberal constitution. All the blessings of freedom from the tyranny of conscription and many benefits fought for by generations of effort in this country were enforced by the victors upon the defeated Germans and were, for that reason, odious in their eyes. But, as I say, it may be that it will work differently this time.

I must comment first this afternoon upon two or three special questions which are likely to cause trouble and are, indeed, already causes of disquiet. I have nothing to add to-day to the statements which I have made on previous occasions about Egypt and Palestine. No one can say that His Majesty's Government have not done their best to meet Egyptian wishes. Indeed, many of us thought that they had gone too far and had adopted the wrong methods in stating, at the outset of their negotiations, that they were willing to evacuate the Canal zone, which zone is secured to us for the next few critical years

---

*Dr. Hugh Dalton speaking to the Bankers & Merchants of the City of London, Mansion House, on 16 October 1946, said: "The British taxpayer is being called upon to find more than eighty million a year to feed and to supply the Germans in the British zone, many millions of whom for many years followed their leaders with intense and unashamed ardour until their wicked plans were finally frustrated."

to come by the Anglo-Egyptian treaty of 1936. The result has been what was then predicted, namely, that their maximum offer was taken as the starting point for new discussions, and these discussions now even involve the whole sovereignty and future of the Sudan. I remind the right hon. Gentleman the Prime Minister of his statement on 7 May, when he said that, obviously, if negotiations break down the original treaty still stands. I hope that His Majesty's Government will act in this sense.

Before we separated for the Autumn Recess, I spoke about Palestine. I must refer to that subject, linked as it is with all other questions of the Middle East. If we are not able to fulfil our pledge to the Jews to create a national home for the Jewish people in Palestine—which is our undoubted pledge—we are entitled and, indeed, bound in my view—because it is our duty, to lay our Mandate at the feet of the United Nations Organisation. The burden may yet be too heavy for one single country to bear. It is not right that the United States, who are so very keen on Jewish immigration into Palestine, should take no share in the task, and should reproach us for our obvious incapacity to cope with the difficulties of the problem.

At present, we have no policy as far as I can make out, nor have we had one for more than a year. The amount of suffering which this indecision in regard to a question which, I admit, may well be called the "riddle of the Sphinx", is causing to all concerned, simply cannot be measured. From the moment when we declare that we will give up the Mandate—giving proper notice, of course—all our difficulties will be considerably lessened, and if other interested Powers wish us to continue, it is for them to make proposals and help us in our work. We have at this moment a large proportion of our overseas Army in Palestine engaged in a horrible, squalid conflict with the Zionist community there. This is a disproportionate exertion for us, a wrong distribution of our limited forces, and the most thankless task ever undertaken by any country. If we stand on the treaty with Egypt about the Canal zone, we have no need to seek a new strategic base of very doubtful usefulness in Palestine, and we can present ourselves to the world organisation as a totally disinterested party. Superior solutions may then, for the first time, become open. I strongly commend this course of action to His Majesty's Government and to the House.

I was very glad yesterday to hear what the Foreign Secretary said about Greece. The result of the Greek plebiscite upon the return of the King fully vindicates the course pursued by the National Coalition Government, by the interim Government of which I was the head, and by His Majesty's present advisers. We have always said it was a question for the Greek people to decide freely for themselves. This they have done under conditions which impartial foreign observers have pronounced not unfair, and which are incomparably more free and valid than anything that has been seen in that part of the world for a very long time. That pronouncement ought to be the end of our special wartime responsibilities towards Greece. I was glad to hear that our troops will be brought home as soon as possible. [*An Hon. Member: "When will that be?"*] I am not pressing for details. There is a kind of guerilla warfare on the Northern frontier of Greece which does not arise out of internal Greek affairs. It arises out of very much larger complications. But still I am most anxious that our troops should come home. I am tired of hearing it said that we are in Greece for something which we wish to get out of the country, or for some advantage. I know of no advantage that we gain or seek in Greece except those ordinary advantages enjoyed by all nations, of trade and friendship, which we ourselves enjoyed before the war.

The future safety and independence of Greece, like many other vital matters, lie in the hands of U.N.O. Our ancient friendship with Greece will never flag or die, but here, as elsewhere, we seek no gain or benefit of a selfish character for ourselves and, as I have just said, we have no desire for any advantages which we did not possess before the war. I hope that all Greeks who wish for the survival of their country will help the new régime and Government, and that the Government will be continually broadened to include all who prefer the life and freedom of Greece to its ruin and absorption in a Communist Balkan *bloc.* I hope fair play will be given to the new régime and the new Government of Greece, and that every step taken will not be the target for sharp arrows of carefully barbed, poisoned propaganda. It is very easy for foreign observers in a position of perfect detachment, to abuse a Government which is struggling against a Communist conspiracy, fomented and supported by outside intrigues. An armed Communist advances upon you, you react against him; therefore, you are a reactionary.

I must now speak about Poland. Here, indeed, an unhappy scene is unfolded to our eyes. In my opinion, the Soviet Government have departed, I am sorry to say, in the spirit and in the letter from many of the agreements and understandings into which we entered with them before Yalta, and at Yalta. It was my firm belief that Marshal Stalin would rest content with the Curzon line, and with a Poland friendly to Russia, and permanently divorced from Germany. On that, I offered on many occasions my counsel to the House. It was agreed that, on this basis, there should be free elections in Poland and that the Polish Republic should be an independent Power. What has happened now? A Government has been set up in Poland which in no way represents the Polish nation. That Government is incapable of holding free or fair elections. The Peasant Party are to be given no full and free opportunity of voting in accordance with their convictions, and of having their votes counted in accordance with their numbers. We must be very careful to distinguish in our minds between the present Polish Government, and the heart of the Polish nation, to whose sorrows and sufferings there seems never to be an end.

I presume that the most delicate and difficult situation at the moment is that which exists around Trieste, where British and American divisions confront the very much larger forces which Marshal Tito has kept under arms and assembled there. Gratitude does not seem to be the outstanding feature of Marshal Tito's character. I am sure every one here was shocked at the brutal and callous manner in which American aeroplanes and their passengers were shot down by the air force of a country whose liberation and independence would never have been achieved but for British and American aid and exertion, or without the victorious campaigns fought in Italy and Germany by the Western Allies. The whole attitude of the Yugoslav Communist Government towards this country, and even more towards the United States, is far from friendly. Considering that the United States is the main contributor to U.N.R.R.A., and that scores of millions of pounds of supplies have been poured into Yugoslavia since the end of the German war, the murder of the American airmen and passengers presents itself in a singularly repulsive light.

Conditions in Yugoslavia are sinister and melancholy. The whole country is being converted, as far as possible, into a Communist area. Communism is being taught in the schools, and every effort is being made to create a Soviet Socialist Republic in the closest association with Moscow. It is not for us to interfere in the internal affairs of another country. [*Laughter*]. Well, I am afraid I make my principle of general application. The Catholic Church and clergy in Croatia are being persecuted with the greatest severity, and the strictest measures of police government are applied to political dissentients. The circumstances of the trial and condemnation of the Archbishop of Zagreb have created widespread regret. There is growing discontent in Serbia, to whose peasant proprietors Communist doctrines are unwelcome.

The course followed by His Majesty's Government has, throughout, been wise and correct, and I am glad to see it has been taken in the closest harmony with that of the United States. I earnestly trust that this policy towards Yugoslavia will be pursued by His Majesty's Government with perseverance, and that the great city of Trieste will be preserved as an international port, an outlet upon salt water for the commerce of all the States and peoples in the Danube Basin. I trust, also, that large Italian populations will not be transferred against their own will to Communist rule, contrary to the whole principle of the Atlantic Charter. I was very glad to hear from the Prime Minister to-day, when he referred to the speech made by my right hon. Friend the Member for Saffron Walden, that the British troops would not leave the Trieste area until the treaty has been fully signed and accepted by all States who are likely to be party to it.

Now I am going to look back a little, in fact, I am going to look back for a year almost to the day, when on 22 October, 1945, I pressed for more rapid demobilisation. I made the following statement, which, I venture to think the House will permit me to read, as I copied it from *Hansard:*

I must, however, make one very serious reservation. In my calculations and estimates I have definitely excluded the possibility of a major war in the next few years. If His Majesty's Government consider that this is wrong, then it would not be a case of demobilisation at all but of remobilisation, because what has taken place and is going on has already woefully impaired the immediate fighting efficiency of the enormous Forces we still retain. I believe, however, it may be common ground that this possibility of a major war may rightly be excluded, and that we may have an interlude of grace in which mankind may be able to make better arrangements for this tortured world than we have hitherto achieved. Still, I make that reservation.

On this basis, I also gave the minimum figures to which in my judgment—a judgment without official information—the reduction should be made, and I stated the figures. Those figures were: Royal Navy, 150,000; Army, 1,000,000; Royal Air Force 400,000; total men, 1,550,000. The figures to which His Majesty's Government announced in February they are working are considerably less than this total, especially in respect of the Army and Air Force; the Navy is a little larger. These are the Government's figures to be obtained by 31 December this year, in the next ten weeks: Royal Navy, 175,000; Army, 650,000, instead of 1,000,000; Royal Air Force, 275,000, instead of 400,000; total in the Services, taking only the published figures, 1,100,000 as against 1,550,000. I believe there are 100,000 recruits additional in training. The Government, therefore have gone much farther in reducing our military strength, notably in the Army and Air Force, than the figures I put forward on the basis of getting down to our minimum figure, whatever it was, as quickly as possible. I am not to-day treating this issue as controversial, as a matter of quarrel between the Government and the Opposition. The Government have the power and responsibility, and they ought to have the knowledge. I am, however, forced to examine the question whether the situation has deteriorated in the year that has passed.

Eight months ago, I made a speech at Fulton in the United States. It had a mixed reception on both sides of the Atlantic, and quite a number of hon. Members of this House put their names to a Motion condemning me for having made it. As ˎevents have moved, what I said at Fulton has been outpaced and overpassed by this movement of events, and by the movement of American opinion. If I were to make that speech at the present time and in the same place, it would attract no particular attention. At that time, I said that I did not believe the Soviet Government wanted war. I said that what they wanted were the fruits of war. I fervently hope and pray that the view which I then expressed is still correct, and on the whole I believe it is still correct. However, we are dealing with the unknowable. Like everyone else, I welcome the recent declarations of Marshal Stalin, and I always welcome any signs of affability which M. Molotov may display. I know him quite well, and, as the right hon. Gentleman the Foreign Secretary will corroborate, he is not nearly so spiky in private relationship as he appears in his public declarations. In these matters, it is not words that count, it is deeds and facts.

This afternoon I am not going to examine the likelihood of another war, which would, of course, be total war. In the Foreign Secretary's calm, assured and measured review of the world situation yesterday, it was evident that various differences of policy exist between the Soviet Government and what are called, for want of a better name—and it is not a bad name—the Western democracies. There are differences in the Far East; there are disputes about Persia; there are various grave and serious questions connected with the Dardanelles; above all, there is the situation at Trieste, there is Poland and its elections, and there are others. The right hon. Gentleman found it necessary—and he was quite right—to survey the whole far from cheering panorama, and touch upon all those points of view; and though his language was diplomatically correct in every respect, one could not help seeing those points of direct difference emerging as between the great Powers which are involved. It would be most unwise to ignore those differences, and every effort should be made to adjust them. I am sure every effort will be made by patient, friendly and, I hope, occasionally secret discussions between the principal Powers and personalities involved.

It was easier in Hitler's day to feel and forecast the

general movement of events than it is now. Now we have to deal not with Hitler and his crude Nazi gang, with anti-Semitism as its principal theme; we are in the presence of something very much more difficult to measure than what was set out so plainly in the pages of *Mein Kampf*. We are in the presence of the collective mind, whose springs of action we cannot define. There are 13 or 14 very able men in the Kremlin who hold all Russia and more than a third of Europe in their control. Many stresses and pressures, internal as well as external, are working upon them, as upon all human beings. I cannot presume to forecast what decisions they will take, or to observe what decisions they may have already have taken; still less can I attempt to foresee the time factor in their affairs. One of our main difficulties in judging all these matters is that real intercourse and intimacy between our peoples are, to all intents and purposes, very much discouraged and prevented by the Soviet Government. There is none of that free comradely life and mixing which very soon would bring immense changes in the relationships of these vast communities, and might sweep away suspicion, without relaxing vigilance.

The Prime Minister referred just now in his speech—he used the expression and I noted it down at the time—to "the total mobilised forces which may constitute a positive danger to peace". That is certainly a serious remark, coming as it does from the head of His Majesty's Government. Now, I am going to ask a question—it is all I have to say before I sit down—on which, I feel, the House, the nation and, indeed, the world should be told the truth as far as it is known to His Majesty's Government, and should be reassured, if it is possible, and as far as possible. To make it easier for the Government to give a brief and general answer, to make it possible for them to give an almost monosyllabic answer, I will put my question in a constructive form. Here is the question: Is it or is it not true that there are to-day more than 200 Soviet divisions on a war footing in the occupied territories of Europe from the Baltic to Vienna, and from Vienna to the Black Sea? There is the question which I am asking, and it acquires particular significance in view of the Prime Minister's reference, which I heard only this afternoon in the House, to "total mobilised forces which may constitute a positive danger to peace". I am not referring to the armies of satellite Powers which, in Poland, are numerous but reluctant, and in Yugoslavia and Bulgaria are less numerous but more ardent.

I shall be very much relieved if I can be told in the course of to-day's Debate that the figures I have given—which I have not given without prolonged consideration and heart-searching, or without discussion with colleagues—are altogether excessive, and if His Majesty's Government can relieve our anxieties in the matter I am quite ready to accept their statement, but I feel bound to put the question. When we think of all the helpless millions and hundreds of millions struggling to earn their living, toiling along the uphill path, hoping for the future, doing their best, one cannot but feel that they ought to know the main outlines, at least, of what is going on around them, which may so vitally affect them. That is all I wish to say to-day. We shall have further opportunities of discussing the whole position in the new Session and, of course, during the Debate on the Address.

Later in the Debate Mr. Hector McNeil, Under-Secretary for Foreign Affairs, said "I am unable to say whether the information of the right hon. Gentleman about the number of Russian divisions in occupied countries between the Baltic and the Black Sea is correct, or what proportion of these divisions is on a war footing; but it is, of course, well known that there are very considerable Russian forces in these countries."

DEBATE ON THE ADDRESS

A SPEECH TO THE HOUSE OF COMMONS
12 NOVEMBER 1946

---

27 October—General Elections in Bulgaria result in victory for the Government bloc. Communists gain an absolute majority in the National Assembly.

27 October—Great Britain and the United States protest against the Bulgarian Govenment's unfair electoral practices.

27 October—Over 40 killed and 300 injured in four days' communal rioting in Calcutta.

28 October—Third instalment of the American Loan is drawn.

28 October—Marshal Stalin replies to a questionnaire submitted by Mr. Hugh Baillie, President of the United Press of America. Asked what in his opinion is to-day the most serious threat to world peace, Marshal Stalin replies, "The instigators of a new war; in the first place, Churchill and people of a like mind in Britain and the United States." He states that there are 60 Soviet divisions in Germany, Austria, Hungary, Bulgaria, Rumania and Poland.

30 October—House of Commons approves a motion for a Royal Commission into the Control and Ownership of the Press.

3 November—150 Moslem refugees are massacred by Hindu mobs in Bihar.

8 November—It is announced that since 1 September, 510 persons have been killed and 1,600 injured in riots in Bombay.

11 November—General Elections in France result in the Communists being returned as the largest single party. They win 159 seats in the National Assembly.

12 November—New session of Parliament opens in London.

[12 *November* 1946

THE extensive armoury of the English language has frequently been ransacked on these occasions, in order to find new and unhackneyed terms of compliment and congratulation which can be applied by the Leader of the Opposition to the hon. Members who have been chosen by the Government to move and second the Address. I confess that I should have found myself baffled, in the selection of any new terms or any new features, but for the remarkable fact that neither of the two hon. Gentlemen is wearing uniform or Court dress. Here, at any rate, is one of the really broad advances of democracy, and it may be some comfort to hon. Gentlemen below the Gangway, if their thirst for blood is not slaked in other ways. But here I must utter a word of warning to Ministers opposite. They must remember that, in this direction, they are moving contrary to the general tendencies of the Soviet Government, which has distinguished itself throughout the world by the gold-laced glory of its official uniforms, and by the punctilio which it observes on all occasions. We may, therefore, possibly regard this innovation either as an advance of democracy, or as a demonstration on the part of the Government of their differences with the Communist régime.

But I do wholeheartedly congratulate both hon. Gentlemen on their speeches, on the unexceptionable character of the sentiments to which they have given vent, and on the form in which they have cast their arguments. I was particularly pleased to hear the Mover of the Address, the hon. Member for the Acocks Green division of Birmingham [Mr. Usborne], speak with favour of the United States of Europe, and I trust that if ever we are able to come to practical action in that field, he will not fail to enrol himself as a servant of that cause, for a regional consciousness of Europe, while certainly vital in itself, is an essential of the United Nations. I also give my compliments to the hon. Member for Leith [Mr. Hoy], and thank him for his very kind references to me. He commanded the universal assent of the House in his tribute to Scotland, and to the work done at Leith in pursuance of the war. The efforts of Scotland and the contribution of Scotland are entitled to world-wide fame; and I must remind the House that they also voted extremely sensibly at the General Election.

This is the second King's Speech of the Socialist Government. They have been 16 months in office. We have had one of the most laborious and protracted Sessions—fruitful, hon. Members may say, but at any rate productive of something which is on record. At this moment, in reply to the second King's Speech, we may profitably attempt to take stock of the position. The world situation has not improved. The Prime Minister, at the Mansion House, drew a sombre picture from which I cannot dissent. At the General Election, we were assured that a Socialist or Left-Wing Government would get on especially well with the Soviet Government of Russia, but relations have steadily deteriorated. The British and American Forces in Europe have melted away, as was inevitable in the case of governments resting upon the popular will, after a great victory. The Russian Armies, based on a despotic form of Government, have been maintained in Europe in vast strength, and mostly on a war footing. More than one third of Europe is held under the Russian Soviet control. The Soviet military frontier is on the Elbe, and it is impossible to forecast what the future and the fate of France will be. No fruition has yet attended the peace negotiations even about the smaller satellite enemy Powers—perhaps the Prime Minister will be able to make some statement on this point to-day.

The United Nations organisation, as he has so forcibly pointed out at the Mansion House, has not, so far, fulfilled our hopes; it remains however our citadel, and we are in full accord with His Majesty's Government in their loyal and faithful support of this institution, whose reign and ascendancy are an earnest of the desire of the overwhelming majority of mankind. To record these melancholy facts which we see around us, is not necessarily to blame His Majesty's Government. The difficulties have been enormous, and the forces which confront them are intractable. British influence abroad has greatly diminished since wartime days. It is not to attack the Government that I mention these facts, but in order to survey our own position. The Foreign Secretary has done his best, and we on this side have given him whatever support was in our power—we have even sometimes supported him to an extent which caused him embarrassment in other quarters. We cannot charge the Government with being responsible for all the evils of the situation abroad. They have certainly not been guilty of any wrongful or provocative action. We readily believe that their motives are as innocent and virtuous as those which are set out in the mellifluous language of the gracious Speech, with large parts of which we are in full agreement. It was the duty of the Socialist Government to take office when called upon to do so so decidedly by the electors. It is not their fault if they are not equal to the job, though it may be our misfortune.

It cannot be claimed, moreover, that even a National Coalition Government would have successfully surmounted all the adverse tides which have been flowing. The Conservative Party cannot of course accept any responsibility for Potsdam, as matters were taken out of our hands in the vital phase of those discussions. [*Hon. Members: "Oh."*] These are facts, but I am sure, whoever had conducted Potsdam, it would have left behind it many grievous legacies for the future of Europe. Nevertheless, the fact remains that 18 months after the surrender of Germany, and more than a year after that of Japan and in spite of the firm, helpful attitude of the United States based on the joint action—what they call "bi-partisan"—of their two historic parties, the world scene is still dark, anxious and confused. No decisive improvement can be recorded, except, of course, that in the mercy of God the cannon have ceased to fire.

In the forefront of any survey of the world stands Germany, a vanquished nation. "Stands", I said—no, prostrate, shattered. Seventy or eighty millions of men and women of an ancient, capable and terribly efficient race are in a ruined and famished condition in the heart of Europe. This confronts us with problems which at present are quite unsolved by the victors. We and the Americans continue to rule and administer the German people in our zones at extravagant and almost unbearable cost to ourselves—I think in this I carry the Chancellor of the Exchequer with me—and with increasing dissatisfaction to the Germans. We have not been told, and I will not attempt to discuss what is happening in the Russian zone. We are all agreed that the proper course is, as I said before we separated, to make the Germans earn their own living, and make them manage their own affairs as soon as possible, and to give them all possible aid while preventing every form of re-armament. If we are agreed on that, let us enforce it. Let us stick to it and enforce it on every occasion as opportunity serves. Though we have not been informed of any attempt which has been made to forecast the form of the peace treaty with Germany, surely it is urgent to make a peace with the German people, or as many of them as lie within our spheres of responsibility. There must be an end to vengeance and retribution.

I am told that Germany must be punished. I ask: When did punishment begin? It certainly seems to have been going on for a long time. It began in 1943, and continued during 1944 and 1945, when the most frightful air bombardments were cast upon German cities, and when the general exhaustion of their life under the cruel Nazi régime, had drained the last ounces of strength from the German race and nation. The Nuremberg trials are over, and the guilty leaders of the Nazi régime have been hanged by the conquerors. We are told that thousands yet remain to be tried, and that vast categories of Germans are classed as potentially guilty because of their association with the Nazi régime. After all, in a country which is handled as Germany was, the ordinary people have very little choice about what to do. I think some consideration should always be given to ordinary people. Everyone is not a Pastor Niemoller or a martyr, and when ordinary people are hurled this way and that, when the cruel hands of tyrants are laid upon them and vile systems of regimentation are imposed and enforced by espionage and other forms of cruelty, there are great numbers of people who will succumb. I thank God that in this island home of ours, we have never been put to the test which many of the peoples of Europe have had to undergo. It is my hope that we shall presently reach the end of the executions, penalties, and punishments, and that without forgetting the hard lessons of the past, we shall turn our faces resolutely towards the future.

Coming now to the affairs of the British Empire, or former British Empire, with its Commonwealth possessions and mandated territories, I was struck by a statement which was reported to have been made by Mr. Clayton, an official of the United States Government, about Imperial Preference. The statement was made at the end of last week. This subject has often been thrashed out and the facts are common knowledge to every Member who studies our affairs with due attention. Everything is on record. We were repeatedly assured by His Majesty's Government, notably at the time of the acceptance of the American Loan—for which we must not be ungrateful—that no commitments to the prejudice of Imperial Preference had been entered into by His Majesty's Government, and that we are entirely free in any discussions which may take place on the future of world trade or world economy. I ask the Prime Minister to say, when he replies in due course, if he is in a position to renew these assurances on the present occasion in order that we may consider, on this side of the House, what action we should take. I thought it right to give the right hon. Gentleman, whose official position alone prevents me from describing him as "my right hon. Friend", due notice of the question which I have asked on this point.

I may, however, hazard, for my own assurance, and that of some of my hon. Friends on these benches, the personal opinion that it would be a great surprise, to me at least, if a Republican Congress were to embrace Free Trade so whole-heartedly, completely, and passionately, and to promote such a casting-down of tariff walls of all kinds as to call in question, even as a matter of discussion, the comparatively small, modest Preference duties which have been built up in the British Commonwealth of Nations, which have become part of our supreme common life and which are even more important to us as symbols of our indissoluble union than for their commercial advantages, which are, none the less, considerable. However, I await the declarations of the Prime Minister upon this point.

I will content myself to-day with one remark, one passage, designed to illustrate the gravity of the events which are now in progress in India. Suppose Europe had been ruled for several generations, I may even say many generations, by a European Council, and had dwelt in internal peace and safety from external aggression, without any wars, with hardly anybody killed during all that time by steel or lead, except common criminals in the course of crime. Suppose peace and order had been maintained by an impartial organisation seated, let us say, at Geneva, and that it had required to maintain its authority only fifty to sixty thousand armed council or international troops, and had carried on all its work with little more than 1,200 officials.

Supposing this long reign of peace had endured, that nearly a century had passed, and immense increases of population had taken place meanwhile, and that equal laws and justice had been given to all and observed by all the many nations, races, and religions of Europe, so that the Russians and Poles, French and Germans, Austrians and Italians, Protestants and Catholics, Communists and Conservatives, had managed to get along for 60 to 70 years without flying at each other's throats.

That certainly would have been regarded as a blessed era, a kind of Age of the Antonines in Roman history. And that impression would not have been destroyed even though there were admittedly many shortcomings, and also, admittedly, boundless need and hope and means for further improvement. Suppose now, that, in the name of progress, it were decided to remove the elements of stability and impartiality which had rendered an all-European organisation possible and had conferred such inestimable blessings upon the masses of the European peoples, that would be a most serious step; it would be a milestone in the history of Europe, and, not only of Europe, but of the world, because we must remember how everything is connected with everything else, especially nowadays. Suppose, moreover, the preparations for the withdrawal of the central power and guiding hand had already released many of the disruptive and rival forces which lurk in every continent and that these were stirring again with age-old animosities, long buried, so long held in neutrality; and suppose, in particular, that the wars of religion in Europe between Catholic and Protestant, which formerly ravaged Europe and which were the cause of the Thirty Years War, again threatened to break out; suppose that already in the last few months in Europe 10,000 Protestants and Catholics had murdered one another.

I have spoken on recent occasions at length on the proposed abrogation of the Anglo-Egyptian Treaty and the abandonment by British Forces of the Canal zone. I do not know whether the Prime Minister has any further information for us on the negotiations which have been lately conducted in Cairo and the conversations which have taken place over here, but if he feels that the moment is not suitable, we should not demur to his view, or press him in any way.

235

About Palestine, however, it is impossible to avoid expressing deep regret at the many changes of tactics and method, at the needless disappointment created throughout world Jewry by the failure to fulfil the hopes which the party opposite excited by their promises and convictions at the General Election, and above all, at the lack of any policy worthy of the name. This absence of any policy or decision on these matters, which have become more complicated as they proceed, has allowed havoc and hatred to flare and run rife throughout Palestine for more than a year—and no one knows where we are to-day. I have nothing to add to what I have previously advised. Here, perhaps, I may speak for myself, because I have always supported the Zionist movement, and many of my friends here took a different view of it at the time, before the war. I cannot, in any way, recede from the advice which I have ventured to give, namely, that if we cannot fulfil our promises to the Zionists, we should without delay place our mandate for Palestine at the feet of the United Nations, and give due notice of our impending evacuation of that country. If this offer is accepted, a burden, which has become too heavy and too invidious for us to bear alone, will have been lifted from our shoulders and placed in international safe-keeping.

If, however, the United States, which is so keenly interested in Jewish immigration, would deprecate such a course on our part, it will be for them to help us in the most effective way, not only with money but with men, and with all that flows from a concerted policy advanced by two great English-speaking Powers. I am not at all deterred in recommending this course by the fact that it has been demanded by the Soviet Government. I was rather glad to find that our minds are flowing in the same direction in one aspect of international affairs. I am convinced that this procedure would either relieve us from the most thankless of all human tasks, from the reproach which attends our ill success, and infirmity of purpose, and from the physical and practical difficulties of the task, or, on the other hand, that it would secure us the support necessary from Jewish and American sources by which alone our work can be accomplished and our mission fulfilled. To abandon India, with all the dire consequences that would follow therefrom, but to have a war with the Jews in order to give Palestine to the Arabs amid the execration of the world, appears to carry incongruity of thought and policy to levels which have rarely been attained in human history.

I leave these external issues in which, in spite of their melancholy features, there is much common ground between the two main parties—after all, we are all in the same boat in the result of many of these things—and I come to the administration and political topics which are at home. Some of these are referred to in the Gracious Speech. The hon. Gentleman who moved the Address spoke of his great desire to demobilise all the Armed Forces after proper conditions had been established, and I am sure that is a widespread desire—but not yet; like the cynical saying, "We all want to get to Heaven but not immediately". The decision of His Majesty's Government to continue compulsory national service for the Armed Forces for an indefinite period after 1949 is one which they would certainly not have reached without good and grave reasons. In a matter like this, which affects in a vital manner the safety of our country, by avoiding one-sided disarmament, and the maintenance of peace, it will be the duty of the Opposition to support the Government, and we shall certainly do so not only in this House but out of doors.

No one can say there is anything undemocratic about national service for the defence of the country and for the preservation of our free island life, and I assume, of course, it will be imposed equally and universally upon all British subjects in Great Britain, without any distinction being drawn between rich and poor. There is a question of some difficulty about Northern Ireland. That must be discussed in a temperate spirit, in view of all the past history of that question. I hope, however, that with the least possible delay we shall be placed in possession of the Government's scheme, especially in regard to the Army, so that we may know the part in our future system which the Territorial Army and voluntary enlistment of all kinds will play, and how these features will be reconciled with permanent national compulsory military service. I hope we can also be assured that there is no question of extending compulsory national service in the Armed Forces, which defend the life of the State, to compulsory service in the industries of the country. In time of war, this sacrifice may be made, and was freely and voluntarily made, by the trade unions and by the people of the nation, but anything in the nature of industrial conscription in time of peace would be intolerable, and all tendency in that direction must be resisted by all who wish to avoid the serfdom of totalitarian régimes.

Here I must frankly deplore the mismanagement and maladministration of the Armed Forces during the last year. All of the three Ministers responsible have been removed, promoted or dismissed, and new men have been appointed. The former First Lord [Mr. A. V. Alexander] has now become Minister of Defence. I would like to take the occasion of offering him my hearty congratulations and of saying that we look forward with confidence to his discharge of these duties. The right hon. Gentleman has a very special ability and experience, and I, personally, have always felt the warmest regard for him on account of the very rough times we went through together during the war. But what with his long journey to India and his protracted work on the Paris Conference, which was also quite good—I much preferred it to his work on his previous excursion—he cannot have given much thought to Admiralty business. We are told the Admiralty runs itself. I am not so sure. To-day we are told the Navy is undermanned. I saw placarded in the newspapers about recent Fleet exercises—that the Navy was undermanned, one battleship, or something like that, was all they could manage. Yet the figures presented to us in February gave them no fewer than 175,000 men on Vote A, or far more than were required for the very large Fleets which were fully manned before the Second World War began. There must be some mismanagement here, and although partial explanations may be forthcoming, I should particularly like to know what is the proportion of men in Vote A of the Navy who are seaborne to-night, and how many of them are employed on shore, and to have comparisons between that and the Navy in previous phases of its administration. A very searching and severe review of naval establishments is undoubtedly required, and I trust this will be undertaken during the Estimates Debates of this year. I recognise, of course, that the

Fleet Air Arm is an addition to the pre-war Navy, and also may be counted as part of our air power.

The former Secretary of State for Air, Lord Stansgate, also has been so much abroad, negotiating for our evacuation of Egypt and the Canal zone, that he has not been able to bring his commanding talents to bear upon the intricate problems and clamant problems of post-war military aviation. Lord Stansgate has gone, and we now have a new Secretary of State for Air [Mr. Noel Baker], but he has gone, too, to the United States.

Finally, there is the War Office. The former Secretary of State for War [Mr. J. J. Lawson] is deservedly popular and respected in all sections of the House. His many good and charming qualities, high patriotism and public spirit, are admired by all. That, however, does not in any way efface the fact that he was not qualified to discharge, or capable of discharging, the extraordinary and complicated tasks with which the War Office is cumbered and pressed in the transition period at the end of a great war. There is great importance in having a political Minister constantly making his influence felt in each of the Service Departments. It is one of the cases where that much abused class, the politicians, is indispensable. Left to themselves, the Service chiefs will not be able to produce solutions of many of the difficulties which occur, and they would be the first to say how much they stand in need of political guidance. This guidance they have not had, I think, in any effective form—in any form worth speaking of—for more than a year, and we have paid pretty dearly in all sorts of directions for the lack of this essential element in our organisation.

Take the Kluang court martial, and all that business there. With my immense Army experience, with all the Secretaries of State for War I have seen criticised or applauded, I cannot understand how any Secretary of State for War, coming into his office one morning and, presumably, reading some of the newspapers, would not have said to the Army Council, "Here you are going to try men—since when has there been a mass court martial like that? Look up the precedents. The Cabinet would have to settle a question of that kind." Nothing of this sort seemed to occur, and so we got into an extremely tiresome and vexatious muddle which did not reflect very well upon the smooth and imperturbable administration of our military law and justice, although I take this occasion to say that I thought the first entrance of the new Secretary of State [Mr. J. G. Bellenger] to the House and his remarks upon this subject were by no means unbecoming.

I am sure that if he feels that he has to stand between the Army and criticism and see that justice is done, there will be many opportunities for him to make his tenure of the office praiseworthy and possibly even memorable. Far more serious is the total failure to produce a policy or scheme in respect of the Army which can be explained to Parliament and which, once understood by the country, can become a powerful aid to voluntary recruitment. Failure, and failure worthy of censure, is applied to the Government administration of the three Service Departments since they came into power, and this failure has been demonstrated beyond contradiction by the dismissal of two out of the three Ministers involved.

I have only a few more topics which I must touch upon, and these leave the military, foreign, colonial, and Imperial spheres and come a little nearer to our own affairs. We are relieved to hear that Ministers will

> prosecute with the utmost vigour the task of providing suitable homes for My people.

This is a day of rejoicing. Is this really true? Have they made up their minds to turn over a new leaf?

MR. SHURMER [Birmingham, Sparkbrook]: Which is more than ever you did.

MR. CHURCHILL: I have passed more social legislation in this House than any man alive. I guarantee that it would have been possible to give a far greater impetus and movement to the house building programme. I have more than once appealed publicly to the Minister of Health, and I am sure that if he chose from now henceforth to be animated by the instruction and statement in the Gracious Speech and let nothing stand in the way of the largest number of homes of all kinds in the shortest possible time by all methods for the largest number of people, he could even now regain a great deal of the position and the hopes which were founded upon his accession to office with his many undoubted abilities. Instead of that we did not get the homes. We got insults every time. Every kind of insult was flung out, not that we seasoned politicians mind what was said about us by people for whom we entertain no respect. But it is maddening for the people who need the homes and houses merely to see the right hon. Gentleman working out his little party spites, as well as personal and class spites which in the great position he now occupies he ought to have outlived. I have heard him described as a new Lloyd George. Good gracious me, it was certainly not by this kind of contribution that this former great Welshman made his name a household word, which will long endure and be remembered in the homes of Britain.

We are also told that it will be the constant endeavour of His Majesty's Ministers to alleviate the hardships and inconveniences of the housewives. This again will certainly be a welcome change. Let me repeat the old adage, "It is never too late to mend". There may still be a moment

> Betwixt the stirrup and the ground.
> Mercy asked, mercy found.

So far during their tenure of power, in spite of the great power which they wield and of the very severe measures that they are able to force upon the working people, who have just voted for them in large numbers, and, therefore, give loyal obedience to much which they would otherwise not have sustained and endured, they have in many ways made things actually worse than they were in the war years. There have been arguments about food. In the first year of peace it is worse than it was in the last year of war. I am told that that will bear statistical and searching examination. By all means let it be examined, and let us see what the figures are. I will even put a question on the Paper, if desired, to elicit a written answer. It is very gratifying to hear the Ministers in the King's Speech admitting their intention to break with their evil past and to go forward and endeavour to alleviate the lot of the housewife. But what is the substance behind these declarations? The change of heart is very good, but what are the acts and deeds by which it is to be accompanied? What is the first remedy for all these misfortunes and for all these difficulties? What is the first step of alleviation which we are promised in the Gracious Speech.

It is the nationalisation of the railways and of inland transport.

MR. SHURMER: You said that 20 years ago.

MR. CHURCHILL· I am not going to pretend I see any-thing immoral in the nationalisation of the railways provided fair compensation is paid to the present owners. I professed myself, as the hon. Gentleman has reminded the House, in favour of this policy in 1919, but what happened? [*Interruption.*]

MR. W. J. BROWN [Rugby]: Hon. Members on the Government benches must not get so rattled.

MR. CHURCHILL: Sir Eric Geddes was placed in complete charge of the railways with all the facilities and power which would have accrued to a State-aided nationalised system. What happened? All that he produced in four years was a very bad service for the public, heavy loss to the shareholders, and the worst railway strike ever known except the one preceding the General Strike.

I must admit that this practical experience of nationalisation—and we do learn by trial and error provided we profit by our experience—damped, I cannot say my usual, my early enthusiasm for this project. But the railways are only part of the problem. They were a very clearly marked-out public service, and one finds it difficult to see why the arguments which have been applied to the Post Office could not equally be applied to the railways; but now the whole problem is changed. [*Hon. Members: "Why?"*] It is changed by the enormous developments in road transport and haulage. Here is a field of complications of the most extraordinary variety. Why the Government should choose this particular moment to throw all this new sphere into confusion and disturbance and make a large addition to the National Debt in order to thrust the clumsy butter-fingers of the State into all this intricate apparatus cannot be imagined, still less explained. And that it should be represented as a Measure for alleviating the incon-veniences and hardships of the housewife—that at any rate is a preposterous fraud. The same is true of their projects for electricity and gas. We can assure the Government that we shall meet the proposals for the nationalisation both of inland transport and of electricity with strenuous and uncompromising opposition.

ROOSEVELT MEMORIAL FUND

BROADCAST, 18 NOVEMBER 1946

---

17 November—The Franklin D. Roosevelt Memorial Fund is opened in London. The required amount of £15,000 is fully subscribed by 23 November.

[18 *November* 1946

I AM very glad to be invited to support the Prime Minister in calling for subscriptions to the British memorial to President Roosevelt. The House of Commons would gladly have voted all the money needed but it was thought better that the Fund should be made up by small subscriptions so that very large numbers of people could have a chance to take their share. In the great republic across the Atlantic the head of the State is also the head of a Party, in the midst of all the controversies of partisan politics. But over here, in Britain, we only knew him as a world-statesman who was a friend in need and a friend indeed to our country and to the causes of freedom and civilisation which were our cause and which were his cause. For more than five years I worked with him in true comradeship. We sent each other, on each side, nearly a thousand long telegrams and so kept commanding unity of purpose and policy amid the innumerable perplexing problems of war, which in its intimacy and in its practical effectiveness surpassed any tale which history tells of the alliances of great nations with common aims and in equal peril.

I conceived an admiration for President Roosevelt as a statesman, a man of affairs and a war leader. I felt the utmost confidence in his upright and inspiring character and outlook and these ripened in my breast a personal regard and affection for him which will dwell with me as long as I live. His love of his own country, his respect for its constitution, his power of gauging the tides and currents of its free, mobile, public opinion were manifest. But added to these were the beatings of that generous heart which was always stirred to anger and to action by spectacles of aggression and oppression by the strong against the weak. His physical affliction lay heavily upon him. It was a marvel that he bore up against it through all the years of Party controversy in his own country and through the years of world storm. As I said to the House of Commons not one man in ten millions, stricken and crippled as he was, would have attempted to plunge into a life of physical and mental exertion, of hard and ceaseless political strife. Not one in a generation would have succeeded in becoming undisputed master of the vast and tragic scene.

There is no doubt that the late President foresaw the dangers closing in upon the pre-war world with far more prescience than most well-informed people on either side of the Atlantic. There never was a moment's doubt on which side his sympathies lay. The bearing of the British nation in that time of stress when we were all alone filled him and vast numbers of his countrymen with the warmest sentiments towards our people. Even while the United States was nominally neutral he advised the extraordinary measure of assistance called "Lend-Lease", which will stand forth as the most unselfish and unsordid financial act of any country in all known history. He was one of those men about whom one could feel that the worse things got, the better he would be. It is not for us in this island to appraise his position in American history, but we have a right to proclaim that he played a decisive part in the fortunes and the future of mankind, that he was the greatest American friend Britain has ever known and the most powerful champion of freedom who has ever brought help and comfort from the new world to the old.

Now in war-scarred London we raise a monument to his memory and to his fame. It is the heartfelt tribute of British gratitude. To the pleasant ceremonial garden, with its fountains and trees and flowers, of which the Prime Minister has spoken, in which this monument will stand, all sorts and conditions of men and women will resort and if Franklin Roosevelt's inspiration lingers there none will take away any thought which does not arouse fearless resistance to tyranny in all its forms and which does not harmonise with the broadening hopes and higher humanities which may some day reign over all the land and sea.

INDIA

A SPEECH TO THE HOUSE OF COMMONS
12 DECEMBER 1946

---

22 *November—Georgi Dimitroff, the Bulgarian Communist Leader, forms a new "Fatherland Front" cabinet in Sofia.*

27 *November—Lord Pethick-Lawrence, Secretary of State for India, announces that since the Interim Indian Government took office on 2 September, some 6,700 people have been killed in communal riots.*

 1 *December—New York State announces formation of a "Disaster Military Corps" to handle "grave domestic disturbances and disasters" arising from "the possibility of atomic weapons in the form of bombs, rockets or guided missiles".*

 2 *December—Mr. Byrnes and Mr. Bevin sign the Anglo-American agreement on the economic fusion of British and American zones in Germany.*

11 *December—Jugoslavia and Albania announce a Customs and Currency Union.*

12 *December—Conclusion of the Council of Foreign Ministers' Meeting in New York. Mr. Bevin says: "The sun of peace is rising." Mr. Molotov says that the results are "as satisfactory to the Soviet delegation as they are to the other delegations".*

12 *December—The General Assembly of the United Nations adopts a resolution condemning the Franco régime in Spain and debarring Spain from membership in the United Nations. The General Assembly recommends all members immediately to recall their Ambassadors and Ministers Plenipotentiary from Madrid.*

[12 *December* 1946

THE House is indebted to the President of the Board of Trade [Sir Stafford Cripps] for the careful, lucid and comprehensive statement which he has made, and we all associate ourselves with him in his appeal to the leaders of the various parties in India to abstain from violent propaganda or invective against each other, which may have the effect of bringing about a recrudescence or intensification of the grave disorders which have occurred. The right hon. Gentleman deplored, in moderate terms, the fact that we were having a Debate on this subject to-day. But it would be a pity if the British Empire in India passed out of life into history, without the House of Commons seeming to take any interest in the affair, and without any record, even in *Hansard*, of the transaction.

It is several months since we have even discussed the Indian drama which is unfolding itself remorselessly. So far, in this Parliament, we have never voted in a Division on these issues, momentous though they be to Britain, to the British Commonwealth of Nations, to the world at large and, even more, to the 400 million who dwell in the Indian Continent. Words are almost inadequate to describe their vastness. But memorable as these issues may be, we have never divided the House on them, nor shall we do so on this occasion. We must still indulge the hope that agreement will be reached between the two great Indian religions and between the political parties which give modern expression to their age-long antagon-isms. We should, however, be failing in our duty if we in this House gave the impression to India that we were inattentive, or even indifferent, to what is happening, and what is going to happen out there. For many generations, Parliament has been responsible for the government of India, and we can only relieve ourselves, or be relieved, from that burden by the passing of a solemn Act. While we are responsible, it would, in my opinion, be disastrous and be discreditable to the House if the whole Session passed away, with nothing but a casual reference being made to these tremendous and immeasurable events which are taking place.

There is another aspect. If we remained silent after all these months, it might be thought that we were in agreement with His Majesty's Government, and that the policy which they were pursuing was a national policy and not a party policy of the forces which they represent. It might be thought that this was a policy of Britain as a whole, and that the execution of it was endorsed by the

British people as a whole, whereas, for good or ill, the responsibility rests with His Majesty's Government. On their heads lies the responsibility, not only for the execution of the policy, but for the powerful impulse they have given to a great many tendencies which are dominant in this matter to-day. I say nothing to derogate from any utterances or statements which have been made by the Members of other parties. They are all excellent, but I should be very sorry indeed, to feel that, as matters unfold in India, there is any question of our being held accountable at the present moment, for the course of events. Therefore, we are bound to take an opportunity to challenge the Government on this matter by bringing the affair to the light of day.

The newspapers, with their alluring headlines, do not do justice to the proportion of current events. Everyone is busy, or is oppressed by the constant cares and difficulties of daily life. Headlines flicker each day before them. Any disorder or confusion in any part of the world, every kind of argument, trouble, dispute, friction or riot all flicker across the scene. People go tired to bed, at the end of their long, bleak, worrying days, or else they cast care aside, and live for the moment. But, all this time, a tremendous event in Asia is moving towards its culmination, and we should be unworthy of the times in which we live, or of the deeds which we have done if, through unduly careful restraint, we appeared to others unconscious of the gravity, or careless of the upshot of events which affect the lives of vast numbers of human beings who, up to the present, have dwelt for well or ill beneath our protecting shield. My colleagues and I were convinced that if we put off all notice of Indian affairs until the end of January—because that is what it would have come to—or, possibly, February of next year after all these months of silence, the immense accountability of the House of Commons and of the British nation might slip, with so much else, uncared for, away. For these reasons, I am sure that we ought not to separate without making at least a passing comment, to put it mildly, upon the main new features of the Indian problem which have presented themselves to us so prominently in the last few weeks.

There are three main new features to which I would

247

direct the attention of the House this afternoon. There was, and there still is, a general measure of consent here and throughout the island to the final transference of power from the House of Commons to Indian hands, but also it is agreed that that transference, if it is to take place, must be based upon the agreement and the co-operation of the principal masses and forces among the inhabitants of India. Only in this way could that transference take place without measureless bloodshed out there, and lasting discredit to our name in the world. Those who are content with the general movement of our relations with India over the last 20 years have hoped that the desire of many Indians to be rid for ever of British rule and guidance would have brought about a melting of hearts among the vast populations inhabiting the Indian continent, and that they would have joined together to maintain the peace and the unity of India, and stride forth boldly into their independent future, on which we impose no bar.

Those are not my views; they are the views of a very great number of people. But it is necessary to place on record the undoubted fact that no such melting of hearts has, so far, occurred. I think that that would be considered in harmony with the habit of understatement which has often received acceptance in this House. On the contrary, all the facts and all the omens point to a revival, in an acute and violent form, of the internal hatreds and quarrels which have long lain dormant under the mild incompetence of liberal-minded British control. This is the dominating fact which stares us in the face to-day. The House will probably be of the opinion that it is too soon for us to accept this melancholy conclusion, or to regulate our conduct by it. To me, however, it would be no surprise if there were a complete failure to agree. I warned the House as long ago as 1931, when I said that if we were to wash our hands of all responsibility, ferocious civil war would speedily break out between the Muslims and Hindus. But this, like other warnings, fell upon deaf and unregarding ears.

I have always borne in mind the words my father used when he was Secretary of State for India 60 years ago. He said:

> Our rule in India is, as it were, a sheet of oil spread out over a surface of, and keeping calm and quiet and

unruffled by storms, an immense and profound ocean of humanity. Underneath that rule lie hidden all the memories of fallen dynasties, all the traditions of vanquished races, all the pride of insulted creeds, and it is our task, our most difficult business, to give peace, individual security and general prosperity to the 250 millions of people—

there are now 400 millions—

who are affected by those powerful forces, to bind them and to weld them by the influence of our knowledge, our law and our higher civilisation, in process of time into one great united people and to offer to all the nations of the West the advantages of tranquillity and progress in the East.

That is the task which, with all our shortcomings and through all our ordeals, we have faithfully and loyally pursued since Queen Victoria assumed the Imperial Crown. That is the task which we have now declared ourselves willing to abandon completely, provided that we have such assurance of agreement between the Indian races, religions, parties and forces as will clear us from the responsibility of bringing about a hideous collapse and catastrophe. We have no such assurance at the present time. Agreement in India, which was the basis of all our policy and declarations, was the indispensable condition. It was the foundation of the Cripps Mission in 1942; it was the keynote of the Cabinet Mission sent out this year, but there is no agreement before us yet; I stress "yet". There is only strife and bloodshed, and the prospect of more and worse. That is the first point of which we must take note—the absence of agreement which, it was common ground between us, should stand as the foundation of the future transference of power in India.

The second point to which I would like to draw the attention of the House is the cardinal error of His Majesty's Government when, on 12 August, they invited one single Indian party, the Congress Party, having made other efforts, to nominate all the members of the Viceroy's Council. Thereby they precipitated a series of massacres over wide regions, unparalleled in India since the Indian Mutiny of 1857. Indeed, it is certain that more people have lost their lives or have been wounded in India by violence since the interim Government under Mr. Nehru was installed in office four months ago by the Viceroy, than in the previous 90 years, or four generations of men, covering a large part of the reigns of five Sovereigns. This is only a foretaste of what may come. It may be only the first few heavy drops before the thunderstorm breaks upon us. These frightful slaughters over wide regions and in obscure uncounted villages have, in the main, fallen upon Muslim minorities. I have received from high and credible witnesses, accounts of what has taken place, for instance, in Bihar. The right hon. and learned Gentleman gave us his report. What happened in Bihar casts into the shade the Armenian atrocities with which Mr. Gladstone once stirred the moral sense of Liberal Britain. We are, of course, cauterised by all that we ourselves have passed through. Our faculty for wonder is ruptured, our faculty for horror is numbed; the world is full of misery and hatred. What Mr. Gollancz, in a remarkable book—which, I may say, shows an evident lack of peace of mind—has called "our threatened values", do not stir us as they would have done our fathers or our predecessors in this House; nor, perhaps, after all our exertions and in our present eclipse, have we the physical and psychic strength to react against these shocking tidings, as former generations and earlier Parliaments, who have not suffered like us, would certainly have done.

The official figure of the lives lost since the Government of India was handed over to the Interim Administration of Mr. Nehru is stated at 10,000. I doubt very much whether that figure represents half the total racial and religious murders which have occurred up to date. An outbreak of animal fury has ravaged many large districts, and may at any time resume or spread its devastation through teeming cities and Provinces as big as England or the main British island. It is some comfort to recall, and I was glad the right hon. and learned Gentleman reminded us of it, that both Muslim and Hindu leaders have joined together to arrest, or at least mitigate this appalling degeneration. I have been informed that it was Mr. Nehru himself who gave the order which the Provincial Government of Bihar had been afraid to give, for the police and troops to fire upon Hindu mobs who were exterminating the Muslim minorities within their midst. That was certainly to his credit and may be taken, so far as it goes, as an encouraging sign.

Nevertheless, I must record my own belief, which I have long held and often expressed, that any attempt to establish the reign of a Hindu numerical majority in India will never be achieved without a civil war, proceeding, not perhaps at first on the fronts of armies or organised forces, but in thousands of separate and isolated places. This war will, before it is decided, lead through unaccountable agonies to an awful abridgement of the Indian population. Besides and in addition to this, I am sure that any attempt by the Congress Party to establish a Hindu Raj on the basis of majorities measured by the standards of Western civilisation—or what is left of it—and proceeding by the forms and formulas of governments with which we are familiar over here, will, at a very early stage, be fatal to any conception of the unity of India.

The right hon. Gentleman gave us some account of the differences that had arisen about the declaration of 15 May, as between the two parties and so forth. But the technical and procedural points now in dispute in Delhi are not the issues at stake; they are only the tactical and argumentative counters; they are only the symbols of passions and hatreds deep in the soil of India, and measured by the standard of a thousand years. The unity of India is of superficial appearance, imposed by many generations of British rule, upon a mighty continent. It will pass away for long periods of time, once the impartial element of guidance from outside is withdrawn. Whatever may be thought of these conclusions—and I have no doubt there is great difference of opinion about attempts to draw conclusions in regard to matters of such vast, vague and obscure a character—the facts upon which they are based should, I am sure, at this stage not pass without occasional mention in the House of Commons, which, as I have said, until other arrangements are made bears a lawful, legal and inescapable responsibility for what happens in India.

The third new and important fact, of which we must this afternoon take notice, is the declaration by His Majesty's Government—made, I think, by the Prime Minister last week. Let me read the last paragraph of the declaration:

There has never been any prospect of success for the Constituent Assembly except upon the basis of an agreed procedure. Should a Constitution come to be framed by a Constituent Assembly in which a large section of the Indian population has not been represented, His Majesty's Government could not of course contemplate—as the Congress have stated they would not contemplate— forcing such a Constitution upon any unwilling parts of the country.

If this is at last the settled policy of His Majesty's Government it will carry them far. It comprises within its scope, it seems to me, the discharge of our obligations, both to the inhabitants of India and to those who are called the Scheduled, or Depressed classes, or the Untouchables as they are regarded by their fellow Hindus, to which obligation we have long been pledged in honour. How this policy will be carried into effect it is not possible to foresee, and still less to foretell, at this moment. It is indeed a formidable programme after so many slowly-grown loyalties have been repudiated, and so many bulwarks cast away. I take note of that declaration, because it seems to me to be a most important milestone in this long journey, which combines the pangs of uphill progress with the evils which beset us upon downhill progression.

The Muslims, numbering 90 million, some in separate States and the rest intermingled in an extraordinary manner with the Hindus, comprise the majority of the fighting elements in India. The Untouchables, for whom Dr. Ambedkar has the right to speak, number, as I contend, anything from 40 to 60 millions. It is to them that His Majesty's Government owe a special duty of protection. At present in these negotiations they are not regarded, in a technical sense, as a minority, so I understand. There is a technical sense. If you are a minority, certain treatment is open to you; but if you are not a minority, then you are denied that treatment. They have been outwitted and out-manœuvred in various ways, through the Poona Pact form of the elections, as the right hon. Gentleman admitted with candour and sincerity, and the affectation or pretence is put forward that they are merely a part of the vast Hindu community, and are not entitled to be considered as a minority entity in India's life. I must particularly ask the Prime Minister, or whoever is to speak for the Government, to state the Government's view and intentions upon this point. Are the 60 million Untouchables to be considered as an entity by themselves, entitled to the consideration which is to be given to entities, or are they merely to be used to swell the numerical size of those whom they regard as their oppressors? I should be very glad if a clearer pronouncement could be made upon that point. I do not anticipate that it will be an unfavourable one.

I have already remarked, earlier in the Session, that the word "minority" has no relevance or sense when applied to masses of human beings numbered in many scores of millions. When there are many scores of millions the word "minority" really does not apply. We are only 46 million in this island, but we do not consider ourselves a minority; we consider ourselves an entity—at least so far. Ninety million Muslims and sixty million people of the Depressed Classes are not relative facts, but actual and absolute facts. The Depressed Classes are fully entitled to be considered as an entity, and I repeat my request to the right hon. Gentleman that a very clear statement should be made on this point.

I must now draw the attention of the House to the character of the Constituent Assembly, which apparently is to proceed to make a republic for India, and engage upon it at once. I have not to-day the intention of scrutinising the electoral foundation upon which this rests—30 millions out of 400 millions.

THE PRIME MINISTER [MR. ATTLEE]: Not 400 millions in British India.

MR. CHURCHILL: They are dealing with the fortunes of all India. Large parts of it are not represented at all. There are 30 million electors, who have not much experience with modern political methods, and that is the foundation. I say that is not necessarily capable of giving a complete democratic verdict such as would be required in other more advanced communities.

MR. COVE [Aberavon]: Is the right hon. Gentleman in favour of extending the franchise?

MR. CHURCHILL: Yes, certainly. I have always been in favour of extending the franchise. I believe in the will of the people. I do not believe in the perversion of the will of the people by actively organised and engineered minorities, who, having seized upon power by force or fraud or chicane, come forward and then use that power in the name of vast masses with whom they have long lost all effective connection. I say that as to the general foundation. A decision is to be taken, as a result of which the British connection with India will come to an end. I am not at all admitting that that decision represents the wish or expression of the people of India; nor do I admit that the minorities who are going to utter that expression can claim the democratic title which, in modern days, attaches to those who speak for the large majorities of universal suffrage elections. The Cabinet Mission's proposal of 15 May for the setting up of a Constituent Assembly was essentially a proposal that the main political parties of India should meet, and through their representatives—70 Muslims, 220 Hindus, in which were absorbed the unfortunate Untouchables, and 4 Sikhs—endeavour to work out the proposed Constitution. Do His Majesty's Government consider that the meeting now taking place in New Delhi, which the Muslim League are not so far attending at all, is in any sense the meeting of a valid Constituent Assembly? The fact that the Muslims are refusing to attend remains a fact, whoever is to blame for it, and a meeting of one side without the other is not a conference. Indeed, the text of the proposals of the Government and the right hon. and learned Gentleman, whose ability has been devoted with such disastrous effects to furthering this policy——

MR. SORENSEN [Leyton, West]: Shame.

MR. CHURCHILL: I remember well when the right hon. and learned Gentleman went out as representative of the Government of which I was the head, and how we had to pull him up because—— [Interruption.] I do not want to say anything——

SIR S. CRIPPS: If the right hon. Gentleman intends to disclose what passed between me and the Cabinet on that occasion, I hope he will disclose it all.

MR. CHURCHILL: The right hon. and learned Gentleman is quite right in what he says, and I shall not pursue the point. [Laughter.] What is all this laughter? No one impugns the conscientious integrity and virtue of the right hon. and learned Gentleman, but I must say that in the Cabinet Mission, of which we have the results published, which has taken place under the present Government, his influence has, I have every reason to believe, been used for an altogether undue emphasis being placed upon the advantages being given to the Hindus. At any rate, the right hon. and learned Gentleman can defend himself. No one more than he has taken responsibility in this matter, because neither of his colleagues could compare with him in that acuteness and energy of mind with which he devotes himself to so many topics injurious to the strength and welfare of the State.

To return to the validity of the present Constituent Assembly, on which I trust we shall have some statement, the document of 15 May states that if the President of the Assembly should decide that a matter raised is not "a major communal issue", the party which objects and maintains that it is a major communal issue, may claim that the matter is referred for the opinion of the Federal Court. How is it possible that this procedure can work if the party which objects is not there at all? The meeting in Delhi is not, therefore—I wish to hear a statement from the Government on this—the proposed Constituent Assembly which they put forward. Let me take a more homely analogy. If the bride or bridegroom fails to turn up at church, the result is not what, to use an overworked word, is called a "unilateral" wedding. The absolute essence of the matter is that both parties should be there. While we hope that this may still be the case, it is still pertinent to inquire if His Majesty's Government consider that their conference of a Constituent Assembly has begun.

I am grateful to the House for listening to me after we have had so full an account from the responsible Minister of the Crown. I feel bound, however, to end upon a positive conclusion, although I will express it rather in terms of negation. In all this confusion, uncertainty and gathering storm, which those who have studied the Indian problem over long years might well have foreseen, there appear at the present time to be three choices—the proverbial three choices—before the British Parliament. The first is to proceed with ruthless logic to quit India regardless of what may happen there. This we can certainly do. Nothing can prevent us, if it be the will of Parliament, from gathering together our women and children and unarmed civilians, and marching under strong rearguards to the sea. That is one choice. The second is to assert the principle, so often proclaimed, that the King needs no unwilling subjects and that the British Commonwealth of

Nations contemplates no compulsory partnership, that, in default of real agreement, the partition of India between the two different races and religions, widely differing entities, must be faced; that those who wish to make their own lives in their own way may do so, and the gods be with them; and that those who desire to find, in a variety of systems, a means of association with our great free Commonwealth may also be permitted to take the course which, ultimately, they may show themselves ready to take.

It follows, of course, from this second alternative, that anarchy and massacre must be prevented and that, failing a measure of agreement not now in sight, an impartial Administration responsible to Parliament, shall be set up to maintain the fundamental guarantees of "life, liberty and the pursuit of happiness" to the millions, nay, the hundreds of millions, of humble folk who now stand in jeopardy, bewilderment and fear. Whether that can be achieved or not by any apparatus of British controlled government that we can form from our dissipated resources, is, again, a matter upon which it is now impossible to form a final judgment.

One thing there is, however, that, whatever happens, we must not do. We must not allow British troops or British officers in the Indian Army to become the agencies and instruments of enforcing caste Hindu domination upon the 90 million Muslims and the 60 million Untouchables; nor must the prestige or authority of the British power in India, even in its sunset, be used in partisanship on either side of these profound and awful cleavages. Such a course, to enforce religious and party victory upon minorities of scores of millions, would seem to combine the disadvantages of all policies and lead us ever deeper into tragedy, without giving us relief from our burdens, or liberation, however sadly purchased, from moral and factual responsibility. It is because we feel that these issues should be placed bluntly and plainly before the British and Indian peoples, even amid their present distresses and perplexities, that we thought it our bounden duty to ask for this Debate.